MW00715479

WANDERING
HEART

WANDERING HEART

The Work and Method of Hayashi Fumiko

SUSANNA FESSLER

State University
of New York
Press

Watashi No Chiheisen by Fumiko Hayashi, copyright © 1931 by Fukue Hayashi.

Bungaku, Tabi, Sonota by Fumiko Hayashi, copyright © 1936 by Fukue Hayashi.

Watashi No Shigoto by Fumiko Hayashi, copyright © 1937 by Fukue Hayashi.

English translation rights arranged with Nihon Bungei Chosakuken Hogo Domei through Japan Foreign-Rights Centre

Published by
State University of New York Press, Albany

© 1998 State University of New York

All rights reserved

Production by Susan Geraghty
Marketing by Patrick Durocher

Printed in the United States of America

No part of this book may be used or reproduced in any manner whatsoever without written permission. No part of this book may be stored in a retrieval system or transmitted in any form or by any means including electronic, electrostatic, magnetic tape, mechanical, photocopying, recording, or otherwise without the prior permission in writing of the publisher.

For information, address State University of New York Press,
State University Plaza, Albany, N.Y. 12246

Library of Congress Cataloging-in-Publication Data

Fessler, Susanna.
    Wandering heart : the work and method of Hayashi Fumiko / by Susanna Fessler.
        p.   cm.
    Includes bibliographical references.
    ISBN 0-7914-3907-0 (alk. paper). — ISBN 0-7914-3908-9 (pbk. : alk. paper)
    1. Hayashi, Fumiko, 1904–1951—Criticism and interpretation.
I. Title.
PL829.A8Z64 1998
895.6′344—dc21   97-41204
                                                                        CIP

10 9 8 7 6 5 4 3 2 1

CONTENTS

NOTE TO THE READER

Japanese names are given in Japanese order, that is, family name first, then given name. Exceptions are those names given in the preface and the names of those individuals whose cited works were published in English.

I have used the Hepburn romanization system for Japanese terms, the Pinyin romanization system for Chinese terms, and the romanization system designated by the American Library Association and the Library of Congress for Russian terms, with the exception of bibliographic notes of Russian works in translation, which are given as they appear.

Unless otherwise noted, all translations in the text are my own.

PREFACE

There is a large pool of writings on Hayashi Fumiko, most of which focus on the life of the author or on one or two of her most famous works. Indeed, so much has been said about *Diary of a Vagabond* that I hesitated to say as much as I did in this study, but I could not deny its importance in Fumiko's writing career. In any case, it seemed clear to me that a general, encompassing study of the author with attention given to the lesser-known works would be a valuable addition to the field. Fumiko was immensely popular in her day, and it seemed odd to me that a writer whose work is almost always included in collections of modern Japanese literature would have had so little serious academic work done on her outside of studies of *Diary of a Vagabond* and *Drifting Clouds*.

Recently some new studies and translations of Fumiko have appeared in English: of note, Janice Brown has published a translation of *Ao uma o mitari* and portions of *Diary of a Vagabond* (*I Saw a Pale Horse & Selections from Diary of a Vagabond* [Ithaca, N.Y.: Cornell University East Asia Program, 1997]) and Joan Ericson has published a book on Hayashi Fumiko, that includes a translation of *Diary of a Vagabond* (*Be a Woman: Hayashi Fumiko and Modern Japanese Literature* [Honolulu: University of Hawaii Press, 1997]). Noriko Mizuta has also written on Fumiko's *Drifting Clouds* ("In Search of a Lost Paradise: The Wandering Woman in Hayashi Fumiko's *Drifting Clouds*," in *The Woman's Hand: Gender and Theory in Japanese Women's Writing* [Stanford, Calif.: Stanford University Press, 1996]). In addition, there are a few Hayashi Fumiko short stories in translation (see bibliography), as well as a partial translation of *Drifting Clouds*. Still, for the English-bound reader, little is available on this dynamic writer. There has been a number of articles and books published in Japanese, the most notable by Professor Eiichi Mori of Kanazawa University. His research is thorough and thoughtful, and his assistance to me on this project has been greatly appreciated. In addition to Professor Mori, other scholars who have contributed significantly to the study of Hayashi Fumiko include Eiko Imagawa, who compiled the chronological history (*nenpu*) in the *Hayashi Fumiko zenshū*, and Taiko Hirabayashi, a close friend of Fumiko's and author of *Hayashi Fumiko* (Tokyo: Shinchō sha, 1969). A careful reading of my footnotes should give the reader an idea of whose work has contributed most.

I myself was drawn to Hayashi Fumiko not, as many people assume, because she was a *joryū sakka* (woman writer). What attracted me to her writing was the independent spirit of the early works, a spirit that expressed a profound faith in the individual's ability to shape his or her own life. This faith contrasts sharply with the determinism so common in Japanese Naturalist writing of the time, and it struck me as quite significant that Fumiko wrote about the same downtrodden underclass that many Naturalists chose to portray, but with the distinct difference that she believed the lower classes had the ability to work their way out of poverty.

Fumiko's attraction and deep attachment to travel also appealed to me. Travel has been a significant and important part of my life, so an author who gave travel and travel imagery special status naturally caught my attention. Her travelogues were a joy to read and provided a fresh format change from her novels.

In the course of my work there have been many individuals and organizations who have helped make it all possible. I thank Yale University and the Yale University East Asian Council for funding provided during my graduate career. I would also like to thank the Japanese Ministry of Education for providing me with a scholarship during the year I spent researching in Japan at Keiō University.

For their academic assistance in Japan I thank Professor Teruhiko Hinotani at Keiō University and Professor Eiichi Mori at Kanazawa University. For their academic assistance stateside, I thank Professor Edwin McClellan and Professor Edward Kamens at Yale University, both of whom provided immeasurable assistance and encouragement. Professors Charles Hartman and James Hargett at the University at Albany also patiently provided helpful comments and suggestions on the manuscript. Zina Lawrence at the State University of New York Press was very supportive of this project, and made the preparation of the manuscript less fearful than I anticipated.

Many of my friends, both inside academia and out, have been integral to the completion of this study. Here I would like to single out and thank Rina Someya, for her patience in answering so many questions, and Professor Akira Miyata and his wife, Sachiko, for being my benefactors in Japan throughout my academic career. Finally I thank William Thomas, who patiently read the manuscript and provided many helpful suggestions. There are many others who have helped along the way, and although a comprehensive list here would grow too long, I would like to express my appreciation for all the advice and interest my friends and colleagues have given me concerning this project.

INTRODUCTION

Among the names regularly included in the canon of modern Japanese literature is that of Hayashi Fumiko (1903–1951), a successful writer from the early 1930s until the time of her death. Very little of her work is read today, although paperback editions of her three most famous works, *Hōrōki* (Diary of a Vagabond, 1930), *Ukigumo* (Drifting Clouds, 1949) and *Meshi* (Food, 1951) are still readily available in most bookstores, and on occasion a collection of her works is published in a one-volume set, as was recently done by Chikuma shobō in its collection of Japanese literature.[1] Except for these publications, though, Fumiko's writing has fallen into relative obscurity; when her works are mentioned by scholars, it is either to note her treatment of the lower classes in *Diary of a Vagabond* or because she falls into the category of *joryū sakka* (woman writer).

The world of modern Japanese literature had already passed through a number of phases by the time Fumiko appeared on the literary scene in the early 1930s. During the early Meiji period (1868–1912), writers such as Futabatei Shimei (1864–1909) and Tsubouchi Shōyō (1859–1935) had concerned themselves with the issue of whether a novel should be didactic, realistic, or a combination of the two. These men, along with their successors, were responding to the Western influence that flooded into Japan during this period of rapid modernization. In Futabatei and Shōyō's wake came writers such as Natsume Sōseki (1867–1916) and Mori Ōgai (1862–1922), who helped create a paradigm for the modern Japanese novel, one that would combine the Japanese psyche and a Western concern for the individual.

Political ferment and rapid economic growth in the early twentieth century influenced writers to express their social views through fiction; the 1920s in particular saw a burgeoning of "proletariat literature," along with other politicized literature following in the Dadaist, anarchist, feminist, and Marxist traditions. Concomitant with these trends was the growth of the Naturalist school—remotely reflective of the French Naturalists—who endeavored to portray man in as realistic a manner possible. Characters' unremarkable lives were carefully depicted, each action minor, with an emphasis on the banality of life. The unfortunate result of this was that the Naturalist novel left the reader not only wanting more action, but also some sort of affirmation that life itself was not meaningless. The focus on the individual, present in fiction from Futabatei on down, all too often concentrated on his inability to function. It was on this point that Hayashi Fumiko's writing differed, and that is why it was so popular.

Fumiko's writing drew a wide audience of both men and women, rich and poor, from all walks of life. What was it that attracted these readers? Overall—and this is particularly true of her earlier works—it was her overwhelmingly positive sense of life. Faced with hardship and misery, Fumiko responded with optimism and strength. Her works provided inspiration for those who shared her lot, as well as a glimpse (for those who did not) of what human determination could do. In an age when the influence from Western philosophies had painted a depressing, deterministic view of mankind, Fumiko portrayed the wonder and beauty of human beings, expressing in a straightforward style a confidence in man's abilities to control his life. This confidence contrasts sharply with the determinism so common in Japanese Naturalist writing of the time, and it struck me as quite significant that Fumiko wrote about the same downtrodden underclass that many Naturalists chose to portray, but with the distinct difference that she believed the lower classes had the ability to work their way out of poverty. This is not to say that Fumiko approached her work with a specific political agenda. Throughout her career her writing displayed a virtual allergy to complex ideologies and philosophical constructs. Rather, she exhibited a kind of naive common sense, one that an audience disgruntled with the petulance of Dadaism, the didacticism of Marxism, and the determinism of Naturalism, found refreshing and honest.

Fumiko's early writing also attracted readers because it crossed social boundaries and provided the wealthy and well-to-do with a window to life in the lower classes. In a society heavily influenced by Confucian values (albeit Japanese-style Confucianism) where interpersonal relations and the maintenance of one's proper position in society played a weighty role in life, Fumiko gave her audience a chance to "mingle" with those people they would otherwise never meet. All these factors, combined with her carefree style and accessible prose, made her a writer of immense popularity.

This book covers my areas of interest; it does not exhaust the possible topics concerning the author. I hope that it will help break new ground, far away from the constant hum of *Diary of a Vagabond*–related commentary, where one can read about Fumiko's lesser known works as well as some of her more famous ones. Some may fault me for not including anything beyond passing mention of some well-known works such as "Nakimushi kozō" (Crybaby, 1935) and "Bangiku" (Late Chrysanthemum, 1947), but I hope that my discussions of some heretofore unknown works will compensate for this. My ultimate goal is to provide a general study of Fumiko that would help introduce the new reader to her works. Although still few in number, studies and translations of her works have begun to appear in Western languages, and the present book is an effort to respond to an increased interest in the writer.[2]

My methods included a thorough reading of all readily available (and some not so readily available) works by the author and then a methodical sorting process to compile a selection of works that would demonstrate the points I wished to make. Of course, there is much input from secondary sources, although I tried to focus more on the works themselves in order to avoid undue influence from others' commentary. There is quite a number of critical articles written on Fumiko (for a selected list, see the bibliography), some of which have interesting theses but most of which are quick rehashes of Fumiko's life and writing career. In order to understand Fumiko's place in the literary world, a cursory reading of these articles is necessary, but the interested student should be cautioned that few of them offer new insight. I shall refrain from specifically recommending any, as such recommendations would have to depend on the individual student's area of interest.

Chapter 1 gives a brief biographical overview of the author's life, something that I felt was necessary in order to understand the changes that affected her writing. A writer is rarely able to completely divorce herself from the context in which she lives, and it was this fact that prompted me to write this chapter. Also, so much of Fumiko's literary reputation is based on her impoverished upbringing that without some attention given to the subject it is hard to appreciate what many of her critics said about her. Where appropriate, discussion of specific works is included to help illuminate the influences that her life had on her work.

The remaining chapters provide a more in-depth look at specific topics that are prominent in Fumiko's works. Chapter 2 discusses *Diary of a Vagabond* and some of the earlier short stories; it focuses on Fumiko's struggle with what writing meant to her and what her mission was as a writer. It includes a short history of the publication of *Diary of a Vagabond*, discussion of the possible influences of other writers on Fumiko's writing, the optimism expressed in the text, whether *Diary of a Vagabond* follows in some of the traditions of classical Japanese literature, and finally a comparison of *Diary of a Vagabond* and some other early works in search of enduring aspects of Fumiko's writing.

Chapter 3 addresses the importance of travel and travel imagery in her writing. In it, I discuss the importance of nostalgia and loneliness in Fumiko's travelogues, and how the former is necessary for the latter to be experienced. I also examine the expression of those emotions in

Fumiko's fiction, and how the travel motif informs much of her work.

Chapter 4 discusses the topic of marriage and other family relationships, and how Fumiko's treatment of them emphasized the importance she attached to freedom of choice. Whereas the earlier works, such as *Diary of a Vagabond*, rarely went further than to express a simple belief in the existence of free will, the works discussed in this chapter address how important it is that one be permitted to exercise that will, unfettered by societal restraints.

Chapter 5 examines the later works in Fumiko's career. These works show a marked change in her writing: they carry the dark, depressing message that man may not control his fate. Her characters in these works exhibit a resignation heretofore unseen, and many of them believe that, given their helplessness to change their lives and the world around them, there is little point in placing much importance on the complexities of ethics.

In the appendices I have included the translations of three essays that are heavily quoted in the main text, so that the reader may see for himself the full text. Reading Fumiko's essays can be a trying exercise, as she rarely followed a logical train of thought. After reading a host of them her meaning becomes clearer to the reader, but to the uninitiated eye these works may seem quite confused. In my analysis of these essays I have imposed what I take to be the implicit logical structure of Fumiko's thoughts, and have duly noted that in the text.

Hayashi Fumiko produced hundreds of works during her short life. The pace that she set for herself—one that most probably contributed to her early demise—suggests that, had she lived longer, a collection of her works could have been twice the size it is today. And while the nature of her writing changed over the years, the literary quality did not diminish; her first and last novels are both regarded as masterpieces.[3]

CHAPTER 1

Life of and Influences on the Author

CHILDHOOD

Hayashi Fumiko[1] was born in Moji, a small town on the Shimonoseki Straits, in 1903.[2] Her mother, Hayashi Kiku, and father, Miyata Asatarō, were not married, so Fumiko was registered in her maternal uncle's (Hayashi Hisayoshi) family registry. Fumiko never expressed negative feelings about the fact that Kiku bore her out of wedlock—for her, lineage or birth was of secondary importance. Some of her fictional characters are illegitimate children, but their illegitimacy is never something with which they struggle in any psychological way. Illegitimacy is presented as more of a social barrier than anything else. This will be discussed in more detail later, but suffice it to say that Fumiko did not let her illegitimacy become a disruptive concern in her life.

Kiku was born on November 28, 1868, the eldest daughter of her mother, Fuyu, and her father, Shinzaemon. Her family ran a drugstore in Kagoshima, and then later a hot-spring inn in Sakurajima.[3] Kiku had a daughter, Hide, out of wedlock on July 13, 1898. A man by the name of Matsuyama Kojirō acknowledged paternity, but did not marry Kiku. In his biography of Fumiko, *Hayashi Fumiko: Hito to sakuhin* (Hayashi Fumiko: The Writer and Her Works, 1966), Fukuda Kiyoto frankly notes that Hide and Fumiko were most likely not the only children that Kiku bore, and that there is no way to know how many other siblings by different fathers Fumiko may actually have had.[4] In *Diary of a Vagabond*, Fumiko writes that she had a total of six siblings but that she had only ever met one, a sister—presumably Hide. She says she has bitter memories of that sister, and that she did not like the way in which the sister treated Kiku.[5] Reading Fumiko's other autobiographical works, however, one gets the impression that she was an only child; obviously her siblings, however many there may have been, did not play a very important role in her life.

Fumiko's father, Asatarō, was born in 1882 in Ehime Prefecture, the oldest son of a middle-class farming family. His family also ran a silversmith shop, and he had an uncle who made a specialized kind of paper—Iyo paper—in the prefectural capital, Matsuyama. Asatarō helped his uncle by peddling the paper, and this was the beginning of his career as an itinerant peddler. Later Asatarō struck out on his own peddling lacquerware and cutlery. This work took him to Sakurajima, where he often stayed at Kiku's family's inn.[6] It was there that the two met and became romantically involved.

Kiku was fourteen years Asatarō's senior—quite an age gap—and Fukuda Kiyoto says that this, and the fact that Asatarō never registered Fumiko in his own family register, would suggest that Asatarō never had any intention of marrying Kiku; he was simply interested in a short affair, but the birth of a baby caused him to stay seven years with Kiku before finally abandoning her and Fumiko for another woman.[7] Fumiko says in *Diary of a Vagabond* that her mother was chased out of town for becoming involved with someone from another province, but it seems more likely that Kiku's infidelity itself, not the foreignness of her lover (Asatarō), embarrassed her family enough to ask her to leave. Kiku and Asatarō moved to Yamaguchi Prefecture.[8]

Sometime between September 1899 and May 1901, Kiku and Asatarō left Sakurajima and went on the road together as itinerant peddlers. The couple rented a house in Moji, and it was there that, after a labor induced by a fall down a flight of stairs, Kiku gave birth to Fumiko.[9] At the time of Fumiko's birth Asatarō was working in Shimonoseki as an assistant in a pawn shop, but by 1904 he had set out in his own independent business and moved the family from Moji to Shimonoseki, where he ran an auction house. Business was brisk due to the outbreak of the Russo-Japanese War, and Asatarō soon opened branch stores in the cities of Wakamatsu, Nagasaki, and Kumamoto. To run these branches he enlisted the help of some friends, one of whom was Sawai Kisaburō, the man who would eventually adopt Fumiko as his own daughter. Kisaburō came from a farming family in Okayama Prefecture, and was twenty years Kiku's junior.

In 1907, Asatarō moved the headquarters of the store from Shimonoseki to Wakamatsu. Located near the ferry crossing (Wakamatsu is located in the Gotō Archipelago off the coast of Kyūshū), the shop sold such things as gold-leaf screens, Buddhist altars, cigarette cases, cloth, textiles, and pocketwatches. The shop also served as a residence for Asatarō, Kiku, Fumiko, Kisaburō, and other shop employees. For three years the family lived this way, until Asatarō's philandering caused too much strife for the family to stay together. Asatarō had a mistress named Hama, a geisha whom he had been seeing for years and who followed the family to Wakamatsu when they moved there. Asatarō set up Hama in her own apartment nearby, but Kiku, who was quite aware of the circumstances, objected to the idea of so much money being spent on her husband's mistress, so Hama was moved into the shop residence with the family. As one may imagine, this caused quite a bit of tension among family members. By this point Asatarō was eager to find an excuse to end his relationship with Kiku. He also realized that Kisaburō felt empathy for her, and he used that as a pretext to throw them both out of the house: he sent Kiku out on a business errand on New Year's Eve, 1910, and when she failed to return in good time he sent Kisaburō out to look for her. When the two of them finally came home, he accused them of having an affair and told them to leave the house.[10] Fumiko was called before her father, who asked her if she wanted to go with her mother or stay with him. Fumiko replied firmly that she preferred the former, so Kisaburō, Kiku, and Fumiko moved to Nagasaki.[11] Fumiko's parents' unhappy union apparently left a deep impression on her; although she recorded remarkably few bad memories from her childhood, the topic of soured marriages began appearing in her fiction quite early.

Over the course of the next ten years, Fumiko changed residences and schools numerous times, as Kisaburō's work as a traveling salesman required relative mobility. In April 1910, Fumiko was enrolled in the Katsuyama Elementary School in Nagasaki. Sometime shortly after that she transferred to the Hachiman Girls' Elementary School in Sasebo. In January 1911, she transferred from the Hachiman Girls' Elementary School to the Naike Elementary School in Shimonoseki, where she remained until October 1914. Her transcripts from this period show average marks and a total of twenty-five absences during the four-year period.

While Fumiko was living in Shimonoseki with Kiku and Kisaburō, Asatarō moved from Wakamatsu to Moji and opened a new store there. He married Hama in June 1911, but they divorced not long after in February 1914. Inoue Takaharu, in his biography *Hayashi Fumiko to sono shūhen* (Hayashi Fumiko and Her Environs, 1990), says that while Asatarō and Hama were married Fumiko visited them often, sometimes staying the night at their house.[12] However, this information conflicts with some other accounts in which Fumiko is said to have rarely seen her father and to have not felt much warmth toward him.[13] Two of the main causes of this belief are the semi-autobiographical novel that Fumiko wrote in 1939 entitled *Hitori no shōgai* (One Person's Life), and an essay she wrote in 1941, "Chichi o kataru" (A Discourse on My Father). In the novel, the narrator tells of her lack of affection for her father, such as in the following statements: "Perhaps it was because I had been separated from him for a long time, but in any case I could not feel even a little love toward my father";[14] and "I must confess here that

I have nothing but hard, cold feelings toward my father, who threw out his own wife and child."[15] The events in *One Person's Life* so closely resemble events in Fumiko's life that it is easy to assume that the former is a true account of the latter, but there is no corroborating evidence that Fumiko truly felt that way about her father. Indeed, there are other events described in *One Person's Life* that apparently never happened in Fumiko's life, such as an affair with a man named Koizumi while she was in Paris.[16] Takemoto Chimakichi addresses this issue in his biography, *Ningen: Hayashi Fumiko* (The Person: Hayashi Fumiko, 1985) and concludes that Fumiko felt strongly about her father, but not in a negative way.[17]

In other works, Fumiko recalled this period of her childhood as a happy one; she harbored no animosity toward Hama and seemed to enjoy her visits to Moji. Kiku and Kisaburō did not object to her spending time in Moji, either. Even after Asatarō and Hama separated, Fumiko is thought to have visited her father often. Some sources even say that Asatarō helped pay for Fumiko's later schooling in Onomichi.[18]

Fumiko thus shuttled between parents, but in October 1914, Kisaburō's clothing store failed and he and Kiku decided to try itinerant peddling again. Kiku left Fumiko in the care of her niece, Tsuru, in Kagoshima. Consequently, Fumiko changed schools again, this time to the Yamashita Elementary School in Kagoshima. Fumiko did not stay long with Tsuru before she was shunted to Kiku's mother's house, also in Kagoshima. Fumiko did not get along well with her grandmother, Fuyu, and she did not attend school often during this time. Details of her life between October 1914 and May 1916 are unclear, but after that period she joined Kiku and Kisaburō on the road, helping them to sell their goods.

In May 1916 the family rented a house in Onomichi, which they used as a base for their peddling business. Fumiko was enrolled in the fifth grade class of the Second Municipal Elementary School in Onomichi. It was at this school that she came under the guidance of a teacher, Kobayashi Masao, who would remain an important figure in her life. Kobayashi was the first teacher to recognize Fumiko's literary talent; he encouraged her to pursue studies in literature, music, and painting. The following year Fumiko asked her mother for permission to continue her education, and Kiku agreed. After passing the entrance examinations, Fumiko was enrolled in the Onomichi Municipal Girls' High School. She paid her own tuition out of money she earned working evenings at a local sail factory and working weekends at a noodle shop. It was also around this time that Fumiko made the acquaintance of a boy named Okano Gun'ichi, a student at the Onomichi Commercial High School. Gun'ichi was Fumiko's first love, and when he graduated in 1921 and moved to Tokyo to attend Meiji University, he wrote to Fumiko and encouraged her to come to the capital after she finished school in Onomichi.

Fumiko did well at painting and composition but she struggled with mathematics and science, so she took remedial lessons from Kobayashi at his house. Kiku and Kisaburō, busy working, were often absent from the house when Fumiko came home from school, so to escape the loneliness at home Fumiko would spend time in the school library, where she eagerly read such works as Jack London's (1876–1916) *White Fang* (1906) in translation, and Suzuki Miekichi's (1882–1936) *Kawara* (Tile, 1911). After her reading comprehension improved, she progressed to such works as Abbé Prévost's *L'Histoire du Chevalier des Grieux et de Manon Lescaut* (The History of Chevalier des Grieux and Manon Lescaut, 1731), Prosper Mérimée's *Carmen* (1847), and Johann Wolfgang von Goethe's *Die Leiden des jungen Werthers* (The Sorrows of Werther, 1774), all in translation. When she became a second-year student she came under the tutelage of Imai Tokusaburō, a Waseda University graduate, who introduced her to the poetry of Heinrich Heine (1797–1856), Walt Whitman (1819–1892), Joseph Freiherr von Eichendorff (1788–1857), Novalis (aka Friedrich von Hardenberg, 1772–1801), Karl Busse (1872–1918), and others. It was also during this time that Fumiko began writing lyrical poetry.

One should note that Fumiko never learned any foreign language well enough to be able to read foreign literature in the original; she read all of the above works in translation.[19] She studied English in school, but she never gained proficiency. She studied French at night school during the time that she spent in Paris in the early 1930s, but her French remained rudimentary. She learned a little Chinese when she visited China in the late 1930s, but it amounted to no more than isolated phrases. Likewise, she learned fragmented Malay while in Southeast Asia in the early 1940s, but never became fluent. Learning words and expressions in foreign languages was entertaining for Fumiko, but she never showed enough interest to continue her studies to an advanced level. In her work she only occasionally comments on her foreign language ability, most notably in "Pari (no) nikki" (Paris Diary, 1947) and "Shiberiya no santō ressha" (Third Class on the Trans-Siberian Railroad, 1932). In the former piece, she records her enrollment in night school in order to learn French, but she says that her French never amounted to much. In the latter, she has stilted but enjoyable conversations with her compartment companions (presumably in English) and also struggles to understand the many foreign languages she encounters throughout the train trip. Itagaki Naoko says that Fumiko did well in language-related subjects in school, and that she enjoyed English, but there is no record of her actual ability in the subject.[20]

She was quite fond of inserting foreign phrases in her text, especially in French, English, and Chinese. With French and English, either she would write the phrase in *kanji* (Chinese characters) and gloss the characters with the pronunciation, or simply write the word phonetically in *kana*. With Chinese, she would write the word in *kanji* and gloss it with Chinese pronunciation. In either case, mistakes were frequent, even allowing for pronunciation changes due to Japanese phonetic limitations. The use of foreign terms was more for decorative emphasis than for anything else. Accuracy was secondary, as long as there was a taste of the foreign language to give the reader a feel for the atmosphere of the story.

The teenage Fumiko was fond of reading, and it is possible that reading books was more enjoyable than reading blackboards, for she was quite near-sighted. Fumiko started to wear glasses from an early age, but she was self-conscious about them and wore them only when absolutely necessary.[21] Many photographs of her show her without her glasses, looking vacantly toward the camera (which must have been but a blur in her vision). Later in her adult years, this myopia translated into a focus on the olfactory as opposed to the visual or aural. Landscapes, people, rooms, and so on are described by their scent. Some works mention scents more than others, but olfactory descriptions are found in almost every piece, both fiction and nonfiction (i.e., travelogues and essays). Some examples follow below:

a) [In a letter to her distant lover:] Even now, your scent remains on my hands. (*Ten Years* in *Shinchō HFZ* vol. 21, 13)

b) "Well, grandmother comes from a family of doctors, so she smells like medicine." (*Ten Years*, 30)

c) Rikue brought the fountain pen up to her nose. It had a sour smell. When she gave it a good sniff, it smelled like a man's hair. Soon that sourness spread like steam and surrounded her on all sides. Rikue turned around and around, trying to blow away the hateful smell. (*Ten Years*, 49)

d) When Yukiko brought her sleeve to her lips, in some way it smelled like Tetsuo. (*Ten Years*, 59)

e) "In [the box] of incense that was sent from Hatoi Temple there is a scent that I like. Whenever I smell that scent, I remember the time when grandmother passed away and there is no stopping the loneliness and nostalgia that ensues."[22] (*Ame* [Rain, 1942] in *Shinchō HFZ* vol. 21, 167)

f) I had become a waitress right down to the smell . . . (*Diary of a Vagabond* in *Shinchō HFZ* vol. 2, 149)

g) When I opened the closet doors I suddenly smelled the odor of a lonely woman living alone. (*Diary of a Vagabond*, 160)

h) "I like *sensei*, she is a good teacher, that's why I like her. I love her smell, too. But, I don't like her smell very much now." (*Kawa uta* [River Song, 1941] in *Shinchō HFZ* vol. 20, 174)

i) The smell of medicine was as refreshing as mountain air. (*Ten Years*, 15)

j) I went outside. A smell of fish wafted through the village. (*Diary of a Vagabond*, 166)

k) It was an evening that spoke of the coming of spring, fragrant with the smells of incense and women. (*Diary of a Vagabond*, 175)

l) Having just come from the bath, my skin smelled strongly of soap. Somehow when I smelled the smell of soap I felt like I wanted to go to France. (*Diary of a Vagabond*, 195)

m) In the theater, dusty from human breath, the smells of tobacco, dried fish, mandarin oranges, and the stench of the toilet all filled one's nose. (*River Song*, 30)

n) When she passed through the Kaminari Gate onto Nakamise Way, her bosom was boiling over with the smells of Asakusa. (*River Song*, 277)

o) Rikue washed her face and opened the window—there must have been a chestnut tree or something somewhere, as she had the sense of a melancholy smell wafting with the breeze into the room. (*Ten Years*, 32)

p) The room was cold and smelled of medicine, and there was a loneliness that stimulated a sense of sadness as one might experience on a journey. (*Ten Years*, 125)

q) Perhaps it was the wind, or the driving rain hitting the bamboo blinds, that evoked a feeling something like the sadness felt on a journey. Mixed with the smell of the incense that had been burning for many days were the smells of dirt and of the kitchen. (*Rain*, 166)

r) Michiko lay her face down on the book of poetry and pressed her eyes against it. The nostalgic smell of the printed paper rose to her nose. (*Rain*, 197)

s) I embraced the smell of the dear wooden box to my bosom and thought warmly of the New Year's gifts I would send home. (*Diary of a Vagabond*, 163)

These passages can be divided into three groups: first, those that use smell to describe characters; second, those that describe settings; and third, those that relate smells to emotions. The first group includes (a) through (h). A person's smell, be it their perfume, their perspiration, or some other odor, brings their image to mind without a visual description. Fumiko does not describe the character's appearance; rather, she describes his/her scent and that often indicates his/her appearance. What is also notable is that although the memory must be partially visual—it would be hard to remember a person without seeing some sort of image of their physical appearance—the vision is omitted from the narrative. In passage (c) Rikue does not see the man from whom she wants to escape, in passage (d) Yukiko does not see Tetsuo, in passage (f) Fumiko does not appear with a soiled apron. Yet all those images pass through the reader's mind with nothing more than the description of the smell.

Sight and smell are different from the other senses in that they do not involve an action by the perceiving actor: touch involves an action by definition, taste necessarily involves the act of consumption, and sound can only be created by an action (i.e., nonaction does not produce sound). Only in the case of sight and smell can an actor be doing nothing else but exercising that sense. Therefore, in order to conjure up an image without an action, the writer has only two choices, sight and smell. The former is much more commonly chosen by writers in general than the latter, so the emphasis that Fumiko puts on smells offers a fresh change. Also, a sight can be described without associated smells entering the reader's mind (the image of a telephone does not bring to mind a certain smell), but smells invariably cause one to envision the object that gives off the odor (the smell of fresh bread immediately brings to mind the image of a hot loaf). Fumiko's scent-based descriptions thus have a richness lacking in purely visual descriptions.

The second group of passages are those that describe settings through smells instead of views. This group includes (i) through (n). Like those passages that describe characters, these passages also usually bring to mind both the smell and the sight of the landscape. Passage (m) particularly does so, as one imagines the thick air swirling in the theater air and the audience lighting and smoking their cigarettes, peeling oranges and popping the sections into their mouths, ripping pieces of dried fish with their teeth and chewing laboriously, and finally getting up to go to the squalid toilet. These actions are not in the passage itself, but they are undoubtedly those that spring to the reader's mind, as the description of the smells of these actions cannot be divorced from the actions themselves in one's mind.

The final group of passages are those that relate smells to a sense of loneliness, melancholy, or nostalgia. A detailed discussion of Fumiko's use of loneliness and nostalgia in her travel imagery follows in chapter 3, but passages (e) and (o) through (s) demonstrate here how she combines smells with these emotions.[23] For example, in passage (o), the smell itself is described as melancholy; this is technically impossible, but the implication is that the smell of the chestnut tree reminds her of something that makes her sad. In passage (e), the smell of incense brings back the memory of a lost grandmother, a memory that causes the speaker to feel nostalgic. In (r), Michiko has no past experiences with the printed page to make her feel nostalgic about the smell of ink, but rather it is the poetry written in such ink that evokes her emotions. In these and the other examples, the smell brings forth a memory that is directly associated with an emotion. Fumiko's use of smell did not change over the years; there are similar passages in works from the earliest days of her writing career and in those she wrote decades later.

YOUNG ADULTHOOD

In 1921, as a fourth-year student at the girls' school, Fumiko had some of her poetry published in *San'yō hinichi shinbun* (The San'yō Daily Newspaper) under the pen name Akinuma Yōko. She also published three poems—"Haien no yūbe" (Evening at the Superannuated Estate), "Kanariya no uta" (Canary's Song), and "Inochi no sake" (Elixir of Life)—in *Bingo jiji shinbun* (The Bingo Current Events Newspaper). Fumiko graduated from the girls' school with poor marks, ranking 76th in a class of 85 students. The combination of not doing well in the sciences and working nights and weekends took its toll on her academic record but it did not prevent her from graduating. Because of her humble origins and the relatively spotty nature of her early education, Fumiko is often thought of as one who never finished school, but this is simply not the case. While her education was not particularly advanced, it did provide her with the basic skills she needed to become the popular writer that she was. It would be an exaggeration to say that she was an extraordinarily gifted child who taught herself to write; Kobayashi and Imai both encouraged and helped her learn more about literature. However, while she continued to read widely as an adult, her literary curiosity never extended into philosophically complex academic questions. Furthermore, her vocabulary never displayed the depth and variety that one would associate with the precocious child she is often said to have been. In sum, she was neither a child genius nor an elementary school dropout; she was a secondary school graduate of average, or perhaps slightly above average, intelligence.

Fumiko decided to take Gun'ichi's advice and move to Tokyo in April 1922. The city held two promises for Fumiko: first, the chance to live happily ever after in a marriage with her childhood sweetheart; second, the opportunity to advance in the literary world. The majority of writers in Japan at the time lived and worked in Tokyo, and it was generally considered the place one should live if one wanted to establish oneself as a writer.

Once in Tokyo, Fumiko had to support herself while she waited for Gun'ichi to graduate from university. She went through a gamut of jobs: public bath attendant, shoe attendant, electrical factory worker, celluloid toy factory worker, parcel wrapper, office worker in a stockbroker's, and more.[24] Soon after Fumiko had moved to Tokyo, Kiku and Kisaburō also moved there and set up a second-hand clothing store in the Kagurazaka area. Fumiko then worked with her mother transporting goods for the store.

In March 1923 Gun'ichi finally graduated, but things did not go as Fumiko had planned. Gun'ichi's family objected to his marrying Fumiko, presumably because of her dubious background, so he ended up breaking his engagement to her. It was a great disappointment for her, but she stayed on in Tokyo working in a café and living in a rented apartment in Shinjuku, not far from where her parents were living. When the Great Kantō Earthquake hit on September 1, 1923, Fumiko fled the city along the coast to Ōsaka, then went to Onomichi, where she stayed at her former teacher Kobayashi Masao's house. It was during this time that Kobayashi suggested she use the pen name "Fumiko."[25] She later went to Shikoku, where she met with her parents who had fled there from the devastated Tokyo area. From about this time on, she began keeping the diary that was the basis for her first novel, *Diary of a Vagabond*.

In 1924, Fumiko returned to Tokyo, where she worked for two weeks as a maid for the writer Chikamatsu Shūkō (1876–1944). She may have intended to stay longer, but two weeks were all she could stand of such work. As she did a few years earlier, she went from low-wage job to low-wage job—celluloid factory worker, salesperson in a wool shop, scrivener's assistant in the city district office, office worker, sushi shop assistant, waitress, and so on—to support herself, but the wages were not sufficient and her parents had to send her money from Onomichi (where they were living) to cover her cost of living.

During this time, she got to know the poet and modern theater actor Tanabe Wakao (1889–1966). She moved in with him, but the relationship did not last long. One day Fumiko found a savings passbook with a balance of 2,000 yen and a love letter from another woman in his bag. Fumiko had been working to support the both of them and barely making ends meet, so the realization that he was hording money plus having an affair was enough to make her leave him after only two or three months.[26] Through Tanabe, Fumiko had met the poet Tomotani Shizue and through her consequently got to know a group of anarchist poets who met on the second floor of a French restaurant in Hongō. The regulars included Hagiwara Kyōjirō (1899–1938), Tsuboi Shigeji (1897–1975), Okamoto Jun (1901–1978), Takahashi Shinkichi (b. 1901), Ono Tōzaburō (b. 1903), Kanbe Yūichi (1902–1954), Tsuji Jun (1884–1944), and Nomura Yoshiya (1901–1940). It was here, too, that she met the nineteen-year-old Hirabayashi Taiko (1905–1972), with whom she became good friends.

The above-mentioned anarchist poets are described by Fukuda in the following way:

> In the literary world [following the end of World War I], emphasis was placed on "labor literature" and the periodical *The Sower* was started as one of the first pieces of proletarian literature [in Japan]. Among the people in this movement [which focused on Proletarian literature], the anarchists composed a faction that strove for the utopian extremes of nineteenth-century European liberal thought. These Japanese anarchists sought the nihilistic pleasures that had arisen in Germany. They were baptized in the surrealist hues of Dadaism. And they were a bit Bohemian on top of it all.[27]

Other accounts describe this group in a similar fashion; the consensus is that the writers who met at the French restaurant composed a group who, in the political turmoil following World War I, were interested in a broad spectrum of leftist movements. But while anarchism, liberalism, nihilism, and Dadaism do not share identical ideologies, they do have one thing in common: they are all antiestablishmentarian. It was this unifying aspect that seems to have interested these poets. Certainly this would have attracted Fumiko too, for she was as far distanced from the establishment as possible. The poets' rhetoric soon wore thin on Fumiko, though, and a few years later she decided that their ideas were too extreme for her tastes and she withdrew from the group.[28]

In July 1924, Tomotani and Fumiko began publishing a pamphlet entitled *Futari* (The Two of Us), which contained poetry by both of them.[29] Funds for publishing *The Two of Us* were provided by Kanbe Yūichi, the publisher of the Dadaist magazine *Damudamu* and one of the anarchists who met regularly at the French restaurant. Fumiko's poetry, particularly her poem "O-shaka-sama" (Lord Buddha, 1924) was highly praised by Tsuji Jun, but *The Two of Us* was discontinued after only three issues. Fumiko had enough confidence in her writing skills, though, to visit and consult with two well established writers during this time: Uno Kōji (1891–1961) and Tokuda Shūsei (1871–1943). Uno Kōji gave her advice on how to write, and Tokuda Shūsei gave her financial assistance.

After separating from Tanabe, Fumiko lived briefly in a boarding house with a young student from Tōyō University who also wrote poetry. Shortly after that she became intimate friends with Nomura Yoshiya (one of the leftist writers mentioned above) and ended up moving into his boarding house with him. Nomura was the critic Chiba Kameo's (1878–1935) nephew and had published an article in a supplemental issue of *Chūō kōron* (Central Review) in June 1923, entitled "Puroretaria sakka to sono sakuhin" (Proletarian Writers and Their Works). He later published two poetry anthologies, *Hoshi no ongaku* (Celestial Music, 1924) and *Sankakukei no taiyō* (Triangular Sun, 1926). Fumiko describes Nomura in *Diary of a Vagabond* as a violent man who beat her.[30] In addition to that, he was a sickly man who could not contribute much to supporting the two of them, which left the brunt of the burden on Fumiko.[31] Eventually he, like Tanabe before him, took up another lover and Fumiko left him in 1926 to move in with Hirabayashi Taiko, who had also recently parted with her lover, Iida Tokutarō (1903–1933).

Fumiko's difficult childhood and experience with Nomura were undoubtedly behind her tendency to write with brutal frankness. Especially in her earlier works, Fumiko often depicts her characters' actions and dialogue with a bluntness not often seen in Japanese literature from the period. She prefers her characters to have clearly defined opinions and behavior rather than vague responses and ambiguous references. The result may have shocked some contemporary readers, as Fumiko does not shy away from depicting psychological and physical violence. The following passage, from her novel *Inazuma* (Lightning, 1936), demonstrates this. The two characters involved are the heroine, Kiyoko, and Takakichi, a man whom her family wants her to marry. Kiyoko does not want to be party to an arranged marriage, but Takakichi is persistent. It is near the end of the story, and Takakichi has come to Kiyoko's place searching for his sister, Mitsuko, who has disappeared. Kiyoko is vexed by his presence:

> Takakichi had a boil-like abscess under his right ear, and he had a dark plaster stuck on it. His face looked oddly inhuman, and there were frightening dark circles under his eyes. He put an Asahi cigarette between his pale swollen lips and gestured for a match. Kiyoto feigned disinterest; she found the whiteness of the cigarette between Takakichi's lips pathetic. Takakichi wetted the end of the cigarette and said, "Hey, gimme a match." Kiyoko disgustedly gave him a match, promptly took her suitcase out of the closet and began changing her clothes.
> "Hey!"
> There was no reply.

"Kiyoko . . ."

"What?"

"How stupid! What are you doing in such a huff?"

Again there was no reply. Kiyoko stood in front of the full-length mirror and began arranging her hair, but she found the scar above her own lip terribly ugly. Takakichi suddenly stood up. He threw the cigarette out the open window onto the street below and stood next to Kiyoko, but he smelled so of the plaster that she said, "What are you doing?" and pushed his body away. Takakichi pushed Kiyoko down on the *tatami*, breathed heavily and brushed her hand away from her chest. She had lied [about Mitsuko's whereabouts] and now having been pushed down like this made her see the poplar tree outside her window like a cloud of blue smoke. The sun was high in the sky, and the dizzying warmth spread through the *tatami*.

"Ba . . . Bastard! What are you doing?! I'll scream, you idiot! Damn you!"

The thread in her shoulder seam was ripped and threatened to tear off. Takakichi's arm closed on Kiyoko's neck like a piece of steel. Dirty spittle gathered on his lips as he glared at her, but she glared back and brought both her hands up to his jaw.

"Stop it! I said stop it . . . Idiot!"

"So I'm stupid and full of shit, eh? You brazen . . ."

Takakichi pushed Kiyoko against the wall with his brawny strength. Pressed underneath Takakichi's thick, heavy chest, Kiyoko shut her eyes, resignedly curled up her body and listened intently to the hot-tempered pounding of his heart. Takakichi's breath was stifling as he brought Kiyoko's face up to his own, but she suddenly drew in her chin and bent backwards, like an owl righting itself, and bit his left cheek with a sharpness that drew a spray of blood.[32]

This violent passage is not unique in the novel. The relatively civilized conversation that Kiyoko has with her neighbor, Kunimune, a few pages later would be unremarkable in a different setting but surrounded as it is by such violence it stands out from the page.[33] The characters seem to take such brutality in stride as an unpleasant but unavoidable part of life.

Another particularly violent passage can be found in the short story "Kuroitseru Sonata" (Kreutzer Sonata, 1949) in which a husband, Kōji, and wife, Namiko, try to deal with their hopeless marriage. The two dislike each other intensely, as is clear in this scene in which they fight about whether to separate:

Namiko stood up and went into the sitting room to close the door to the kitchen. Kōji shook both his hands with rage and said harshly, "You are not human."

"Well, if I am not human, what are you? Less than an animal?

You'd best start thinking about working instead of torturing the weak [maid] with your wild delusions."

Namiko stood up suddenly. Kōji tripped her and slapped her face as she lay toppled on the floor. She staggered on her knees toward the alcove and pressed her hands to her nose.

"See? See? You are demented. It's you who's the animal." Blood ran from between her fingers. Kōji kicked her firmly in the back at this retort.

"Who's demented? Before you start talking back to me you should consider your own state of affairs. You keep telling me to get to work, get to work—don't you think I want to? It makes me so angry when you act as if work is just out there rolling around like a bunch of loose potatoes!"

Namiko stood up and took a piece of tissue from the dresser to wipe the blood off her fingers. "I'm sure you'd be at peace if you killed me, but I can't be killed so easily. I will hate you the rest of my life."[34]

A few pages later the two fight again with equal ferocity:

Namiko violently grabbed Kōji's hair as if she meant to tear it from his head. Kōji had his hand around Kiyoko's shoulders and would not let go. Namiko thrust her leg out in the direction of the children and hastily tried to wake them. When her leg thumped into them they cried out as if someone had set fire to them.

Kōji got up suddenly without saying a thing, but he stepped on the hem of the mosquito netting and it came down heavily on his head.

"What're you doing? If you're going to kill me, then please do so! What an outrage! What's all this sweet talk of yours?" Namiko cried.

Kōji kicked Namiko's hip violently as she moved at his feet. An uncontrollable, furious anger boiled up inside of him. He kicked her forcefully two or three times. He stomped on her shoulder and her face with his feet and kicked her some more. The mosquito net came loose on all sides. Namiko howled like a beast and did not fight back. The two children sat and cried frantically in the dark, terror-stricken at their parents' fighting.[35]

The violence here, as in the passage from *Lightning*, is blunt and raw. There is no subtlety in the confrontation, there is no word play, there are no actions that imply a hidden meaning. These scenes have shock value; they are simultaneously so frightful and so seductive that the reader cannot help but be drawn to them. If used too often, they would become distasteful, but Fumiko is generally careful to use them sparingly enough to prevent repelling her readers.

This tendency to describe scenes in a rough manner may be due in part to the influence of Fumiko's impoverished childhood; being the daughter of itinerant peddlers would hardly have taught her refined diction. It may also be due to her experiences as a young woman, particularly those while she was living with her abusive lover, Nomura Yoshiya. Certainly the scenes in which she describes the fights she had with Nomura are quite similar to those above; such as the following scene from *Diary of a Vagabond*:

> When I told him I didn't want him around where I worked, Nomura picked up an ashtray and threw it at my chest. Ashes flew into my eyes and mouth. I felt like my rib bones had been snapped. When I ran away out the door, Nomura grabbed my hair and threw me to the floor. I thought maybe I should pretend to be dead. He kicked me over and over again in the stomach.[36]

Despite the immediate unpleasant sensation the reader may experience when reading such passages, this lack of subtlety, allusion, or innuendo also makes the work more accessible to a general audience, as one need not meditate on possible intricate nuances, nor wade through pages of psychological introspection. This is not to say that all of Fumiko's writing is a litany of blunt narrative; both of the heroines in *Drifting Clouds* and "Late Chrysanthemum" are noted for the subtlety with which Fumiko portrays their emotions, and of course there are plenty of other works in which she displays similar writing skills. However, I think that her avoidance of rumination and adherence to straight description of physical events without the interjection of character's thoughts probably accounts for a good deal of her popularity. Readers who had little patience for pages of intellectual meditation could find immediate gratification in reading Fumiko's fast-paced novels.

Fumiko's blunt language also leaves little room for differing reader interpretations: there is no question that the characters heap abuse and violence upon one another, and that this is what the author wants to convey. She makes no attempt to metaphorize these events, to make them in some way poetic, soft, or lyrical, or to depict them in an abstract manner. Instead, she presents them in the most ingenuous manner possible, her frank voice presenting her audience with the naked truth.

After Nomura left her in 1926, Fumiko supported herself by selling manuscripts and working as a café waitress, but Hirabayashi soon decided to marry Kobori Jinji (1901–1959), a colleague of hers, which left Fumiko without a roommate. She temporarily moved back home to Onomichi and lived with her parents, where she wrote the first draft of the short story "Fūkin to uo no machi" (The Accordion and the Fish Town), which is about her childhood in Onomichi. She soon returned to Tokyo and rented a room with money she earned working as a waitress in Shinjuku. It was then that, while visiting Hirabayashi Taiko's former lover Iida Tokutarō at his home in Hongo, she met a painter named Tezuka Rokubin (1902–1989), the man she would eventually marry.[37]

Rokubin was born January 6, 1902, the second son of a farming family in Nagano Prefecture. When he met Fumiko, he was studying Western-style painting in Tokyo while receiving an allowance from home. He was a quiet and friendly man, quite a contrast to Fumiko's previous lovers. The two were married in December 1926. Years later Rokubin would change his family registry to Fumiko's and take her surname, Hayashi. He also later abandoned his painting career—although he continued to paint recreationally—and devoted himself to promoting his wife's writing career. He managed the family's finances shrewdly enough to amass quite an estate; even after Fumiko's early death in 1951, Rokubin continued to live off estate funds until his own death in 1989. Rokubin was a patient and good-natured man who was able to live with Fumiko's habit of disappearing for days at a time when she set off on trips by herself. All records indicate that the two of them had a happy marriage, despite the amount of time they spent separated; Fumiko almost never traveled with her husband, and she spent quite a bit of time on the road.

In January 1927, Fumiko and Rokubin rented an apartment in Shinjuku. At the time, Rokubin had not quit working yet and was painting theater backdrops. Then in May, they moved again to another rented house in Wadahori. Fumiko's short story "Seihin no sho" (A Record of Honorable Poverty, 1931) was based on the couple's life during this time. In July 1927 Rokubin went to his hometown in Nagano, after which he passed through Onomichi, where he met up with Fumiko, who had arrived there earlier on her own. They went together to visit Okano Gun'ichi (Fumiko's first love), then went to Takamatsu and visited there with Fumiko's parents, Kiku and Kisaburō, for about three weeks.

In October 1928, Fumiko published *Aki ga kitan da* (Autumn Has Come), the first installment of what would later be the novel *Diary of a Vagabond* in the magazine *Nyonin geijutsu* (Women and the Arts). The magazine had been founded in 1928 by Hasegawa Shigure (1879–1941), a playwright and poet.[38] Hasegawa's husband and sponsor of *Women and the Arts*, the writer Mikami Otokichi (1891–1944), had admired a poem of Fumiko's that Hasegawa had earlier published in *Women and the Arts*. Fumiko had given the manuscript of *Autumn Has Come* to an editor in the cultural affairs division at *Yomiuri shinbun* (The Yomiuri News), a man by the name of Hayashi Jōji, but he had thrown it in his desk drawer and not looked at it further. Upon hearing this, Mikami made arrangements for *Women and the Arts* to acquire the manuscript, which was subsequently published and received quite favorably by the readership.[39] More details on the publication history of *Diary of a Vagabond* follow in chapter 2, but here I should like to note that the appearance of *Diary of a Vagabond* marked Fumiko's true debut as an author. Up until that time she had published a half-dozen poems and short stories in various magazines and newspapers, but few of them were of lasting consequence.[40]

In June 1929, Fumiko published an anthology of her poetry entitled *Ao uma o mitari* (I Saw a Pale Horse). It was the first of eight anthologies she would publish between 1929 and 1939, and it was perhaps the most well known. Fumiko's interest in poetry started when she was quite young, but it was not for her poetry that she later became famous. She persisted in writing poems, though, and perhaps more of her poetry was read as part of her fiction—she often inserted poetry into her prose—than independently. Of the thirty-four poems printed in *I Saw a Pale Horse*, eighteen were originally published as part of *Diary of a Vagabond*.[41] She noted in the prologue of *I Saw a Pale Horse* that all the poems had been published elsewhere before being included in the anthology, but the details of that remain unclear.[42] In any case, *I Saw a Pale Horse* was the result of ten years of writing.[43] The favorable response that both *I Saw a Pale Horse* and *Diary of a Vagabond* received prompted other publishers to solicit Fumiko's manuscripts.

In January 1930, Fumiko made the first of many trips abroad: she and several other women writers went on a lecture tour at the invitation of the Government-General of Taiwan.[44] The travelogues that Fumiko wrote about this trip, "Taiwan fūkei" (The Taiwanese Landscape, 1930), "Taiwan no subuniiru" (A Souvenir from Taiwan, 1930), and "Taiwan o tabi shite" (Traveling in Taiwan, 1930) were the first of many travelogues that she would write in the course of her career. Between 1930 and 1943, Fumiko would make no fewer than a dozen trips abroad and her experiences on those trips became important material for both her travelogues and fiction.

In August 1930, *Diary of a Vagabond* became a bestseller when it was published as part of the *Shin'ei bungaku sōsho* (A Collection of New Literature) series by the publishing house Kaizōsha. With the proceeds from that, Fumiko set off in mid-August on a solo journey to mainland China. She traveled throughout Manchuria and then on to the region around Shanghai, visiting the cities of Harbin, Changchun, Mukden, Fushun, Jinzhou, Sanshili, Dalian, Qingdao, Nanjing, Hangzhou, and Suzhou en route.[45] She returned to Japan on September 25, 1930. Many sources cite Fumiko's later trip to Paris in 1931 as the treat she gave herself after receiving the proceeds from the publication of *Diary of a Vagabond*, but although the Paris trip was certainly partially financed by those proceeds, it was the trip to China in 1930 that was the immediate reward of her literary success.[46]

Fumiko spent the beginning of 1931 traveling in Japan with her mother and grandmother, publishing various short stories including her famous "The Accordion and the Fish Town," and attending various conferences. In the end of the year she decided, rather on spur of the moment, to take a trip to France.[47] In early November 1931, at the age of twenty-eight, Fumiko set out on her rail journey to Paris via Korea, Manchuria, Siberia, and Eastern Europe. She arrived in Paris on December 23, 1931, where she stayed, except for a monthlong sojourn in London (January 23–February 25), until May of the following year.

While in Paris, Fumiko attended night school to learn French, although her travelogues from the time indicate that she skipped class often and was not serious about her studies. She also spent a considerable amount of time being a tourist, traveling about to see various famous places in the Paris and London areas. She attended the theater, concerts, and films, and visited art museums, where she was particularly impressed with paintings by Paul Gauguin (1848–1903), Pierre Renoir (1841–1919), Jean Corot (1796–1875), and Maurice Utrillo (1883–1955).[48] Her friends were predominantly from the Japanese expatriate community in Paris, which meant that while she was not very lonely she did not have many native acquaintances. Her fellow expatriates kept her supplied with recent Japanese publications and she took advantage of the free time she had to do considerable leisure reading. She continued to write and send manuscripts to her publishers while she was in France. She generally enjoyed her time in Paris, but the inability to communicate in French beyond the rudimentary level and the strict budget on which she had to live made her want to leave after six months.

By early 1932 she had run out of money and Europe had ceased to interest her all that much; she wrote to her publisher at the magazine *Kaizō* (Reconstruction) and asked for money to pay for passage home. The money was sent, albeit after a small delay. The return trip was also booked on third-class, but this time aboard the Japanese oceanliner, *Haruna-maru*. The ship made stops in Naples and Shanghai, and in the latter port Fumiko had the opportunity to meet the Chinese novelist Lu Xun (1881–1936), about whom she later wrote an essay.[49] Fumiko arrived home in Japan on June 16, 1932.[50] It was quite an adventure; as discussed earlier, Fumiko's foreign language capabilities were limited at best. Moreover, in keeping with her opinion that travel should be done alone, she set out by herself, which is extraordinary considering her gender and the general conservative attitude toward women at the time.[51]

When Fumiko returned to Japan, her writing was very much in demand. Donald Keene notes that, "Indeed, it is probably no exaggeration to say that she was the most popular writer in the country."[52] From her return to Japan to September 1933, she also spent much time traveling domestically, both on lecture tours and for recreation.[53] This period also marks the first time that Fumiko was financially secure. Proceeds from her writing were finally sufficient to support her and her family; previously she had given what she could to her stepfather, Kisaburō, to support his business ventures, but these had invariably failed, so at this point Fumiko set him up in retirement.[54] She writes in her essay "Chiisaki kyōchi" (Little Viewpoint, 1934) that the feelings she had for her stepfather were not those she had for her mother:

> If I had to make some sort of decent distinction about it, I suppose more than "like" or "dislike" I would have to say that I have begun to feel pity for my stepfather. It is not that I am bothered by the thought of him, but there is nothing I can do about the fact that my affections for him do not match those I have for my mother.[55]

Kisaburō's repeated failures in business, which caused the family to live hand-to-mouth and which later caused Fumiko to feel obligated to send money home even when she herself was living on an extremely constrained budget, contributed to the negative feelings that she had toward him.[56] She had tried to encourage him to retire earlier, but to no avail; Kiku and Kisaburō continued to start new businesses and fail at them until finally they accepted her offer to support them in retirement in early 1933.[57] Mere months later, in November, Kisaburō contracted an acute and fatal case of pneumonia. Kiku moved in with Fumiko and Rokubin, and they lived together—although they moved from residence to residence—until near the end of Fumiko's life.

On September 4, 1933, Fumiko was taken into police custody on suspicion of having promised financial support to the Communist Party.[58] She remained in custody for eight days; it was an experience that she wrote about later in the short story "Yume ichiya" (A Night of Dreams, 1947), in which the heroine is imprisoned for ten days for "thought crimes," although she does not know what she did to bring such a fate upon herself. Through the voice of the heroine, Fumiko ruminates on what "thought" is:

> Just what is "thought"? Is it something you get from someone? Do people have their own thoughts? The thoughts that people have, that's not "thought," but rather each individual's interpretation. Just what is thought?[59]

This shows that Fumiko was thinking about and questioning the legitimacy of the charges against her. Being taken into custody must have been a rude awakening for her, who up until that time had only dabbled in political and philosophical thought. Even during the days when she spent time with the leftist poets, she was never a proponent of one particular school, nor was she ever politically zealous, so being arrested for her political patronage would have been a shock.[60]

One thing which may have lead to and perpetuated her reputation as a political radical was her habit of alluding to big questions or issues in her writing without fleshing out the details of the concern. It is dangerous to try to analyze Fumiko's underlying intent with any great depth, as the author herself was not concerned with the details of the allusion; rather, she was satisfied if her writing contained simply a suggestion of the issue at hand, not a discussion of it. It was as if she wanted the reader to be aware of larger questions in a vague way, a way that would give the illusion of depth and richness without the complication of precise details. She seemed to have a fear of structured ideology, something that may have been a reaction to her earlier days spent associating with the leftist poets, an association that helped get her jailed. Fumiko was not one to be truly interested in academic discussions, but she seemed to take comfort in the knowledge that such discussions existed. She made reference to these discussions through two methods: first, the use of literary and religious allusion; second, the use of broad questions that ask the reader to reconsider commonly held truths.

Fumiko made plenty of literary allusions in her fiction; sometimes characters read famous works, sometimes they recall some lesson they learned while reading foreign works. Like almost any author, Fumiko wrote about what she knew, which means that the literary allusions she made were from books that she herself had read. She mentions in her essays that she was fond of Russian literature, particularly the works of Tolstoy, Anton Chekhov (1860–1904), and Fyodor Dostoyevski (1821–1881), and she also enjoyed the works of the French writer Guy de Maupassant (1850–1893) and the German poet Heinrich Heine. Consequently, many of Fumiko's fictional characters read these authors' works. But nowhere in her essays does she explain in detail why she enjoyed these writers' works, nor do her fictional characters demonstrate clearly why they read what they read. Rather, the simple fact that the characters are reading a certain author's work itself satisfactorily demonstrates for Fumiko's purposes what sort of people they are. There is an assumption on Fumiko's part that the reader will appreciate the meaning of the reference without further explication.

A good example of this can be found in the novel *Mukuge* (Rose of Sharon, 1949), in which much is made of the titles of the books that the characters read, but little is said of the books' contents. *Rose of Sharon* is the story of a young woman, Yōko, who has many different lovers but never seems to be content with any one of them. The one with whom she spends the most time, Nogi, is too intellectual for her tastes. She dislikes sitting at home and waiting for him to come home late from work, so one day as he is leaving for work, he suggests that she read a book while she waits:

"It's raining," Yōko said.

"Uh-huh."

"Why don't you go to work a bit late?"

"I still have time to make it. I'm not going to be purposely late. I'll be back early. If you're bored, try reading those books over there."

"Alright."

"There's Schnitzler's *Life of a Woman*—try reading that. Have you ever read Maupassant's *Life of a Woman?*"

"Yes, I have."

"That's alright, too. Schnitzler's is much more interesting. It would be perfect reading for you."

"Yeah, but I don't feel like reading. I just sit around and wait for you all day. . . ."[61]

They continue their conversation about Yōko's dissatisfaction with being home alone all day, until Nogi has to leave for work. He places the book in her hands and leaves without breakfast. Yōko's younger brother, Tomoji, comes to visit a short while later:

Tomoji took *The Life of a Woman* in his hand and started leafing through it.

"Hey Sis, there wouldn't be a book called *The Life of a Man*, would there? If there were, I'd sure like to read it," he exclaimed.

"The life of a man is nothing but roasting and eating food by the fire," Yōko said laughing, as she put some rice in a basket and took it and a cooking pot downstairs.[62]

In these passages, it is the title of the books, *The Life of a Woman*, which is important; the contents of the novels are not discussed here or later in the text. The original title of Maupassant's novel is *Une Vie* (A Life), the original title of Schnitzler's novel is *Theresa: Chronik eines Frauenlebens* (Theresa: The Chronicle of a Young Woman). In their Japanese translations, both titles are rendered into *Onna no shōgai* (The Life of a Woman), which makes it convenient for Fumiko to draw a parallel where there may not be one.

Nogi seems to be trying to say something important by pressing the book on Yōko, but because he does not explain why he recommends Schnitzler's book over Maupassant's, nor why Schnitzler's would be "perfect reading material" for Yōko, the reader is left suspecting that the passage is meaningful, without knowing exactly why. Later in the novel, we see Tomoji reading the book with fervor, but we never hear his thoughts on it, nor does the narrator tell us why he finds it so interesting. Both Maupassant's *Une Vie* and Schnitzler's *Theresa* are not easily dismissed works; both contain strong social commentary that is hard to ignore. The former is the story of an upper-class woman, Jeanne, who must deal with a lascivious husband and criminal son. The latter is about a poor woman, Theresa, who has dozens of jobs and many different lovers—one by whom she bears an illegitimate son—but who never finds happiness. If one knows this, then Nogi's recommendation to Yōko of Schnitzler's book over Maupassant's makes more sense; Theresa bears more resemblance to Yōko than Jeanne does. But Theresa's frustrations in life are still relatively different from Yōko's, and *Rose of Sharon* as a whole would have benefited if Fumiko had fleshed out Nogi's reasoning.

A similarly vague literary reference appears in the novel *Hatō* (Billows, 1939). This is the story of a young woman, Kuniko, who escapes life in the boring countryside by stealing some money from her father and moving to Tokyo. Unlike Yōko in *Rose of Sharon*, Kuniko is interested in reading and reads quite a collection of works, but the most prominent book in her collection is Maupassant's *Une Vie*. Fumiko gives the reader a little more to contemplate in *Billows* than she does in *Rose of Sharon*, though; Kuniko reflects that her drive to strike out on her own and reject her parents' arrangements for her marriage may be due to having read the book:

> To set out on her own life, to hold the ideal of finding her husband on her own, to think so clearly about feeling such happiness—it must have been due to reading about the miserable life of Jeanne in *The Life of a Woman* . . .[63]

This passage tells us at least that the life of the protagonist of *Une Vie* is not Kuniko's ideal life, but it does not go any further. Fumiko does not give even the most basic details of why Jeanne is miserable—something that would only require a few sentences—and so the unhappiness that Kuniko wants to avoid remains a nebulous concept.

None of this is to say that it would have been better if Fumiko had not mentioned the characters' reading material at all. Certainly we are told something about both Yōko and Kuniko here through their response to the act of reading. The point is that Fumiko baits the reader by mentioning these things in passing but leaving the details out. We do not clearly understand why Yōko refuses to read a book when she has leisure time. We do not clearly understand why Kuniko thinks that Jeanne's life is miserable. All we do know is that the act of reading itself (or not reading, as the case may be) reflects the character's traits.

It is curious that Fumiko made such a point of mentioning other literature, especially foreign literature, if only because such an action is often associated with a writer who has given that literature deep and detailed consideration—the kind of study that would involve reading in the original language of publication and perhaps examining secondary source material pertinent to the literature.[64] A prominent example of Fumiko's unqualified reference to other literature is found in the great admiration she expressed for Lev Tolstoy (1828–1910), especially his novel *Voskresenie* (Resurrection, 1899), for in that novel Tolstoy created clear dialogue—dialogue that is so central to the novel that one can hardly discuss the latter without addressing the former—in which his characters discussed politics, philosophy, and literature. It is difficult to imagine Fumiko reading *Resurrection* without reacting to the arguments laid forth on its pages, yet this is what she did.

Resurrection is about the demise of a young woman, Katusha, who, after having an illicit affair with her wealthy master, Nekhludoff, is discarded and left with nothing but prostitution as a source of income. Because of her low social status, she is convicted of a murder that she did not commit. She meets with Nekhludoff at her trial, where he is a member of the jury. The story is narrated by Nekhludoff, who is mortified by the guilt he feels for instigating the process through which Katusha fell to such depravity. The underlying implication is that Katusha is at the mercy of her environment and is unable to do well once she has been defiled by her master. Nekhludoff believes this, for he feels his own actions were the primary environmental determinants of Katusha's actions. Katusha herself also believes this, for she holds Nekhludoff responsible for what has happened to her.

Compared to Tolstoy's more famous *Anna Karenina* (1877), *Resurrection* is rather didactic in tone; in it Tolstoy expresses his dissatisfaction with both the traditional establishment in Russia and with the leftist ideas that had begun to proliferate at the time. Neither political system was satisfactory to him; the poor were oppressed by the upper class in traditional society but the leftists (who promoted the poor's case) were atheists and Tolstoy was a devout Christian. In order to show the problems inherent in both political systems, Tolstoy created two characters, one from each camp, who often discuss politics and through these two much is said about the pros and cons of each ideology. There is also a considerable amount of meditation on social issues on the part of Nekhludoff.

Fumiko's reading of Tolstoy—one that seems oblivious to the complex ideological and theological issues being dealt with in the novel—shows a disregard for complicated academic argument. What Fumiko did see in *Resurrection* was the story of a poor woman, much like herself in her *Diary of a Vagabond* days. Her affinity with Katusha seems to be the core reason why the work held so much appeal for her, even though the Tolstoy character did not share the anti-deterministic beliefs of the narrator of *Diary of a Vagabond*.

Fumiko wrote a poem in 1928 entitled "Itoshi no Kachūsha"

(Beloved Katusha) in which she says that being called Katusha by someone makes her "happier than being called 'Your Highness.'"[65] The final stanza is:

> Katusha, the daughter of serfs, ended up so unhappy
> Swirling snow, Siberia, prison, hard liquor, Nekhludoff
> But I, who was a poor, naive virgin
> Embraced my vast hopes and like an onion in a hopper
> Was raised and set off into the world, large and round.[66]

In this poem she likens herself to Katusha, but other than the fact that they both come from impoverished backgrounds there is little similarity between the Tolstoy heroine and the real-life Fumiko. Katusha is the representative of the oppressed underclass, the people who are fated to suffer and are incapable of overcoming the difficulties that face them. Tolstoy makes this very clear in the text. Fumiko may have been poor, but in her early works she never expressed resignation to her fate. Even the slightest delving into what Katusha represents would have shown that Fumiko was not fundamentally like her. But Fumiko did not look that far; she saw a poor woman and so she saw herself. She ignored the political and social commentary that Tolstoy wove into the text, and instead chose to focus on surface characteristics.

Fumiko's distaste for detailed examination of academic and philosophical issues can also be seen in her treatment of religion in both her fiction and her essays. She was not a Christian, although she had a certain amount of interest in reading stories from the Bible, and she enjoyed attending church services when she was a young woman living in Tokyo. In *One Person's Life*, she says:

> I started going to church every Sunday [after I moved to Tokyo]. I suppose you could say that I first started thinking about writing when I heard a bit of a sermon on the street one day and thought how it might be helpful. In church, one spoke freely, and I heard things which I had never heard before. It was there that I also learned the names of foreign writers. Judas' betrayal, the story of Abraham, Noah's flood—being a newcomer to the big city I soaked them all up like moss soaks up water. I learned quite a lot, albeit haphazardly, from these free lectures. Despite all this, I still loved the works of Shelley, who had been hounded out of the university for espousing the ideas of atheism. . . .
>
> For me, too poor to pass through the gates of any vocational school, church was like my own university. It soothed my spirit and comforted me, and for that I was grateful. It was at church that I learned about medieval religion and literature. I was not the kind of true believer who would fall to her knees before God, but I felt a strong feeling for faith in something. . . . I must have been a terrible pessimist

toward life before I had faith in God. Whenever I felt uneasy, I would go to church and listen vacantly to the distant, eternal sermon, and it would calm my feelings of peril.[67]

We can see that Fumiko was fond of Christian mythology and that she felt a certain comfort when in church. But the language she uses to describe these things is purposely noncommittal: "faith in something" and "listen vacantly to the distant eternal sermon" do not imply a specific adherence to Christian doctrine. She felt that religion was important, and she had respect for the "true believers," but she did not share their fervor. Rather, the knowledge that there existed some greater power and that there existed a carefully crafted structure of organized religion to communicate the wisdom of that power to the common man was all that Fumiko wanted to understand; she did not want to understand the power or know the actual structure (i.e., Christian doctrine). Her reverence for organized religion was not limited to Christianity, either. She recognized the important role that Shintoism and Buddhism played in Japanese society—a role that bonded the community and provided moral structure—and she was distressed to see that role diminishing. In her journal *Sakka no techō* (Author's Notebook, 1951) she comments on the changes evident in both Buddhism and Shintoism in modern Japan:[68]

> Temples have become just some place where there is a large sitting room. They aren't Sunday meeting places for villagers, but rather they have become buildings that are only useful for funerals. I think that Japanese Buddhism must be reconsidered.[69]

She goes on to note how folk religion has become equally corrupt. She does not say that the Japanese should embrace Christianity; she merely suggests that the Japanese people should take new stock in their religious beliefs, which suggests that she felt a "strong faith in something" would be beneficial to others, as well as herself. Further definition of religious beliefs did not interest her, however. In no place does she discuss individual lessons from the Bible or from the Buddhist *sūtra*, or any details from any religious doctrine.

Fumiko does occasionally question the validity of organized religion, and these questions echo the distrust she displays toward defined structural arguments. In the following passage from *Diary of a Vagabond*, Fumiko hears the cries of Salvation Army volunteers and reacts by questioning the good of organized religion for the poor:

> Poor people don't have the time or energy to believe in Jesus Christ or Shakyamuni. Just what is religion?! [The Salvation Army volunteers] don't have to worry about where their next meal is coming from, that's why they spread out in little groups into the streets.[70]

Fumiko's characters often vacillate on religious questions, unable to make firm statements without doubt, which implies that anything but blind "faith in something" may be too much for men to contemplate, as in the following is a dialogue from *Kawa uta* (River Song, 1941). This is the story of two women, Kikuyo and her former teacher, Hisako. Hisako teaches elementary school and among her students is a girl named Shimagi who is particularly precocious. Hisako takes a special interest in Shimagi and tries to provide her with the guidance that she so desperately needs. One day, Shimagi asks Hisako about the origin of the world:

> "Say, *sensei*, who created the world?" Shimagi said, changing the subject.
> "That would be God," said Hisako. . . . But she herself could not grasp clearly the image of "God."
> "You know, lately I have been thinking all about weird things—I think it will drive me to a nervous breakdown," said Shimagi.[71]

Even though Hisako can assuredly say that "God" created the world, she cannot quite grasp what the concept "God" is. Shimagi dismisses further rumination on the subject by saying that such things are just too much to contemplate. Like the author, the characters display a disinterest in complex issues. This scene is characteristic of the way in which Fumiko deals with all philosophical questions. It is enough for the characters to have vague notions of issues; any more would be too much, as it would require that the characters—not to mention the author herself—take a firm stand on philosophical issues, something Fumiko was not interested in doing.

SUCCESS AS A WRITER

The years 1934 and 1935 saw Fumiko busily traveling around the country giving lectures and paying visits to friends and supporters. She was writing and publishing many short stories, but the main publications from these years were second editions of the works that made her famous: *Diary of a Vagabond* and "A Record of Honorable Poverty." In September 1935, Fumiko published one of her most celebrated short stories, "Kaki" (The Oyster, 1935), about a young man, Shūkichi, whose life is a downward curve into failure. Three things made "The Oyster" different from other stories Fumiko had written up to that point: it has a story line that is not based on the author's personal experiences, it features a male protagonist, and it has mature character development heretofore unseen in Fumiko's writing. Fumiko had written nonautobiographical stories before, but "The Oyster" was a true departure in that its protagonist, Shūkichi, shares nothing in common with Fumiko, save his penury. While "The Oyster" was a successful, popular work, it still had one major fault: in it, Fumiko tries to use political vocabulary to write about the plight of the working class, but her days spent with the leftist poets in the French restaurant were over and her sympathies toward leftist movements were not strong enough to make the political passages convincing.

"The Oyster" is the story of a man who loses his job sewing cheap satchels because his employer mechanizes the shop. He loses self-respect, and gradually goes insane with paranoia. The story is touching in places—Fumiko depicts Shūkichi's faltering relationship with his common-law wife quite well—but didactic. The narrator's emphasis on Shūkichi's oppression is excessive and the leftist lectures are too stilted to fit smoothly into the text. In the following scene, Shūkichi warns a friend and fellow worker, Tomikawa, about what will befall laborers such as themselves in the future:

> Maybe you haven't heard yet, but it seems there's a new factory in Minoda that's started mass production of low grade goods. I guess all that stock stored in Ōsaka will be counted as wasted labor wages. The market will be overflowing with machine-sewn cheap leather. How wretched we'll be! And when the boss-man expands the factory, even hand satchels and *Chiyoda* purses will be spit out by machines. I've got to consider the matter carefully. It's all getting quite perilous, isn't it? I don't like the thought of it, but I suppose I could always start a tempura shop—you know, serve *sashimi* and boiled vegetables—like those stores in Tengin. I can't continue making a big deal about being an artisan of *azuma* satchels.[72]

This language is that of a politically aware Luddite, not that of a timid man who is slowly becoming mentally unstable. Fumiko tried to make Shūkichi both a victim and a mouthpiece, but it does not work well. The reader is expected to sympathize with him, but that is difficult when he persists in self-destructive behavior despite the fact that he has demonstrated a strong political awareness of his plight.

The main problem with "The Oyster" is that Fumiko was writing on something about which she herself had doubts. Shūkichi's thoughts are mechanical, and Fumiko never explains exactly why he is so fond of his low-paying job. He works slowly, and the finished product is mediocre. The reader might expect him to jump at a new opportunity, but instead he regresses into paranoia when the prospect of factory mechanization appears. Being a self-made woman who did not romanticize poverty, Fumiko had difficulty portraying a sympathetic protagonist who did. Moreover, the vocabulary of the leftist movement did not suit her writing style; stiff words such as "wages" (*kōchin*) sound awkward embedded in paragraphs that deal with intense emotion. Two years after writing "The Oyster," Fumiko called the incentive which drove her to write it a "foul wind."[73]

Nonetheless, in response to the success of "The Oyster," Fumiko held a commemorative gathering (*kinenkai*) to celebrate its publication on November 14, 1935. The number of famous writers who attended attests to the fame and acceptance that Fumiko had gained; guests included Uno Kōji, Hirotsu Kazuo, Satō Haruo (1892–1964), Tokuda Shūsei, Hayashi Fusao (1903–1975), Hasegawa Shigure, Yoshiya Nobuko (1896–1973), and Sata Ineko (b. 1904). Fumiko paid for the entire event, a considerable sum of 254 yen.[74] She had arrived on the literary scene.

There was another event that signalled Fumiko's acceptance into the *bundan*.[75] In June 1936, the French writer Jean Cocteau (1889–1963) stopped in Japan while he was on a world tour. Fumiko was selected by Kikuchi Kan (1888–1948), one of the most prominent figures in the *bundan*, to be his representative to go and meet Cocteau at the Kabuki Theater and present him with a bouquet of flowers. Fumiko had met Cocteau before in France, which was probably one of the reasons Kikuchi selected her, but Kikuchi would not have chosen her solely for that reason.

However, even after Fumiko was an established and accepted writer, she was critical of the *bundan* and its tendency to be an old-boy network. In her collection of essays *Sōsaku nōto* (Creative Notebook, 1938) she says that the *bundan* was an curious entity because it gave no consideration to anything published in women's magazines. She went further to say that the reason young writers were unable to write with any freedom was because the literary world refused to extend a helping hand from behind the high walls with which it surrounded itself.[76] The grudge that Fumiko harbored against the establishment did not prevent her from becoming an accepted part of it, but she never seemed eager to build literary friendships for the sake of social connections.

But what provided Fumiko's incentive to write? What was her literary muse? During and immediately after the years that she was writing *Diary of a Vagabond*, Fumiko wrote various essays in which she says that she felt compelled to write, that writing for her was a comfort, and that she simply did it because she enjoyed it immensely. Writing was a difficult task for her, even if she felt naturally driven to do it. In her 1935 essay *Seikatsu* (Everyday Life), she described how she spent her days: she filled the daylight hours with reading the newspaper and doing household chores because she found other people's presence so distracting that she could only work in the early morning hours, when the house was dark and quiet. The structure of the essay reflects the way she spent her day; it jumps from one subject to another, unable to focus on one topic, until finally it settles upon describing the process of writing:

> When the clock strikes ten, everyone in the house says their goodnights. I find it scary with everyone in bed, so I make the rounds of the house, checking all the locks. Then I make a midnight snack in the kitchen and take it upstairs. I'm very happy if we have some salted *kombu* and dried bonito on hand. It's been chilly lately, and there's nothing I can do about the cold taking its toll on my body. I long to write a verse . . . and as dusk comes, I end up sitting in front of my desk, savoring the pain and joy that writing brings to me. I have a Western style chair, so I get cold when I sit writing for hours at a time. The thing that is the most hateful—the most cruel—when I am writing is being held up for hours searching for one word in the dictionary, all the while feeling like I'm overflowing with emotions that I need to get down on paper. My dictionary is a *Student's Practice Dictionary* that I bought for seventy-five *sen* when I was loafing about in Takamatsu in Shikoku, and it's quite dog-eared now. I've bought plenty of dictionaries since then, but ultimately I prefer to use this one, even though there aren't enough entries. When I think about it, I really do live the life of a country schoolgirl. If I were asked to write something about my life, I would begin to feel strange about the fact that my life is so unspectacular.[77]

Often her late night vigils proved unfruitful, as she could be distracted by the slightest of stimuli around her. She expressed this best in a poem, also in the essay "Everyday Life":

> The clock struck one
> Everyone must be asleep
> Their breathing sounds like an avalanche
> > five thousand miles away
> Two o'clock, Three o'clock
> My paper is still blank
>
> As the clock strikes four
> the brazier runs out of coal
> I open the rain shutters and go to the shed for more
> Grasping the coal lightly in my hands is more pleasant
> Than the chore of writing words
> Somewhere a caged warbler cries out[78]

Alone, in front of her desk, Fumiko struggled with the emotional need to write. She tried to explain that need often, although her sentences often end in indeterminate reasoning. She could only say that she felt writing to be extremely pleasurable, and that she wished she could do it better. In her essay, "Literature, Travel, Etc.," she describes what writing means to her:

Although I still cannot believe that someone like me, with mediocre talents and poor education, can support herself writing novels, I find that uncertainty indescribably enjoyable. . . . I also think nothing of staying up all night for two or three days at a time. Once I set in on my work, I can't eat a thing; all I can do is diligently face the paper before me. But perhaps this state of being is one that only other writers can understand. How pleasing it is! Writing a novel is as pleasing as having one's lover waiting for one.

I've enjoyed reading since I was a child, and it is because of this pleasure that I have endured this far, not doing myself in. I am a true optimist and I hate gloomy things; despite that, I dedicate myself to loneliness. I feel I have come this far through the hunger and longing I have for literature. Even now, my goals are constant hunger and constant longing. . . . I am so full of ambition that my selfishness borders on disgusting. . . . I've been keeping a diary for about five years now. I keep to writing one page every day for my newspaper novel, although there are days when I manage to write three or four pages. I cannot simply lounge about until the mood to write strikes me, like the writers of old would do. Lounging about would make me stupid. There is no point in imposing stupidity upon stupidity.

No matter how difficult it may be, I make it a point to sit myself down at my desk at least once a day in an effort to grow accustomed to such a routine. For someone of mediocre ability, there is no recourse but hard work.[79]

There is no doubt Fumiko was determined to become a successful writer, but after she published *Diary of a Vagabond* she was a little overwhelmed by the attention showered upon her. Suddenly she wanted to escape from the life she had created for herself, one of daily forced work, and one that made her self-conscious of her writing in a way she disliked. She comments in an essay on *Diary of a Vagabond*:

Writing fiction is not an enjoyable activity in the sense that other people see what you are doing. Sometimes I think about giving up on writing altogether. It would be great to go back to writing like I used to—naturally inspired and writing what I want to write. And nobody would see what I was doing. I wrote *Diary of a Vagabond* without thinking about publishing it. Many critics have offered their opinions on that piece, but to me they're all ludicrous. *Diary of a Vagabond* was written during a time that I had no publisher. It goes without saying that I had no intention of publishing it. That is why I wrote such a piece in the first place.[80]

THE INFLUENCE OF YOKOMITSU RIICHI

Fumiko did not belong to any writers' group and she contributed manuscripts to almost any publisher or periodical that requested them, which prevented critics from easily placing her in any specific school of writing. We know that early on she was influenced by the leftist poets, but that influence wore thin quickly. Another influence, heretofore given little notice by critics, was that of Yokomitsu Riichi (1898–1947), a writer whose name is predominantly associated with modernism and the New Sensationalist School (Shinkankakuha), a group of writers active in the late 1920s. Yokomitsu experimented with various writing styles during his lifetime, and two of those styles are reflected in Fumiko's writing: the New Sensationalist School style as used in Yokomitsu's short stories "Maketa otto" (The Defeated Husband, 1924) and "Atama narabi ni hara" (Heads and Bellies, 1924), and the dense-text style that he used in his short story "Kikai" (The Machine, 1930).

Yokomitsu himself was greatly influenced by a number of European writers, including Marcel Proust (1871–1922) and Paul Ambroise Valéry (1871–1945), and he was intent upon experimentation that would depart from previously dominant writing styles.[81] He took the New Sensationalist School movement quite seriously and attempted (albeit rather incoherently) to define what the movement stood for and what virtues its writing had.[82]

Yokomitsu's "The Defeated Husband," along with other early works, is described as "marked by short sentences and by 'jumps' from one statement to the next without logical connections."[83] What Yokomitsu was trying to do in this and other New Sensationalist School–style works was to depict a scene solely by recording the sensations experienced by the narrator, without any emotional response or subjective interpretation. The sentences are generally short, even abrupt, and present vivid images of scenery:

> A little girl with perfectly normal legs was limping hurriedly along imitating a cripple. After her came a truck racing along jammed tight with policemen. The load of policemen stood silently protruding above the cab like black stamens. A car followed after them. There was a girl inside who was tired. The wooden bridge shook as the vehicles passed over. He came to the main road and turned right. Several trams flew by shaking their human bundles to the rear. The crammed flesh ricocheted inside the square trams. Whirlpools of sickly fragrant lust, bounding and leaping.[84]

Each sentence presents new stimuli, much like a set of bright, flashing lights before the reader's eyes. There is little to indicate the response of the protagonist to his surroundings; Yokomitsu depends on the stark imagery to give as objective a description of the scene as possible. When Fumiko wrote in a similar style in *Diary of a Vagabond* and some of the travelogues from Paris, she kept the "jumps" but added a lyrical quality to them. The following passage, from *Diary of a Vagabond*, describes the narrator and her friend, Kimi, relaxing after spending the day together:

> The two of us looked out silently at the distant, cold, vast ocean. I want to be a crow. I think it would be nice to go on a trip, carrying a small satchel. Kimi's Japanese-style coiffure was blown about by the wind, and it looked forlorn, like a willow on a snowy day.[85]

Here Fumiko, like Yokomitsu, uses short sentences and jumps from observation to observation, but the difference between this passage and Yokomitsu's is clear; where Yokomitsu tried to write in a style that expressed only objective observations devoid of all subjectivity imposed by a narrator, Fumiko included the desires of the narrator (by using "I want" and "I think") and her impressions of her companion ("[her hair] looked forlorn").[86]

In Fumiko's travelogue, "Rondon no geshuku sono ta" (A London Boarding House and Other Matters, 1932) the narrative makes such jumps as to be nearly incoherent. The paragraph preceding the following passage tells us that Fumiko has bought her ticket to London, and then goes to a little theater where a film of Cocteau's is being run:

> At the time of death, just a little of Jean Cocteau's stories would be good.
>
> Ah, could there possibly be such a selfish novelist in Japan? To write by oneself, to direct by oneself, to recite poetry between acts, to laugh by oneself, to violently jostle the audience, the audience was stupefied.
>
> "What is that?"
>
> "The nonsense of a poet. Foreigners' nonsense is that sort of thing."
>
> "It is an altogether meaningless film."
>
> "I'm stunned. It's really wonderful."
>
> "Oh, writing novels has become so hateful."
>
> Jean Cocteau asked inwardly, "What, are you surprised?"
>
> It was a film with no plot—Venus went out for a walk, a woman on canvas had her lips pecked at, people entered mirrors, slowly they became water, ahh, how frightening . . . I won't be able to sleep. On the other side of the mirror there were five rooms. It was a traumatic hotel, 1) Room for Ascending Teachers, 2) Opium Room, 3) Rendezvous Room for Those Who Had Lost Hope, 4) Suicide Room for Mexican Revolutionaries, 5) Room for Teachers of Thieves—the audience was driven crazy. One realized the quality of the print when the negro angel was seen through from behind. The negro became white, and I had never before seen a movie that dealt so beautifully with black and white.

"But the road is long."
Jean Cocteau appeared from behind the silenced black and silver curtain to recite a poem about a snowball fight.[87]

Even the apparent eclectic nature of the film that she seems to be describing cannot be fully responsible for the "jumps" in this passage, particularly in the dialogue. With no narrative between quotes, the audience's speech stands starkly isolated from the rest of the text, much in the same way that the images of the limping girl and truck of policemen do in the above passage from "The Defeated Husband." Fumiko makes it even more perplexing by writing many French and English words in *hiragana*, not set off from the rest of the text in any way.[88] The section of text immediately following this passage is equally disjointed:

> *N'est-ce pas*!
> I put down the small trunk I had brought with me from Japan and went to the northern parking area. Why is it I am such a stickler about bringing along my baggage? Isn't that waste paper rattling around in the bottom?
> *Adieu*, university students of Paris! I said, and shaking hands, they gave me a photograph of me standing in the middle of a field and told me it was a souvenir.
> Who is solitary? It is because of their solitude that people become likable. Send us a letter when you get back to Japan.
> "Yes, you too" Hayashi. Fumiko. Got it? *Comprends pas*![89]
> "I understand. Your name is *bois*, too many trees."[90]

This is the end of the section; there is no further explanation of the scene. If rearranged on the page, the text would perhaps read better as poetry than as prose, as one is accustomed to incomplete sentences and vague intimations in poetry, where prose generally demands more precise language. This style of writing appealed to Fumiko if for no other reason than it deviated from the norm, and she was the first to try new things simply because they were new. She used this style predominantly in the early 1930s, during which time she also wrote some works that do not share the same qualities—perhaps an indication that she was exploring different styles in search of one that suited her.

The second of Yokomitsu's styles mentioned above, the dense-text style found in his short story "The Machine," was revolutionary when it first appeared. The writer Itō Sei (1905–1969) described his own reaction to "The Machine" as follows:

> In 1930 Yokomitsu Riichi suddenly changed. This was "Kikai" ["The Machine"], which appeared in the September issue of *Kaizō*. . . . I had just bought the magazine and started to read "The Machine" as I was walking along the main street in Ushigome, and the impression it made

> was such that it took my breath away. He had suddenly dropped the jumpy, impressionistic [New Sensationalist School] method . . . and was now approaching a style that was flexible . . . in which the language went forward without intermission and the printed text had hardly an indentation in it, the type literally crammed on the page.[91]

The style that Itō refers to is perhaps most noticeable when the reader first sets eyes on the printed page; paragraph breaks are rare, dialogue is inserted into texts with no punctuation marks, and sentences tend to be longer than normal. Reading such a densely printed text is a tiring activity, but the draw of the narrative pulls one along until, pages later, there is a break in the narrative where one can lift one's eyes from the page.

Fumiko wrote about her own impression of Yokomitsu's writing in the following way:

> Recently I have been reading Yokomitsu Riichi's work. There is no space between his words, nor a wasted breath between his sentences. I was tired upon the first reading. Upon the second reading I felt a sort of attraction toward his work, and upon the third reading, I had great respect for his style. Yokomitsu's style is something that I could not achieve even if I tried over the course of decades. I wonder if there is anybody in the world of proletarian literature who has such a firmly rooted style? I have thought of trying to write my "literature of poverty" in this sort of dense style, using much *hiragana*, but for me it is still quite a difficult task.[92]

This was written in 1931. In the years that followed, Fumiko published many works that used the same tightly packed style of "The Machine," some of which were: "Izumi" (The Spring, 1936), "Meian" (Lightness and Darkness, 1936), "Hototogisu" (The Cuckoo, 1938), "Bangiku" (Late Chrysanthemum, 1948), "Yoru no kōmorigasa" (Evening Umbrella, 1948), "Suisen" (Narcissus, 1949), "Gyūniku" (Beef, 1949), and "Hone" (Bones, 1949). But none of these works copied anything more than the physical structure of the printed page. Like "The Machine," "The Spring" and "Lightness and Darkness" both have tightly packed text with few breaks and both make liberal use of *hiragana*, but this is where the similarity ends.[93] Whereas Yokomitsu wrote in long, flowing sentences, Fumiko could only manage to do so for the first few pages of "The Spring," after which she reverted to her familiar short, choppy sentences. In "Lightness and Darkness" the text begins with short sentences that never change to longer ones. The texts' appearance on the page reflects the dense style in which Fumiko said she wished she could write, but they do not cause the reader to feel pulled along by the narrative, as "The Machine" does, because they lack an important element: stream of consciousness. In "The Machine," there are few convenient breaks for the reader, few places where he can lift his eyes from the page for a moment of introspection; he feels constantly pulled by the narrative to continue reading. The stream of consciousness in "The Machine" does not clearly distinguish one thought from the next; it records a continuous, rather than discrete, series of thoughts. Tanigawa Tetsuzō described Yokomitsu's style in "The Machine" as "'arabesque-like' associationist" writing, referring to the natural flow of the text in which the narrator strings together his thoughts, feelings, and sensations.[94] The smoothness of the flow is partially due to consistent first-person narration and is aided by the absence of dialogue; the resulting text is one constant chain of thought produced by one voice. However, "The Spring" and "Lightness and Darkness" never achieve this "associationist" quality because the narratives are told in the third person and are interrupted by dialogue. When Fumiko set out to write in the style of Yokomitsu, to create a text that would attract her readers the way she describes being attracted by Yokomitsu's work, she did not take the necessity of a first-person narrator or stream of consciousness into consideration. The result is texts that tire the reader (as she said Yokomitsu's did upon first reading) but fail to captivate him.

THE INFLUENCE OF TOKUDA SHŪSEI

Another writer who strongly influenced Fumiko was Tokuda Shūsei. She met Shūsei in 1924 in Tokyo when he was already a firmly established writer and she had yet to publish anything. He gave her a bit of money to help her along, and their long-lasting friendship was established. Fumiko was fond of Shūsei's writing and she complimented him in her essays, saying that she admired the fact that he welcomed her visits despite the fact that she was poor and had no introduction.[95] She does note, however, that he never took a look at her manuscripts in the way a mentor might be expected to do.[96] Their relationship was more of a professional friendship than that of mentor and disciple. Still, there are some similarities in their writing worth noting.[97]

Perhaps their most prominent similarity lay in subject matter; both writers wrote often about people who lived in poverty. Of course, this in itself was certainly not unique during the heyday of proletarian literature (the 1920s), but what made Fumiko and Shūsei's writing different from the rest was the relative lack of leftist political polemics. Neither writer was interested in portraying the lower classes in a way that would promote the Marxist idea of bourgeois oppression of the proletariat. It was simply that poverty was familiar to both writers, and it was natural for them to write about that which they knew best. Shūsei was criticized by Sōseki for writing a novel that "had no philosophy."[98] Fumiko, however, did not totally avoid philosophical statements in her writing; rather, her statements were vague, and when characters who are interested in philosophy and politics speak their minds, they are rarely portrayed in a positive light. In *Shūsei kara Fumiko e* (From Shūsei to Fumiko, 1990), Mori Eiichi notes three other similarities between Fumiko's and Shūsei's writing: temporal layering, the use of onomatopoeic language, and a change in mid-career from autobiographical novels (*shishōsetsu*) to standard fictional novels (*honkaku shōsetsu*).[99] It is certainly possible, as Mori suggests, that Fumiko was imitating the temporal layering in Shūsei's novel *Kabi* (Mildew, 1911) when writing such earlier works as "Obihiro made" (All the Way to Obihiro, 1933), "The Oyster," and "Kareha" (Dried Leaves, 1936), but there were other established writers who used the same method, such as Nagai Kafū and Uno Kōji.[100] It would be hard to single out Shūsei as the single writer who influenced Fumiko to write in this manner.

The same could be said of the use of onomatopoeic language and the change from autobiographical works to standard novels. Shūsei and Fumiko were not the only writers to do either of these things, so it is impossible to say that the latter was directly influenced by the former. In her essays, Fumiko mentions many of Shūsei's works but her admiration is quite general and does not touch on the structural specifics mentioned above. A typical example, from her essay "Master Shūsei," follows:

> I have been reading Shūsei's works since the time that I myself started writing novels. Now that I have a few years under my belt, I have come to appreciate the flavor of his writing. I still savor his *Footprints* or the clique depicted in "The Story of a Prostitute."[101]
>
> Of his short stories, the one I like best is "The Folding Satchel," in which he describes losing his wife; it is brief and lucid.[102] There is no argumentation in Shūsei's writing. I also enjoyed the novel *The Stubby Spirit* written about the time he lived in Hakusan.[103]

There are numerous passages, similar to this one, that praise Shūsei's works but do not describe specifically what it is about the work that is good. This is not surprising, given Fumiko's dislike of detailed analytical thought, but it does not help matters, either, if one wants to pinpoint what it was about Shūsei that Fumiko might have felt worth emulating in her own work. I think that Shūsei indeed had some influence on Fumiko, but it is perhaps most evident in the inspiration he instilled in her, not in specific stylistic mannerisms passed from one writer to the other.[104]

THE EARLY WAR YEARS

In October 1936, Fumiko set out on a short trip to northeastern China, where she met up with Rokubin, who had been in China since May of that year on a sketching trip. They returned to Japan together shortly after that. In November 1937, Rokubin was conscripted into the army and was stationed in Utsunomiya, where he served as an assistant nurse for two years, during which time Fumiko apparently had occasional contact with him. She wrote about the day Rokubin's draft notice came in her essay "Ōshō zengo" (Before and After the Conscription, 1937). Both she and Rokubin expected the draft notice, so its arrival was no surprise, but Rokubin's departure left Fumiko slightly numb and critical of the war. She did not share the pride that Rokubin's father expressed at the thought of his son serving in the army.[105] She did not write much about him during his absence, although she did note that she thought of him while talking with Japanese soldiers in China, and her language indicates warm feelings and affection for her husband.[106] Rokubin remained in the army until July 1939.

By late 1937, Japanese military activity in China had greatly escalated and the fall of Nanjing to Japanese troops in December 1937 prompted Fumiko to travel to Shanghai and Nanjing, this time as a reporter for *Mainichi shinbun* (The Daily News). Other writers also participated in wartime reportage, as Donald Keene notes:

> No sooner had the fighting broken out near Peking than various magazines dispatched war correspondents to China. As early as July [1937] *Chūō kōron* sent the novelists Hayashi Fusao and Ozaki Shirō to Shanghai, and in September *Bungei shunjū* sent the dramatist Kishida Kunio and the critic Kobayashi Hideo. These writers, and many others who followed them to China, normally described their experiences first in newspaper and magazine articles, later in full-length books. . . .
>
> Most of the correspondents, whether sent by the government or by some magazine, spent no more than a month or two in China, just long enough to become accustomed to the sight of Chinese corpses littering the wayside. The reporting of the scenes of war was almost always on a popular level, and the interesting, if ill-informed comments undoubtedly influenced the way Japanese at home thought of the war.[107]

Fumiko was one of these correspondents; she accompanied Japanese troops on the front for one month and was the first Japanese woman in the city of Nanjing after its fall.

The Japanese government began to realize that popular writers could help their cause by glorifying events at the front for those citizens supporting the war effort at home. Keene records:

In August 1938, the Information Section of the Cabinet (Naikaku Jōhōbu) had held a meeting with various literary men to discuss the participation of writers in the projected attack on Hankow.[108] All except Yokomitsu Riichi, who asked to be sent to Peking, expressed their eagerness to serve with the troops. An organization, known as the Pen Unit (*Pen butai*), was formed, but so many writers wished to join that not all could be accommodated.[109]

Fumiko was one of the writers who was accepted into the *Pen butai*, and it was as a *Pen butai* reporter that she went to Shanghai in November 1938. In an event that almost every biographer has recorded, Fumiko was incensed that her rival, Yoshiya Nobuko, had been chosen by *The Daily News* to cover the fall of Hankou in November 1938. She responded by abandoning the Pen butai group and boarding an *Asahi News* truck headed for the front. She was the first Japanese woman in Hankou after its fall, as she had been in Nanjing the previous year. *Asahi News* published her account of the trip in December 1938, entitled *Sensen* (Battlefront), which sings the praises of the Japanese army. A second account, *Hokugan butai* (The North Bank Unit) was published by *Chūō kōron* the next month. Both works express the same emotions; indeed, the two contain many similar passages, indicating that Fumiko was stretching her manuscript to meet demands from two different publishers. Fumiko paid a price for her ambitiousness; she fell victim to the malaria epidemic that ran through the Japanese troops, although it seems her case was a relatively mild one.[110]

THE WAR YEARS

From the time she had arrived in Tokyo in 1922 until late 1939 Fumiko had changed residences at least a dozen times, not to mention the amount of moving that she did as a child. This peripatetic lifestyle was second nature to her, but a turn of events in 1940 changed her situation. At the time she was living in Shimo-ochiai, and when she found herself forced to move she decided to buy a house instead of rent one. She wrote later of her decision:

> I never imagined that in my life I would build a house but then I absolutely had to move out of the rented house I'd been used to for eight years so I took the time to walk around looking for a house to rent. At first I thought I'd like to live in the downtown area of Yanaka but after getting to know the place I couldn't find a house I liked. Thinking again, I found it hard to leave this Shimo-ochiai that I had become so used to and I began to think that it would be nice to get a plot of land in this area and build a little house.[111]

In reality, the building project on which Fumiko embarked was far from "little." She put an enormous amount of time and effort into the construction of the house where she would live the rest of her life. If she was going to build a house, she was going to build it right:

> Finding the money to build the house was difficult so a year went by before we could start construction. In that time I found nearly 200 reference books on house building and gained a rough idea about timber, tiles, and carpentry.
>
> I wanted to choose a first-class carpenter.
>
> First I drew up a plan of my house and showed an elevation of the plot to the builder Yamaguchi Bunshō, who worked on and improved the plan for over a year. I was convinced that it was important for my house to let the four winds pass through it. I also wanted to save money on the spare rooms and spend extra on the tearoom, bathroom, water closet and kitchen.
>
> Even so, we didn't have the money saved up for building the house so it was rather like crossing a dangerous bridge but if it was to be my home for life the greatest thing was to make it a sweet and beautiful one. Well, the knowledge gained from my reference books made me want to find a good carpenter so I spent months studying the work of one who was introduced to me.[112]

The plot of land was purchased in December 1939. The house was a splendid affair with a large garden, a pond where Fumiko raised goldfish, and a separate storehouse. The house itself was divided into two wings, with rooms for Rokubin's studio, Fumiko's study, Fumiko's library, Kiku's room, a guest parlor, and three other general purpose rooms. This house was about as distanced from Fumiko's hardscrabble *Diary of a Vagabond* days as possible; by any definition, it was a wealthy family's estate.[113]

From October 1942 through May of the following year, Fumiko traveled to French Indochina, Singapore, Java, Borneo, and Sumatra as a member of the Japanese News Corps (*Hōdōhan*), a large group of writers sent to the area in 1941 and 1942 "to create friendship and understanding between the local people and the Japanese" as part of the Japanese government's effort to promote the idea of the Greater East Asian Co-Prosperity Sphere.[114] Like other writers in the corps, Fumiko spent most of her time getting to know the natives of the area. The works that resulted, including "Sekidō no shita" (Below the Equator, 1943) and "Sumatora—Seifū no shima" (Sumatra—Island of the Western Wind, 1943), are void of the political agenda seen in *Battlefront* and *The North Bank Unit*; indeed, they almost never mention the war.[115] Fumiko's experiences in French Indochina also became important material for her later novel *Drifting Clouds*, about a young Japanese typist stationed in Dalat during the war. As fate would have it, this trip to Southeast Asia was the last trip that Fumiko would make overseas.

The year 1943 was the last during the war in which Fumiko published. By that time, war privations and government censorship made publishing extremely difficult. The Japanese government placed strict controls on newspapers, magazines, and publishers of books, and although Fumiko was a very popular writer, that did not prevent her from being affected by war; *Diary of a Vagabond*, "Nakimushi kozō" (Crybaby, 1934), and "Joyūki" (Diary of an Actress, 1940) were all banned in 1941.[116]

The next two years found Fumiko and her family evacuated from Tokyo to the countryside where they rode out the remainder of the war. Before she was evacuated, though, Fumiko did one thing of lasting significance: she adopted a son. According to a letter sent from Rokubin to Inoue Takaharu, Fumiko had been thinking about adopting a child for a while, and thought she preferred a daughter over a son.[117] She had spoken to Rokubin about it, but did not tell him when, if ever, she planned on actually adopting. Then, while Rokubin was out of town on a trip to Shinshū, Fumiko received word that there was a baby boy available for adoption. She went with a friend, identified only as Hanzawa, to the hospital to get the baby, but stayed in the car for fear that she would be recognized by the hospital staff. Hanzawa handled the details and returned to the car with the baby whom Fumiko named Tai.[118]

When Fumiko wired Rokubin to tell him that she had adopted a baby, he was surprised to say the least. He returned home immediately to see Fumiko and Tai and apparently was happy with the adoption. After Fumiko's death, some manuscripts of hers were discovered that told of Tai actually being her own biological son. This sent a wave of doubt through Rokubin's mind that was not quelled until 1961, when he heard an account of the adoption from Hanzawa that matched every detail of what he had heard from Fumiko herself. This convinced him that the manuscripts were no more than fictional pieces, although he remained miffed as to why Fumiko wrote them in the first place.[119]

This episode in Fumiko's life reveals two things about her personality: first, that she was wont to do rash things, such as adopt a son while her husband was out of town. Second, that she freely fictionalized events in her life with a realism that fooled even her husband. This event should give all biographers pause, as so much information is based on Fumiko's own accounts of her life. Certainly the earlier mentioned fictionalized events in *One Person's Life* are another good reason to be wary of using Fumiko's writing as fact-based information.[120]

In any case, Fumiko was thrilled with her new son and expressed no disappointment in having a son instead of a daughter. She took great joy in being a mother and spent a considerable amount of time with Tai despite her busy schedule. Fumiko wrote two short stories about the process of adopting a child, one before she adopted Tai and one afterwards. The former, "Fūbai" (The Anemophily, 1941), is about a young, single woman, Sanae, who has her heart set on adopting a child. She does not want to get married, but she does want to be a mother. Sanae lies to the adoption agency and tells them that she is a widow. The agency proceeds with the arrangements and Sanae cannot sleep at night for the joyful anticipation in her heart; she lies in bed thinking about buying milk and baby clothes. Ultimately, Sanae's single status is exposed and she is rejected by the adoption agency. This leaves her heartbroken and angry that she will not be given the chance to prove what a good mother she could be.

The second story about adoption, "Nioi sumire" (The Sweet Violet, 1949) is about an aged woman, Tsuta, who reflects on her life and her relationship with her adopted daughter, Noriko. The two women have markedly different personalities but seem to get along nonetheless. Tsuta has a less than conventional life, having had two lovers and never marrying, but Noriko's presence seems to bring her a sense of stability. "The Sweet Violet" should also be noted for the flashback scene at the midwife's when Tsuta receives her new daughter; the transaction is conducted in a cold and businesslike fashion, much like the situation when Fumiko's friend, Hanzawa, rushed into the hospital to get Tai while Fumiko waited outside.

While "The Anemophily" expresses the fearful anticipation Fumiko must have felt before adopting Tai, "The Sweet Violet" expresses the hopes she had to grow closer to her son as he became an adult. Sadly, Fumiko never had the chance to see her son mature to adulthood; she died when he was only eight years old. Tai himself died a premature death in 1959 when he fell from a train while on his way home from a pleasure outing.[121]

Fumiko and her family spent most of their time in 1944–45 in the countryside in Shinshū. Fumiko kept herself busy writing children's stories for the children in the village where they were staying. Writing children's stories was an ongoing side interest of hers; she had published some stories in 1936 and those she wrote while evacuated in the countryside were later published in 1946 and 1947.[122] In 1950, she published a collection of Hans Christian Andersen's stories that she had rewritten.[123]

THE FINAL YEARS

The end of the war brought the Hayashi family back to Tokyo. They moved back into the big house in Shimo-ochiai in November 1945.

From that point on, Fumiko spent most of her time either in Shimo-ochiai or in the resort town of Atami. On occasion she would travel to other locations in Japan, but her real traveling days were over. Her later writing saw a departure from the optimistic tone so typical of her before and during the war, which I believe was due to a combination of disillusionment after the Japanese surrender and dissatisfaction with her stationary life. No longer was she the representative of the working class, illegitimate children, and liberated women. Gone were the days when she was the champion of the underdogs. Now she was wealthy, married, and quite established in the *bundan*.

She spent the last five years of her life writing almost constantly at a cruel pace, something that may have contributed to the heart attack that killed her at the relatively young age of forty-eight. Her physician warned her in late 1950 that she must rest more to avoid aggravating her chronic valvular heart disease, so she made it a point to spend one week a month convalescing in Atami, but she always took her work with her.

It was during these last years that she published *Drifting Clouds*, generally considered her best work. Other major works she published during this time include *Rose of Sharon*, "Bones," "Narcissus," "Downtown," "Beef," and *Aware hitozuma* (Pitiful Wife, 1950). At the time of her death, she was working on three different novels: *Jokazoku* (A Family of Women), *Sazanami* (Waves), and *Food*, as well as the short stories "Raichō" (Snow Grouse, 1951) and "Kikuobana" (Chrysanthemum Pampas Grass, 1951), all of which were published posthumously.[124]

In May 1951, her heart palpitations grew worse and she became generally weaker, even to the untrained eye. On June 27 she went to the Iwashiya restaurant in Ginza with a reporter and photographer from the magazine *Shufu no tomo* (Housewife's Friend) in order to write an article in the series *Meibutsu tabe aruki* ("On the Path of Famous Dishes"). They then went to a restaurant in Fukagawa to eat some eel, after which Fumiko returned home at 9:30 P.M. She went to bed in her study sometime after 11:00 P.M. Shortly after that she experienced severe pain and Rokubin came from the next room to comfort her. She received treatment from three doctors but to no avail; she died at one o'clock the next morning of cardiac arrest. On July 1, Kawabata Yasunari (1899–1972) officiated at her funeral, which was held at her house.

Fumiko certainly led an unconventional life, a fact of which she was proud. Her lineage was not of primary concern to her and her reputation was something to which she gave little consideration, if any at all. She was constantly trying to write "solid works," but especially in her younger days, she was rarely satisfied with what she produced.[125] She was not a writer with strong political or philosophical convictions, no matter now many critics tried to label her as such. She was happy to live in a rather haphazard manner, taking opportunities when they presented themselves and not worrying much about what would follow them. Fumiko once said of her writing:

> I am not much of a stickler when it comes to holding fast to the plot of a story. Rather, I am a bit cowardly about plot construction. When a coherent, trunk-like idea comes to mind, I enjoy making branches and leaves to adorn it. And I feel successful if major allusions spread out from the text.[126]

I believe she lived her life in much the same way. She did not plan much for the future but rather was content to live on a day-to-day basis, taking turns of events as they came. As she was a "bit cowardly about plot construction," so too was she cowardly about arranging her life; it was much more enjoyable for her to "branch out" toward new opportunities as they presented themselves than to organize her life in any sort of structured manner.

CHAPTER 2

Diary of a Vagabond *and the Optimism of the Earlier Works*

Diary of a Vagabond is the most popular work Fumiko ever produced. Other novels, such as *Drifting Clouds* and *Food*, and some short stories such as "Late Chrysanthemum" and "The Oyster," are invariably mentioned on the shortlist of her works, but more attention has been given to *Diary of a Vagabond* both by critics and her readership than to any other work. *Diary of a Vagabond* has been dramatized in both the theater and film many times, including many productions that were staged years after Fumiko's death, a fact that attests to the novel's lasting appeal.[1] Translations of selected sections exist in English, Russian, Chinese, Korean, and Esperanto. An informal survey of educated Japanese today shows that *Diary of a Vagabond* is the first title that comes to mind when people are asked about Hayashi Fumiko. In the early 1990s, the work experienced a minor revival as Japanese suffering from the national economic recession idealized a simple life—a return to basics— and saw in *Diary of a Vagabond* a romantic notion of poverty. Almost every piece of literary criticism on Hayashi Fumiko mentions the novel, and most dedicate considerable attention to it. Given this, it may seem redundant to dedicate much time and energy to one more evaluation of *Diary of a Vagabond*, but the fact remains that so many elements in *Diary of a Vagabond* are integral to Fumiko's writing that it behooves one to start an examination of the author's work as a whole through this novel.

Hayashi Fumiko wrote *Diary of a Vagabond* based on the diary that she kept from the time she moved to Tokyo in 1922 until 1928. *Diary of a Vagabond* was published serially in the magazine *Women and the Arts* from August 1928 until October 1930. During that period twenty installments were printed in all, although *Diary of a Vagabond* did not appear in every monthly issue of *Women and the Arts*. These installments bore separate titles, but all had the subtitle *Diary of a Vagabond*. Besides the sections of *Diary of a Vagabond* published in *Women and the Arts*, there was also a section published in the October 1929 issue of the magazine *Kaizō*. These installments, along with some others previously unpublished, were compiled into the novel entitled *Diary of a Vagabond*, which *Kaizō* published in July 1930. Shortly after that, in November 1930, *Kaizō* published *Zoku Hōrōki* (Diary of a Vagabond, Continued) as a single volume (*tankōbon*) in their series Collection of New Literature. In 1933 *Kaizō* published *Diary of a Vagabond* and *Diary of a Vagabond, Continued* together in a single volume.[2] From this time on, *Diary of a Vagabond* was reprinted many times both as a single volume and as part of a collection of modern Japanese literature. It is still in print today in paperback, published by Shinchōsha.

The section order in the single-volume version of *Diary of a Vagabond* (i.e., the order in which publishers have printed and continue to print) is not, however, the chronological order in which the sections were originally printed. The single-volume version of *Diary of a Vagabond* does not contain the original section titles, nor are the sections clearly delineated by some sort of punctuation or break. The only indication of a break in the text is the change of month in the diary entries; unrelated incidents appear side by side, and the result is that the reader may occasionally feel lost in the narrative, unsure of how the narrator came to be in her present situation from another, seemingly unrelated situation.

There were also considerable changes made in the language of the single-volume version of *Diary of a Vagabond*. In *Hayashi Fumiko no keisei*, Mori Eiichi charts these changes and gives examples from the text. In sum, he notes that in the single-volume version (as compared to the serialized version), there is an increase of the following: onomatopoeia, vernacular expressions, grammatically complete sentences, words written in *katakana*, present tense (as opposed to past tense), and use of the phrase "I think" (*to omou*). Also in the single volume there was a decreased use of particles. But do these changes alter the effect on the reader? The changes, particularly the increased use of complete sentences, may make the text read more like a fictional narrative and less like a diary, but there is already so much in *Diary of a Vagabond* that makes it unlike a true diary, that I doubt such minor editorial changes would make much of a difference. Ultimately, the ideas being expressed in the text were not profoundly altered by any of these editorial changes.

The title of the work itself, "The Diary of a Vagabond," speaks of a major theme: vagrancy. The word *hōrō* (vagrancy, wandering, roaming) has two meanings: first, to move about without defined purpose, to not reside in one location; second, to do as one pleases or not worry about matters. Both meanings apply to Fumiko. She spent her entire youth moving about, and she describes those experiences in the early sections of *Diary of a Vagabond*. She emphasizes the fact that a vagrant life was as natural to her as a stationary life was to most others, and her statements "travel was my hometown" (*tabi ga furusato de atta*) and "I was predestined to be a wanderer" (*watashi wa shukumeiteki ni hōrōsha de aru*) are often quoted by critics who wish to emphasize the forlorn image so often associated with the author.[3] The dynamics of travel and travel imagery in Fumiko's work are further explored in the next chapter, but here I would like to stress the second part of the definition of *hōrō*: "doing as one pleases."

The lifestyle that Fumiko describes in *Diary of a Vagabond* was certainly an unconventional one. She was a young, single woman living in Tokyo, sometimes with a lover, sometimes on her own, moving from job to job but never finding satisfactory employment. Yet the way that she described her life does not indicate that she felt she was doing much out of the ordinary. She had simply wanted to be allowed to pursue her own goals. Donald Keene notes that, "If one had to judge from [Fumiko's] publications, one would conclude that her chief concern was liberation from financial worries, brutal men, and bothersome gossips."[4]

Fumiko did not become a hermit, but she did distance herself from people to a certain extent, mostly to be free of the judgmental attitudes these people had toward her lifestyle. She enjoyed people's company but treasured the time that she had alone. Her low income forced her to share accommodations with an assortment of people, but she often became dissatisfied with the living arrangement and moved elsewhere after a short period. Even in the later years, she was intensely individualistic and demanded the freedom to act according to her will. Doing as she pleased, for Fumiko, meant moving at will on a regular basis and so the twofold meaning of *hōrō* describes her quite well.

STRUCTURAL ATTRIBUTES OF *DIARY OF A VAGABOND*

As mentioned above, *Diary of a Vagabond* is based on the diary that Fumiko kept as a young woman. The final form of the work has the structure of a diary, with entries separated by dates—albeit vague, as only the month is indicated, and not the day—but at the same time there are many things that make *Diary of a Vagabond* quite unlike a diary. A diary, by definition, is "a daily record of events or transactions, a journal; specifically, a daily record of matters affecting the writer personally, or which come under his personal observation."[5] I would add to this definition the fact that a diary is written by one person, although it may be about events that involve more than that one person. It is also invariably written in the first-person voice, and events are recorded as they are observed by the author, not an omniscient narrator. Finally, as a diary is "a record of matters," that is, a record of past events, one would expect it to be written in the past tense, except for hopes and anticipations, which would naturally be in the future tense.

Diary of a Vagabond is written in the first person, but Fumiko's treatment of dialogue in the text often makes the reader forget that one is reading a diary; dialogue is directly recorded, surrounded by quotation marks, in the same way it would be in a third-person narrative. To give an example, the following is the entry for one complete day:

> The two of us ate, feeling rather crestfallen.
>
> "We've been getting a little lazy lately. You wipe down the staircase, and I'll do the laundry . . ."
>
> "No, I'll do it. You can just leave it here." When I looked at Toki's eyes, puffy from lack of sleep, I found her unbearably pitiful.
>
> "Toki, what's with that ring on your finger?" On her frail ring finger glittered a white stone set in platinum. "What's with that violet coat?" I asked.
>
> There was no reply.
>
> "You're tired of being poor, aren't you?"
>
> The thought of meeting up with the mistress downstairs made my skin crawl.
>
> "Oh Miss! Can't you do something about Toki?" The mistress's words struck painfully, like cold water pouring on my chest.
>
> "Last night on this side of the neighborhood there was a car honking away. This is the head household in this town so it's especially obnoxious when the rumors start flying . . ."
>
> Oh, enough already. I was bent over the laundry, and her words struck my back like so many little pellets.[6]

It is particularly odd that the writer records her own speech in quotation marks. Recording another's speech in this manner can be done naturally in a diary, but the author's speech is not so easily recorded. Generally speaking, there are two normal styles in which speech can appear in diaries: the first is one in which all speech is rendered into narrative and quotation marks are eliminated, as in the following example:

A) John said he did not want to go, but I told him he should consider it.

The second possibility is one in which all speech except the narrator's is recorded in quotation marks:

B) John said, "I don't want to go," but I told him he should consider it.

Both possibilities are commonly used and should be familiar to any reader. However, in the passage above and throughout *Diary of a*

Vagabond, Fumiko chose neither of these possibilities. In *Diary of a Vagabond*, the scene recorded in A and B above would be written as follows:

C) "I don't want to go."
    "Oh, I think you should consider going."

Such dialogue makes the reader forget momentarily that the text is written in the first person, until the narrator voices thoughts outside the quotation marks. Occasionally, Fumiko uses either style A or B, but the overwhelming majority of scenes in *Diary of a Vagabond* use style C.

Besides the treatment of dialogue, there is another aspect of *Diary of a Vagabond* that differs from the expected: actions are described with an attention to detail rarely seen in diaries. As a diary is a record of the events and thoughts in a person's life, unrelated minutiae are rarely included. The author may note her own feelings in detail, but rarely does one see in a diary the sort of long descriptive passages that a novelist would use to portray a setting. But *Diary of a Vagabond* contains many passages in which details—specifically the minor actions of characters—are meticulously noted; the following passage, again the complete entry for one day, illustrates my point:

> Rain. I played with the boy all day. The mistress, a woman with high cheekbones, is called Ohisa. Okimi is much more gentle and beautiful, but fate is a mysterious thing. Why do men do such things?[7]
>
> "Hmm. Things down in the harbor area really seem bad." Ohisa had bared her shoulders and was combing her hair as she applied oil to it.
>
> "What sort of attitude is that supposed to be?" The old woman scolded Ohisa from the kitchen as she scrubbed the pots. It was raining. Gloomy April rain. A vegetable vendor pulled his cart past the houses lining the rain-drenched streets.
>
> "I wonder what food is in season these days?" I said.
>
> In the evening Ohisa and the master went off to town in the rain on some business. The old woman, the children, Okimi and I gathered around the table for dinner.
>
> "They really are fine, going out together in this shower," the old woman said, as if they were really quite fine indeed.[8]

Sentences such as "Ohisa had bared her shoulders and was combing her hair as she applied oil to it" and "A vegetable vendor pulled his cart past the houses lining the rain drenched streets" do not sit well in *Diary of a Vagabond*'s diary format; their detail is too complete to be a simple record of events. Moreover, the passage is dedicated primarily to the visual description of the scene, not description of notable events happening within that scene. Consequently, although this passage would be perfectly normal if it were part of a first- or third-person fictional narrative, in a diary it is awkward at best. Fumiko felt that one of her strong points as a writer was her ability to capture everyday detail. She wrote in a 1949 essay:

> The foundation of my writing lies in my giving life to trifling details. I am interested in details such as the fact that people breathe, no matter where they are. That's what kind of writer I am.[9]

Indeed, the details that she included in *Diary of a Vagabond*, although they did not fit well into the diary format as discussed above, did help make the work a success.

Perhaps the fact that she based the novel on her own journal inspired Fumiko to retain the diurnal format, and thus the pretense of writing a "diary," but the final product bears only a remote resemblance to what the reader would expect of a diary. One advantage Fumiko gained by retaining this format is the appeal that such a text has; it is much the same appeal that *shishōsetsu* (autobiographical novels) have, in that the author's supposed true-life experiences increase reader interest. In Fumiko's case, her loose lifestyle—a single woman supporting herself and assorted lovers—titillates the reader. Through *Diary of a Vagabond*, Fumiko provides readers with the opportunity to be a voyeur of an unfamiliar world, an opportunity that naturally increases the reader's curiosity. Mori Eiichi comments that:

> *Diary of a Vagabond* could be viewed as a work that chronicles a working woman's travels through the world of employment. In its voluminous pages is depicted the itineracy of a café waitress. At the time, when working women had become the subject of conversation in society, a work like *Diary of a Vagabond* that recorded the realities of those women's lives would surely have drawn many readers. [The heyday of *Diary of a Vagabond*'s popularity] was just at the same time as the period when the prosperity of popular literature was on the rise, and there must have been many readers who picked up copies of *Diary of a Vagabond* out of related interest and curiosity.[10]

Mori goes on to quote Furutani Tsunatake, a young man who was in literary circles at the time:

> The young women with whom we young men could most freely associate at the time were the café waitresses. I soon became one of the regulars at the café. My curiosity was strongly piqued about the inner lives, that is, the private lives, of those women, and I wanted to have a peek inside.
> At least as far as employment was concerned, those café waitresses' lives were written about at length in *Diary of a Vagabond*. For me at the

time, perhaps one could say that I was engrossed in [*Diary of a Vagabond*] more to get a glimpse of the lives of those waitresses—a sight they never revealed to their customers—than to read a piece of literature.[11]

Thus both readers who were curious about the lives of the working class and readers who were interested in the private lives of young women were drawn to *Diary of a Vagabond*. It is impossible to know the exact composition of Fumiko's readership—what percentage were which sex, what age, what economic status, and so on—but it seems that her narrative would have appealed to a broad range of people. For those who were outside the protagonist's world, it offered a glimpse of an unknown existence. For those readers who knew the protagonist's world, it was a poignant description of the familiar.

As with most *shishōsetsu*, it is not safe to assume that everything Fumiko wrote in *Diary of a Vagabond* is faithful to reality. Some events in *Diary of a Vagabond* have been recorded elsewhere, and are accepted as true, such as her move to Tokyo and her relationship with Nomura. Others are contradictory to outside sources, such as the date of her birth. It is plain that, although the text is based on real-life events, it is as a whole a work of fiction. Although many scholars use the information in *Diary of a Vagabond* when writing Fumiko's biography, never is *Diary of a Vagabond* itself called an "autobiography" (*jijoden*); it is invariably called a "novel" (*shōsetsu*).

It is tempting here to launch into a discussion of other diaries in Japanese literary history and to compare them to *Diary of a Vagabond*. Certainly one could find similarities here and there, but there is no evidence that Fumiko consciously attempted to follow any sort of literary tradition when she wrote *Diary of a Vagabond*. Hirabayashi Taiko recalls that the first title Fumiko gave to the work that later became *Diary of a Vagabond* was *Poetic Diary* (*Uta nikki*). Mori Eiichi sees this as a significant fact in that it suggests Fumiko was writing a collection of narrative vignettes, much like the early Heian text, *Ise Monogatari* (Tales of Ise). Furthermore, Mori points out, the structure of *Diary of a Vagabond*—prose commentary on accompanying poetry—is similar to the structure of *Tales of Ise*, in which the prose explains how the poems came to be written. Finally, the subject of many stories in *Tales of Ise* is romantic love, and Fumiko writes quite a bit on the same subject in *Diary of a Vagabond*. Nakamura Mitsuo says that

one can understand what sort of unexpected connection that [*Diary of a Vagabond*], written in such an apparently flippant manner, has to ancient Japanese culture if one considers the position that diaries (*nikki*) and poetry collections (*uta monogatari*) occupy in our country's pre-modern canon.[12]

Hirabayashi, Mori, and Nakamura all see the influence of premodern literature on *Diary of a Vagabond*, but while it is true that *Diary of a Vagabond* is a diary of sorts, and it is also true that it combines prose with poetry, these characteristics are too general to specifically identify *Diary of a Vagabond* as a work directly influenced by Heian *nikki*. There is much that is dissimilar about the two: Heian diaries, such as *Tosa nikki* (Tosa Diary) and *Kagerō nikki* (The Gossamer Years), make heavy use of textual allusion and conventional poetic forms; they focus on the melancholy, evanescent nature of the world; they are about the aristocracy. *Diary of a Vagabond* uses no textual allusions and its poetry is free form; it focuses on the energy of the narrator; it is about the lower classes.

If one were intent on identifying premodern texts that influenced *Diary of a Vagabond*, I would suggest Matsuo Bashō's (1644–1694) travelogues, such as *Oku no hosomichi* (Narrow Road to the Deep North, 1702) or *Oi no kobumi* (Essay from a Traveler's Book-Satchel, 1687). Bashō, like Fumiko, moved from place to place and wrote about his travels. *Narrow Road to the Deep North* and *Essay from a Traveler's Book-Satchel* are written as diaries about journeys, just as *Diary of a Vagabond* is, and they contain both poetry and prose in most entries.[13] But where Bashō's works focus on the uniqueness and character of specific (usually scenically famous) geographic locations, *Diary of a Vagabond* focuses on primarily one area—Tokyo—and the emotional state of the narrator. Still, there is more similarity to *Diary of a Vagabond* in Bashō's works than in *Tales of Ise*.

The question remains whether Fumiko actually read Bashō's works; little proof exists to show she did, except the following passage from her essay "Literature, Travel, Etc." (1936):

> I respect people like Bashō, who was full of common sense. He was indifferent to material desires, and had a character that was pure and penetrated by a splendid emptiness. His loneliness reveals his inner spirit and expresses the loneliness that we Japanese have within ourselves. When he set off on his trip to the north, he was embarrassed by all the farewell gifts that his neighbors gave him. For him, it was quite difficult that things had come to that.[14]

This shows that Fumiko respected Bashō as a person, but it says nothing about how she felt about his writing or even if she read his work at all. Fumiko's fictional characters read Western literature more than Japanese literature, and in none of her works do the characters ruminate or comment on Bashō, except in one short paragraph in the novel *River Song*. In sum, although there are some similarities between *Diary of a Vagabond* and other prominent works in the Japanese premodern canon, I find no conclusive evidence that Fumiko was indeed influenced by those works.

Diary of a Vagabond has much of the New Sensationalist School style mentioned in the previous chapter, which makes it a very frenetic narrative. Rarely does the narrator focus on one subject for any longer than a few short paragraphs. Attention jumps from one subject to the next, sometimes without a logical connection. The diary format here helps tremendously: section breaks (i.e., new entries in the diary) help keep the text from seeming too disjointed, as a subject change from one day to another seems natural. Also, within daily entries the text is often broken by blank spaces between paragraphs, as if the narrator had written part of the entry in the morning and part later in the day. Fumiko said that while she was writing *Diary of a Vagabond* she was still trying to understand "what constituted a novel," and perhaps the unconventional style of *Diary of a Vagabond*—which purports to be a diary but reads like a third-person narrative—is a reflection of that.[15]

I think that *Diary of a Vagabond* is best described as a creative anthology, a conglomeration of loosely related vignettes written by a young writer who was learning about creative writing as she was engaged in it. Like the portfolio of a young painter, *Diary of a Vagabond* contains an assortment of creative efforts that displays the artist's range and shows a gradual evolution of style. While it was not until a few years after *Diary of a Vagabond* that Fumiko could construct a full-length novel with a central plot, well-developed characters, and an adherence to theme, *Diary of a Vagabond* was the means by which she first began to understand the dynamics of writing a novel.

PHILOSOPHICAL AND LITERARY INFLUENCES

In some of Fumiko's early essays on her own work, she says that her inspiration to write was provided by both the desire to communicate ideas to a large audience and also by the personal desire to put pen to paper. She does not explicitly state what ideas she wanted to convey, only that she wanted to give her readers a feel for what was then her lifestyle:

> I want to use my own style to describe my own perception of reality. My goal is to reach many readers. There are probably many writers who would feel satisfied if just one or two readers understood what they write, but I am not one of them. I must target a large audience. Even those writers who call themselves "proletarian" write dry, highbrow novels that are difficult to understand. Their message probably goes right over their reader's head. Such writing is exactly like an

advertisement; one reading is more than enough. Those proletarian writers just want to convey a few common ideas to their readers, and I do not think there is one heart-felt emotion contained in their work. The media loves the proletarian writers, but from those writers' opportunistic need to write comes a commercialism and corruption that results in work that fails to draw readers.[16]

This helps explain why Fumiko was so hesitant to define terms, structure arguments, and make a firm statement about her political and philosophical beliefs; for her, the texts that proletarian writers produced were didactic and unappealing, and in an attempt not to write with such dryness, she avoided anything that resembled a structured argument. She preferred a lyrical approach, one that expressed emotions without blaming human constructs for causing the characters to feel such emotions. *Diary of a Vagabond* was very much an attempt to do just this, but it was criticized as something very different. Fumiko's response was:

> A long time ago, a certain feminist critic commented on my work in the following way:
>
> "Because I have criticized Hayashi Fumiko's works (most notably *Diary of a Vagabond*) as *lumpen* pieces, there are many people who think that I speak slightingly of her artistry. Certainly, Hayashi's works lack volition. Despite the fact that her works are studded throughout with poems that shine like gems amidst the prose, they lack the power of real-life situations. For this reason her works are, as far as proletarian literature is concerned, second-rate."
>
> I read her criticism with deep regret. She says that my work lacks volition, but that is probably due to the fact that in the case of *Diary of a Vagabond* I was writing a piece that does not follow in the path of proletarian literature. I never put up a sign advertising *Diary of a Vagabond* as any particular type of literature, or as belonging to any certain artistic school.[17]

Fumiko tried to describe what she felt her writing was, but she failed to make herself clear:

> The term "proletarian literature" in Japanese really means "the literature of poverty." If one talks about the literature of poverty, then my works certainly fit into that category. The foreign word "proletarian" reeks of the intelligentsia and ideology. The literature of poverty! In all its meanings, my work is the literature of poverty. Thank goodness for the Japanese language! But then, the term "literature of poverty" also has a *lumpen*-like quality. The vagueness of language causes a strange chasm of meaning in cases such as these.[18]

What she may have been trying to say was that her writing expressed the emotions that one experiences when one is vagrant—the loneliness, the frustration, the desires—and was not commentary on why one is vagrant in the first place. She never made this distinction clear in her essays and her early reputation suffered as a result.

Fumiko said that she was inspired to write *Diary of a Vagabond* after she read the Japanese translation of the Norwegian Nobel Prize–winning novelist Knut Hamsun's (1859–1952) novel *Sult* (Hunger, 1890). Donald Keene remarks that "apart from the poverty she describes there is little similarity between the two books."[19] More specifically, the narrator of *Hunger* spends most of his time either looking for food or trying to sell his manuscripts; the narrator of *Diary of a Vagabond* does the same thing. Both narrators lament their extreme poverty, and both constantly search for the means to improve their lot. Mori Eiichi theorizes that reading *Hunger* may have convinced Fumiko that her own life could be the stuff of successful fiction, but it was not *Hunger* alone that inspired her to write *Diary of a Vagabond*. Mori also points to Kasai Zenzō's (1887–1928) short story "Ko o tsurete" (With Children, 1918) and Maksim Gorkii's (1868–1936) *Nadne* (The Lower Depths, 1901) as works that convinced Fumiko that poverty could be used as subject material. Up to the time she began writing *Diary of a Vagabond*, she had been struggling with the mechanics of writing a novel and she had been trying to sell her poetry and children's fiction with little success, so the realization that her diary could be the basis for a novel must have been an exciting one for her. Her frustrations with writing a novel are expressed in *Diary of a Vagabond*:

> I don't know what form my novel should take. It isn't just someone's fervent daydreams, is it?[20]

Upon visiting the novelist Uno Kōji to ask him about how to write novels, she finds that his advice does not help her much:

> "Just write the way you speak," he told me. In my heart I thought about how that just wouldn't do it. . . . My problem is that I must write the way I speak, but writing something like "Um, I um," will never do.[21]

In any case, Fumiko knew that she did indeed want to write a novel, and so despite the confusion she felt about how to go about such a project, she set about rewriting her diary. In an afterword she wrote about the process of writing *Diary of a Vagabond*, she claims that she had not clearly thought about writing a sustained novel:

> At the time, I hadn't even thought about what kind of thing constitutes a novel. All I thought about was what kind of thing I wanted to write . . . Today's youth have an understanding of "the novel," but I think I became a writer by natural creation, and not any learned process.[22]

However, the number of passages in *Diary of a Vagabond* about the act of writing and how it should be done suggests Fumiko's sincere concern over the mechanics of being a good writer. She may have felt a natural inclination toward writing, but it was not simply "natural creation" that guided her literary endeavors. It does seem true, however, that she followed no "learned process," if by that she means a consistent set of rules that delineate the proper way to write a novel.

When looking for both traditional and modern influences on *Diary of a Vagabond*, one must keep in mind that Fumiko's education was limited and that there is little possibility that she was well enough read to intertwine Edo period fiction with other modern influences in anything more than a haphazard manner. When she asked herself "What is a novel?" or "What is poetry?" she was not asking whether a *honkaku shōsetsu* (fundamental novel) was a more legitimate piece of literature than an autobiographical novel, or any such academic question, at least not in such concrete terms. Her concept of literature was vague and abstract, and her failure to fully address and answer her own questions about what constituted a novel indicates that, although she succeeded in writing well-received, successful novels, she was never truly concerned with an academic investigation of the nature of "literature."

Diary of a Vagabond was published in the midst of a period of great debate on the nature of "pure literature" (*junbungaku*) and "mass literature" (*taishūbungaku*). Writers and critics could not agree on what separated the two—a debate between Akutagawa Ryūnosuke (1892–1927) and Tanizaki Jun'ichirō (1886–1965) in the 1920s on whether art was for art's sake or should appeal to the readers' interest fueled further debate for the next decades.[23] Fumiko was not involved in these debates, but the nature of her fiction provokes further consideration of the matter. *Diary of a Vagabond* certainly did appeal to a wide audience, but it was also written as an end in itself. She did not anticipate a wide circulation of the work, and was not pandering to audience expectations. *Diary of a Vagabond* was often miscategorized as proletarian, and it was proletarian literature that many writers of the *bundan* saw as displacing "pure literature" from its prominence in daily newspapers and other periodicals.

Such issues defy efforts to classify *Diary of a Vagabond*, although the lack of concern regarding these issues on the author's part could only help push the work into the category of "popular literature," if for no other reason than that writers who wanted their works to be classified as "pure literature" were obligated to publicly theorize why it should be. Did being categorized as "popular literature" lessen the import of Fumiko's work? Hardly. It did, however, change the nature of critical commentary on them. Most critics summarily describe her writing and few push further to examine her character development, writing style, plot structure, or imagery. The assumption is that she avoided complexity, and thus delving into her works carefully would yield little fruit.

Academic concerns aside, no worries about whether *Diary of a Vagabond* was a legitimate piece of literature kept it from being a popular work. Its popularity was partly due to the light, easy language that Fumiko used, and the optimism that the protagonist often expressed. Fumiko's language was usually uncomplicated, which may be due to her limited education; often this meant that she did not employ the vocabulary necessary to describe emotions exactly, and had to fall back on common terms that did not convey ideas with much precision. She did avoid using the same expression repeatedly, however, and the variety of vocabulary in her works makes up for its simplicity.

As a young woman, Fumiko had no agenda for writing other than fulfilling her own spiritual need to put pen to paper. But if Fumiko was unclear on her motives to write, her critics were not; *Diary of a Vagabond* was published during the peak of the proletarian literature movement and because the subject matter was the life of someone in the lower class, many critics saw *Diary of a Vagabond* as another piece of leftist literature that described the plight of the proletariat. As a result, Fumiko spent quite a few years denying any connection to proletarian writing, mostly to deaf ears. As late as 1949, she still saw fit to mention this issue in an afterword for *Diary of a Vagabond*:

> I am not capable of being "left wing" or "right wing." Although I was a member of the poor proletariat, I did not take part in the proletarian movement. I walked my own path. I have no connection whatsoever to such political groups.[24]

Ignoring her protests and angry essays that opposed the categorization of her work as "proletarian literature," critics usually focused on her lifestyle—as separate from her words—and concluded that a writer of the times who lived in abject poverty was necessarily part of the "proletarian" movement. Given the assumption of an authorial proletarian political agenda, it was easy for critics to dismiss her works as "secondrate," all the while missing Fumiko's true inspiration.[25]

There are a few standard terms used by critics when they discuss Fumiko's literature: *runpen* from the German *lumpen* (rag or tattered cloth), which in Japanese means "tramp" or "hobo," but is also used as an adjective to modify *bungaku* (literature), meaning "literature of the poor"; *puroretaria* (proletarian), which also refers to the lower class, but also suggests a distinct politicization;[26] *nihirisuto* (nihilist)—perhaps the most problematic term—which refers more to individualism (see my discussion below) than to the Western concept of *nihilism*;[27] and *anaak-isuto* (anarchist), which is often closely tied with *nihilist*, although Fumiko identified with the latter more than with the former. Fumiko had problems with the first two classifications and preferred to call herself a nihilist, if anything. However, she uses the term "nihilist" so loosely as to prevent anyone from clearly defining what she means by it.

Lumpen literature was a product of the global economic hardships that followed World War I. There were a large number of unemployed, migrant workers in Japan, and *lumpen* literature recorded their plight. Although *Diary of a Vagabond* is unquestioningly about a young woman who moves from low-level job to low-level job after World War I, Itagaki Naoko notes how *Diary of a Vagabond* differs from other pieces of *lumpen* literature:

> *Diary of a Vagabond* does not follow the usual path of spiritless *lumpen* literature, which gets stuck in and buried by the mud. It is penetrated by the aspirations born from dissatisfaction with one's present circumstances.[28]

The aspirations Itagaki speaks of here are the manifestations of Fumiko's optimism, and they provide what Itagaki calls "a sense of health to her *lumpen* literature."[29] The sick man of "spiritless *lumpen* literature," wallowing in self-pity and despair, offered no promise of improvement, but the narrator of *Diary of a Vagabond* does show herself capable of recuperation simply because she believes that it can be done.

In her essay, "My Horizon," (1931) Fumiko does not define *lumpen* literature, but she does attempt to differentiate between it and what she calls "the literature of poverty" (*binbō no bungaku*). She says her work is definitely "the literature of poverty" because the characters are poor, and she denies that her writing is *lumpen* literature. Ultimately, however, she does not pinpoint the difference between the two and leaves the question unanswered, blaming a "strange chasm" (*okashii gyappu*) in language for her inability to do so. She equates affiliation with any literary school—especially proletarian literature—with prostitution of the intellect; she says that if one is made to tow the political line of a given movement, then one must compromise one's individual ideas, and being a strong individualist (what she called *nihilist*—see below), she refused to concede her judgment to others on any point.[30]

Fumiko's equation of nihilism with individualism is a departure from the Western concept of nihilism. For instance, Nietzsche writes:

> A nihilist is a man who judges of the world as it is that it ought *not* to be, and of the world as it ought to be that it does not exist. According

to this view, our existence (action, suffering, willing, feeling) has no meaning: the pathos of "in vain" is the nihilists' pathos—at the same time, as pathos, an inconsistency on the part of the nihilists.[31]

The Western notion of nihilism took on a different character when it entered Japan; there the concept of futility (*tsumaranasa*) was the main focus of literary nihilists, not nonexistence.[32] Fumiko's definition of nihilism was a further departure from futility; when she refers to nihilism, she clearly takes it to mean a sort of individualism, or rebellion against social norms and trends. The logical progression from the concept of futility to individualism, as seen in literature, is explained by Takeuchi Seiichi:

> If one examines the language that expresses [Masamune Hakuchō's] protagonists' pose of acting "in vain"—desolation, monotony, satiation, weariness, uselessness, depression, apathy, dry indifference, mediocrity, repetition, triteness, mechanicality, putrification, etc.—it goes without saying that it is all the language of self-regression, refraction, and negativity. Thus, regarding the conditions that caused this state, Hakuchō can only weakly declare, "Nonsense! This has become old and familiar for millions of people. I'm tired of looking at it."[33]

In other words, Hakuchō rejected what society had become because it was dull and monotonous; the perceptions of the individual, as opposed to those of society, were most important. If we keep this in mind, Fumiko's statement below begins to make sense; her nihilism was not a statement of nonexistence, but rather a rejection of common ideas in preference for her own, individual ideas. She says:

> I must confess that I am a proponent of nihilism. Thus I do not follow the latest trend like everybody else, nor do I suddenly change my mind about things.[34]

But even a cursory reading of Fumiko's works reveals that she was not really a nihilist by any acceptable definition. Further examination of the word 'nihilist' in her fiction shows no discernable consistent usage, as the following four passages demonstrate (transliterations for key phrases are provided in the notes):

> Chiyo spoke frankly about sleeping in toilets and abandoned houses since she came to Tokyo. When she said, "I have no place to go today," Nakayama replied, "You are quite a nihilist."[35] He thought a moment and wrote her a letter of introduction. ("Flowers on a Vine," 1935)[36]
>
> "There is a guy I know who went to London . . ." Tsuneko said, blowing out the match flame.
> "Is he coming back from London?"
> "No, he just went there recently . . ."

"Oh? Is he somebody you are attracted to?"

"That's right . . ."

"Oh, I see. And are you eventually going to marry him?"

"No, I'm not going to marry him. I probably won't see him for three or four years . . . and I don't know what will become of him, nor what will become of me, do I?"

"Yes, well, you can't make promises about the future, but even so you don't have to think so nihilistically about it, do you?" ("Lightness and Darkness," 1936)[37]

At the time [May 1938] I was interested in Confucius, Zhu Xi, Tang poetry, and Tao Yuan-ming's poetry. I have only superficial knowledge of such things and don't really understand them, but as it is written in Zhou Mao-shu's *Tong-shu*, "the Non-ultimate and also the Great Ultimate! The Great Ultimate through movement generates yang. When its activity reaches its limit, it becomes tranquil. Through tranquility the Great Ultimate generates yin. When tranquility reaches its limit, activity begins again. So movement and tranquility alternate and become the root of each other, giving rise to the distinction of yin and yang, and the two modes are thus established. By the transformation of yang and its union with yin, the Five Agents of Water, Fire, Wood, Metal, and Earth arise. When these five material forces are distributed in harmonious order, the four seasons run their course."[38] I have become extraordinarily fond of Zhu Xi's predecessor Zhou Mao-shu's explanation of his comments on the aspects of *li* and *qi*. Chinese literature is totally nihilistic. It can be escapist literature, but in my present state of mind I cannot but feel encouragement when I read this kind of thing. (*One Person's Life*, 1939)[39]

"Sometimes I feel like there is nothing for me to do. I feel no incentive, and there are times when my youth yields to life in the countryside without any objectives. When that happens, I take the children for a walk in the mountains . . . Anyway, maybe I am a nihilist from the root up," said Nakagawa.[40]

"Hmm, but, I don't like nihilists.[41] You have such a great talent, and you are killing it. Isn't it a great waste? Don't you have any desires at all?" asked Rikue. (*Ten Years*, 1940)[42]

Certainly it is possible to describe what Fumiko seems to mean by 'nihilist' in each individual passage, but the meaning is not consistent from one example to the next. Chiyo's nihilism is her willingness to live in a way that society condemns. Tsuneko's nihilism is her decision to not marry immediately when the opportunity arises. Nakagawa's nihilism is his inability to pursue goals of any kind and his flight from responsibility. And the nihilism of Chinese literature is presumably something akin to the Daoist philosophy of inaction, but Fumiko is so vague as to leave the reader puzzled. The text she quotes is a complex scholarly work which purports to "lay the pattern of meta-physics [*sic*] and ethics for later Neo-Confucianism"; how that could be 'nihilistic' and how that nihilism would be related to the 'nihilism' of the other pieces quoted above is a mystery.[43] Yet Fumiko used this and other terms liberally. In her essay "Watashi no oboegaki" (My Memoranda, 1930), she makes similar loose usage of the term 'romantic':

> I went to the zoo recently. I went into the aquarium and gazed at the various goldfish and carp. At the monkey cage I briefly watched the life of the baboons. I think nature is quite a romantic thing. Even while the monkeys fight and howl indiscriminately, the fish swim with their beautiful tails fluttering.[44]

The sentences preceding and following the central statement do nothing to clearly explain what Fumiko means by the term 'romantic.' Both the term 'nihilist' and the term 'romantic' are foreign loanwords written in *katakana*, which makes them stand out from the rest of the text. They are emphasized words, words that carry with them the connotations of multifarious ideologies, words that would best be used discriminately, but Fumiko used them almost irresponsibly. Such nonchalant use of relatively conspicuous terminology opened avenues for critics with special agendas, and it is because of this that Fumiko faced the criticisms she did about being a leftist writer.

Although leftist critics read *Diary of a Vagabond* as an exposé of the plight of the working class, such a reading does not offer much insight into the piece. Throughout the text, the narrator focuses on positive aspects of life, celebrating such things as *ryoshū* (loneliness on a journey) and *kodoku* (loneliness or solitariness) instead of lamenting them. It would have been easy for her to complain about living conditions, or to wallow in self-pity, but she does not; she is inspired by the beauty that surrounds her, even in abject poverty. The opening passage describes her rather odd childhood acquaintances—a prostitute, a miner, and a singer among others—and then comments that her life was more interesting than a circus. These are not the words of one who lives in despair.

Fumiko may have professed to have a personal philosophy ("nihilism"), but her lifestyle proves that she was prone to casually throw this self-professed philosophy to the winds when it proved impractical. She was not in any way a political or philosophical zealot but rather a pragmatist; when she needed food, clothing, or housing, she took the most easily obtained employment available to earn the money for those things as quickly and painlessly as possible. She rejected societal opinion that looked down on single working women, but she also knew that neither nihilism nor any other antiestablishmentarian philosophy would provide the means for survival; in the end she knew she had no choice but to

conform to society's expectations at least enough to survive. This is perhaps best summed up by a passage in *Diary of a Vagabond* in which she
is sorting through her books to decide which ones to sell for money to
buy food. She comes across a collection of Kobayashi Issa's (1763–1827)
poems and thinks to herself:

> Issa was a complete nihilist. But I'm hungry now. I wonder if I could
> sell this book for something.[45]

In another section, a similar sentiment is expressed when she says:

> Oh, neither the idea of 'proletarian' nor that of 'bourgeois' is in my
> mind. All I want is to eat one white rice cake.[46]

A truly philosophically concerned writer may have responded to her
hunger by gaining inspiration from Issa or perhaps expressing the failure of the bourgeoisie to help the proletariat, but not Fumiko. These
desperate situations did not call for ideological responses, they called for
pragmatic, physical action. She knew that adherence to nihilism or
Marxism would not put food in her stomach, but work would.

Probably due to her association with the anarchist poets in the 1920s,
some critics say that Fumiko was influenced by anarchism. I think that the
term 'anarchist' may be more appropriate than 'nihilist' to describe
Fumiko, although the author herself would have probably disagreed with
me. As discussed above, nihilists wrestle with the idea that all is "in vain,"
without proposing what could counter the problem. Anarchists also recognize that societal and governmental restrictions cause actions to be "in
vain," but they propose a solution: anarchy. 'Anarchy' does not mean
chaos; rather, it means a total lack of governmental authority, or an
absence of any cohering principle, as a common standard or purpose.
(While opponents of anarchy claim that this necessitates chaos, anarchists
argue to the contrary.)[47] Given Fumiko's dislike of authority and restrictions and her expressed rejection of the common purpose of leftist writers, 'anarchist' is a more fitting label for her than 'nihilist,' but neither
label is perfect. Hirabayashi Taiko, one of Fumiko's peers, astutely noted
that none of the political or ideological designations assigned to Fumiko
by critics really represented what her writing addressed:

> She broke down all existing rules and standards, and whether one says
> that she was wild and uninhibited, or liberated, or an anarchist, in any
> case she took those ways of life and wove them into her own way.[48]

FREE WILL AND DETERMINISM

It is difficult to make many general statements about Fumiko's writing
because her style underwent a constant evolution during her career. Of

course one can recognize trends, but it is hard to say that any one of them is ubiquitous. In the most broad sense, Fumiko's career can be divided into two parts: early autobiographical works and later non-autobiographical works. The former tend to be optimistic and express a faith in the existence of free will, while the latter tend to be pessimistic and deterministic, and communicate a loss of the idealism found in the earlier pieces. But within these divisions there are exceptions, and of course the overly simple classifications of "early" or "late" cannot possibly adequately describe the hundreds of works that Fumiko produced during her lifetime. There are many variations within each period; Fumiko experimented with style, structure, character development, and more throughout her life.

When I speak of determinism, I refer to "environmental determinism," the belief that "the primary determinants of action are causes in the external environment, primarily the social environment."[49] In other words, the belief that man is subject to outside factors that greatly influence if not completely determine his fate. Fumiko did not hold this to be true—at least in her earlier works—as her characters are usually portrayed controlling their own fate through actions over which they do have volitional control. As a result, the characters remain optimistic in the worst of situations because they feel they have the ability to improve things.

Fumiko's belief in free will contrasts with the deterministic attitude of some of the Naturalist writers of the earlier twentieth century, such as Shimazaki Tōson (1872–1943) or Tayama Katai (1872–1930). Tōson's protagonist in *Ie* (The Family, 1911), Koizumi Sankichi, and Katai's protagonist in *Inaka kyōshi* (Country Teacher, 1909), Hayashi Seizō, both exhibit an inability to act in order to gain a good in their lives; repeatedly they express desires and then extinguish them by stating, "there is nothing one can do" (*shikata ga nai*), indicating that the determinants of action are not caused by the self, but rather by the external environment. They are slaves to their environments, unable to control their futures, relegated to watching their fates pass before their eyes without being able to raise a finger in protest. This fatalistic view of life may have been the result not only of European literary influences, but also a long-standing Japanese literary tradition in which the ineffectual hero is seen as a most sympathetic character. As far back as the Heian period, protagonists such as Prince Genji in Murasaki Shikibu's *The Tale of Genji* suffer in the hands of fate and are more admirable for it. The religious resignation promoted during the medieval period, which focused on the evanescence of life, also served to punctuate the nobility of ineffectual protagonists. In the modern era, many writers continued this tradition, perhaps in an effort to evoke their predecessors—in essence, a work that emphasized the fatalistic or deterministic was a conservative one, and one that emphasized an optimistic outlook was a liberal one. Whatever the incentive, the overwhelming tendency of the writers who are now part of the modern canon was one toward determinism.

Not so Fumiko, whose protagonists may become discouraged at times but who always press on. This is not to say that Fumiko's stories all have happy endings in which the protagonist triumphs over difficulty simply by willing it so. On the contrary, the majority of her protagonists do not rise above their original situations; if they experience a change of social status or financial means at all, the change is not vertical but horizontal, into a different but equally poor situation. Fumiko's faith in man's free will is expressed through the actions of the characters when they attempt to improve their lives; her persistence in creating characters who try, characters who endeavor to improve, characters who believe they can better their situation, is what makes her fiction, especially the earlier works, most notable.

Fumiko did not write much about why she created her optimistic characters, although an early article entitled "Watashi ga moshi Kachiusha de atta naraba" (If I were Katusha) explains how she would have portrayed the heroine in Tolstoy's *Resurrection* differently, had she been the author.[50] The comments she makes reveal her tendency to make characters strong, to portray them finding opportunities instead of dead-ends.

Fumiko says that her Katusha, instead of falling into prostitution, would have possibly become a merchant, or an assistant of some sort, both jobs that hold more promise than prostitution. She also suggests the possibility of Katusha managing a modest inn to support herself. In sum, all of Fumiko's proposed changes involve some sort of change for the better for the heroine, made possible by the heroine's choice to improve her own life, not because some environmental factor changed it for her. Fumiko felt that although Tolstoy had given more thought and consideration to creating Katusha than he had to any other female character, she could not accept the dark, depressing, fatalistic situation in which he placed her.

In contrast to Katusha's resigned acceptance of poverty and degradation, the narrator of *Diary of a Vagabond* most commonly expresses her frustration with poverty by voicing a desire to try harder. She almost never uses expressions like "there was nothing I could do" (*shō ga nai* or *shikata ga nai*); instead her utterances most often end in the volitional (*-tai*). When she does use *shō ga nai*, she uses it to describe the emotions she experiences (e.g., "there was nothing I could do about how sad I felt"), not the situations in which she finds herself.

I believe that it was this particular aspect of *Diary of a Vagabond* and other early works that endeared Fumiko to the public. *Diary of a Vagabond* is invariably spoken about in terms of the struggle of the heroine against her own poverty, not her suffering at poverty's hands. Fumiko's books had heroines and heroes (as opposed to antiheroes), characters whom the reader could admire and from whom they could draw inspiration. Fumiko's writing was never so sophisticated as to clearly communicate complex morals or values, but by choosing to portray her characters as volitional beings she implied to her readers that free will existed, that man functions by exercising his free will, and that failure to do so—expressed through indecision and resignation—was an immoral act. Whether her readers recognized this in so many words is questionable, but it seems that the resultant optimistic quality of her fiction was a drawing point for her audience.

The later works see a shift from a belief in free will to a resignation grounded in determinism. *Drifting Clouds* and *Food*, written in the last years of Fumiko's life, still have heroines with volition, but their underlying messages are less idealistic: Yukiko in *Drifting Clouds* resigns herself to the hopeless relationship she has with Tomioka, even though it seems doomed from its early stages; Michiyo in *Food* endures a positively miserable marriage for no apparent reason. The success of these works lies not in Fumiko's trademark optimism but rather in the mature depiction of the characters and the well-crafted plot. These works will be discussed in more detail later; here I use them merely as examples of those works that expressed deterministic ideas. There are a few exceptions to the trend, that is, early works that are deterministic (or fatalistic), such as "The Oyster" (1935), and late works that are not, such as *Kamome* (Wild Ducks, 1946), but the overall tendency is undeniably present.

What caused Fumiko to lose faith in free will and become deterministic? Perhaps her later wealth brought disappointments. Itagaki Naoko theorizes that Fumiko's deteriorating health—particularly the heart condition that plagued her in her last years—caused her to turn toward darker subjects. Fukuda Kiyoto suggests that perhaps the cause was her realization that women would forever be subordinate to men. Whether it was wealth, sickness, or some sort of personal realization, something definitely caused a change in her later works. In 1946, she commented on her career up until that time:

> *Diary of a Vagabond* was my virgin work but I find rereading it extremely difficult. I have written that reading *Diary of a Vagabond* makes me feel as if I am looking at the vomit of my youth, but I am thankful that my life as a young woman has proved to be so valuable to my literary spirit. At the time, I was living on the strength of self-

abandonment. Since the days of *Diary of a Vagabond*, I have lived a long life as a writer, and I am happy now that, Japan having lost the war, I can bury myself in my work earnestly. . . . I am sick and tired of writing serious novels seriously. I want to return once again to the *Diary of a Vagabond* days of self-abandonment.[51]

If "self-abandonment" (*sutemi*) meant a light, positive style, then Fumiko did not succeed in her attempt to return to those days and that writing style.

The optimism so characteristic of Fumiko's early writing is ubiquitous in *Diary of a Vagabond*, but it has a curious attribute: it is expressed repeatedly without substantiated, concrete goals. As mentioned, the volitional suffix -*tai* is quite commonly used, but without an explanation of how the author intends to accomplish that which she wants to do. For example, although she is constantly struggling to support herself and her lovers, she does not propose how things should change in order for her to have a better life; she knows only that she would like a better life, and that she must find it herself. One day, as she idly leafs through a magazine, she thinks to herself:

> I can't stand this existence. If I don't do *something*, I'm just causing myself to rot completely.[52]

The following day, she continues with:

> I felt like myself for the first time [in a long time] after straightening up the big dining hall. I've really got to do something. But even as I think this day after day, night after night, I simply return to my room, exhausted after an entire day on my feet, and immediately fall into a sleep so deep as to be void of dreams. It's lonely. And truly pointless. Being a live-in servant is a tough life. I keep thinking that one of these days I will find a room to rent and commute to work, but I never have the chance to leave the house for a minute. It seems such a waste to fall asleep at night—I stare into the darkness of my room and listen to the insects chirping in a ditch outside.[53]

The desire to act in some way is expressed repeatedly in the text, to the extent that it supersedes the goal. On occasion, Fumiko says that certain experiences inspire her toward the goal of writing, but in these incidents, it is not the goal of writing but rather the emotion of longing to achieve the goal that is important. Longing inspires her, longing provides a heart to her otherwise bleak existence and gives her a reason to persevere. Longing also gives way to a pleasant anticipation, something that brightens Fumiko's dull life. Again, the importance of Fumiko's belief in free will is crucial if longing is to result in enjoyable anticipation, because if she were resigned to her fate, there would be little reason to anticipate change and possible improvement.

Still, there are many places in *Diary of a Vagabond* where the protagonist expresses doubt about her ability to accomplish what she wants to do. The doubt is not due to a belief that something is physically impossible, however; rather it is due to her uncertainty about whether she has the skills to accomplish her goals. This doubt is most often expressed about her ability to be a good writer, as in the following passages:

> Am I really a poet? I could spit out poetry as fast as a printing press. But it would all be writing in vain. Not one good word would come of it. And the poems would never find their way to the printed page. Nonetheless, I still want to write like crazy.[54]

> I have no hopes of writing anything. I can't master a thing. Writing poetry is the height of folly. How did [Beaudelaire and Heine] put food on the table?[55]

Fumiko was frustrated by constantly feeling the urge to write but never being able to create something she felt was worthy. This constant tension between effort and unsatisfactory results is one of the most important elements in *Diary of a Vagabond*, and certainly the most prominent. It is not always expressed as a writer's frustration; in the first two parts it is most often expressed through the narrator's unsuccessful attempts to find work. Indeed, she does find many different jobs, but they are never to her satisfaction—either the working conditions or the pay is poor—and so she is forever searching for a new job, much in the same way that, in the third part, she is forever trying to write a good manuscript.

Her failures are setbacks, but she does not dwell on them. Past events are almost never remembered with regret. The narrator's childhood, despite all the difficulties experienced in it, is remembered fondly as a positive, cheery time. The people she met would normally be considered a rather ragtag crew, but she describes them as a most "interesting" group:

> In our cheap lodging house, there was a crazy old man whom everybody called "Nutty." He had been a miner, and people in the house said that he got so funny because of a dynamite explosion. He was a nice lunatic, one who got up early every morning and set off to help the women in the town push their carts. He often picked the lice out of my hair for me. He later went to work as a pillar constructor. Besides him, there was a minstrel with one glass eye who had drifted in from Shimane, a couple of miners with their wives, a racketeer who sold *mamushi* liquor, a prostitute who had lost a thumb—the group was more interesting than a circus.[56]

Other memories are recalled with equally positive feelings. Negativity is virtually absent; frustration and other similar emotions are invariably expressed about present events and future possibilities, but never about past accomplishments. So while the object of optimism often remains vague, the presence of the optimism is undeniable. This positive outlook on life is present in almost all of Fumiko's early works; it was not until the last few years of her life that she began to look back on her life with bitterness.

EARLY SHORT STORIES

There are a few works that followed *Diary of a Vagabond* that are worth specific mention here because they exhibit the same optimism so characteristic of Fumiko's early career. The first are two short stories based on events in Fumiko's childhood: "The Accordion and the Fish Town" and "Mimiwa no tsuita uma" (The Horse with an Earring, 1932). The former has traditionally been given more critical attention than the latter, but the latter is equally well written. These stories are about life in poverty, but they are told through the eyes of a child who maintains a joyous outlook on life in the same manner as the narrator of *Diary of a Vagabond*. In "The Accordion and the Fish Town" the narrator, Masako, works hard helping her parents (who are itinerant peddlers) to sell their wares in their adopted hometown of Onomichi. There is little rest for Masako between work and school, but she does not seem to mind. Being a new arrival in town, it was difficult for her to gain acceptance at school, but even in the description of those difficulties there are patches of optimism:

> We had yellow millet rice again. Whenever I eat, my mind invariably runs to the stable. I didn't eat lunch at school. At lunch time I went to the choir room and played the organ. I played that organ well, using the melody that my father plays on his accordion.
> My speech was crude, so I was often scolded by my teacher. The teacher was a fat woman, beyond her thirties. She was always peeking out from behind the canopy of her bangs, a bunch of hairs that look like an old rag.
> "You must use standard Tokyo dialect," she would say.
> So everybody used beautiful language like *"uchi wa ne."*[57]
> And I would forget myself sometimes and say, *"washi wa ne,"* which would make everybody laugh at me. Going to school, I got to see many beautiful flowers and lithographs, and that was fun, but all the other kids would not stop calling me names.[58]

The comical description of her teacher makes the scolding seem not so serious, and the wonders that Masako sees at school make it a fascinating place even if her classmates tease her.

"The Horse With an Earring" expresses a similar optimism; abject poverty takes on an adorable air, as in the following scene in which a girl tries to get a taste of *sushi*:

> On the tray there was some dried fish sprinkled with soy sauce. Yashio got the idea that she'd like to eat the rolled *sushi* that she had seen being made at a restaurant in town. She cut a small piece of newspaper, spread out some rice on top of it, added some dried fish, and just like the *sushi* she had seen, rolled it up, round and round. But somehow, after it was all rolled up, it didn't have the flavor that Yashio had imagined rolled *sushi* would have.[59]

The newspaper is a sorry substitute for the *nori* (dried laver) in which *sushi* is rolled, but the final sentence is humorous, and makes the sad scene of a hungry child surprisingly charming.

This optimistic attitude is found not only in Fumiko's depiction of children; "A Record of Honorable Poverty," and "Shōku" (The District, 1932) are autobiographical works written about Fumiko's life as an adult and they contain the same cheeriness, although it is expressed by characters other than the narrator. "A Record of Honorable Poverty" is often called the sequel to *Diary of a Vagabond* as it is written about Fumiko's life in 1931 right after she married Rokubin. "The District" is about a young woman who is getting used to her newly married life. There are characters common to both works and one of them, Komatsu Yūichi (modeled on Rokubin), is the main provider of optimism in both narratives. The narrator is a gloomy sort, but she cannot help but be swept along with it, faced with the dominating sanguineness displayed by her husband. In both works Yūichi is a painter and the narrator is a housewife. The couple is not well off and must economize to make ends meet. The narrator is despondent and moody, but the source of her unhappiness is not clearly developed; happy married life is an experience to which she has a hard time adapting after some previous abusive relationships. Yūichi is patient—almost to the point of saintliness—and the narrator cannot understand at times how he can maintain his constant cheeriness. Yūchi calls himself a "romanticist," by which he means that he has faith in man's ability to decide his fate, and he seems determined on his part to improve his lot.[60]

In the following scene from "A Record of Honorable Poverty," the wife discovers that they have no rice in the house. Yūichi is out at the neighbor's, and the narrator sits in the house alone, counting coins until she finds enough money to venture out onto the dark streets in search of food for dinner. She buys some rice and vegetables, and on her way home thinks about the meaning of life:

> For what purpose does man live? To work? To eat? Every day I'm just getting by, but it has become even more difficult.

I groped my way through the wooden gate. The house was pitch black, the only visible thing was the charcoal fire, burning like a single eyeball, in the brazier on the concrete kitchen floor.

"Where did you go?" Yūichi said.

"I . . . Well, we didn't have any rice, so I went out."

"To buy rice? Why didn't you say something sooner? Don't move." Yūichi had been spread out on the floor, and as he spoke he rolled up the floor mat.

"I meant to say something earlier . . . I'll get right on cooking it," I said.

"OK. You know, you shouldn't stand on ceremony with me. If we don't have any money, then just tell me so. It's best to be clear. . . . I was thinking I would head off to the exposition at Ueno tomorrow. I figure there should be some extra work with a paint shop. I can't expect to paint paintings without working at all. Right! Art, painting, they are man's comfort. I'll paint a summer panorama, something just right to show to old men and women from the countryside—that would be perfect."

"Hey, are you scolding me?"

"Scold? I'm not scolding you. Give me a break. Stop twisting my words. I told you that poor folks don't beat around the bush. Isn't it best to cast off your reserve and ask clearly for what you want? Sneaky thoughts will only make you depraved."

Tears flowed from my eyes as I washed the rice. His order to me to not be sneaky resounded in my bosom. All the false show I had made about being a virtuous woman now fell pitifully into ruins.

Yūichi cried out in a scathing, thick voice, as if by it he meant to drag himself up from his present state of despair. "You've got to rid yourself of the extravagant feeling that you can't live without being in a state of abandon. We just can't have that."

"What do you mean? Isn't a state of abandon best?"

"Just how many days of starvation training have you chalked up? Could it possibly be a whole year?"[61]

Here Yūichi is both brutally honest and merrily provocative. He tries his best to bring his wife out of her doldrums, and he never lets himself be pulled into her depression. Yūichi in "The District" refuses to let even talk of suicide dishearten him. The narrator recalls:

When I came home after a year overseas, the only gift I brought for Yūichi was the statement, "I'm going to die."

"Going to die?" he had responded. "Well, you must be all excited. Death is so popular in Japan these days—is it the same abroad? But now, take a look around the room. There's your desk, there's my easel, both fine as ever, doesn't that make you feel as if you left here only yesterday? And take a look at Koro. He's gotten pretty big, but he isn't missing a thing. I didn't teach him any tricks, but he's a cute thing, just lying about the place. The garden has become quite nice, hasn't it? It's a shame there's nothing but balsam trees, but still it's quite sharp, isn't it?"[62]

Yūichi first chides her for her defeatist attitude, then launches into the reasons why life is good. Such an attitude is unfamiliar to the narrator— the assumption that her life will be difficult is deeply ingrained in her mind, and she is slow at learning about the ways of a loving husband. In "A Record of Honorable Poverty" the two have the following conversation:

> "How were you reprimanded by your former lovers?" Yūichi asked as he removed some bones from the dried mackerel in his mouth.
> "I was never reprimanded."
> "That's not possible. I think you must have had some hard times."
> I took a look at the bathhouse stovepipe as I chewed on a whole mackerel. "How were you reprimanded?" seemed like such a crude way to ask something, but I quelled the fire that blazed inside me and looked up at Yūichi's face. Yūichi licked the last bit of food from his chopsticks. My stomach felt all sour, and my eyes were swollen. "Why do you say such things even now? Are you trying to torment me? No matter how poor we get, please don't torment me, don't hit me. We will probably never have it better than we have it now, and we will probably see days when we have less to eat than this, but please don't strike me on the excuse that we are poor. If you do ever end up hitting me, I . . . I will have to leave you, too. If I get hit again, my bum right leg will surely break and I won't be able to work any more."
> "Ho . . . were you reprimanded so terribly by the others?"
> "Yeah, they called me a worthless bitch."
> "No wonder you say such things in your sleep. 'Stop or you'll break my bones!' you say, and you cry in your dreams."
> "But—don't you see that I'm not crying because I still love the men I left? Even a dog would whimper in his sleep if he were tormented enough, wouldn't he?"
> "I'm not blaming you. I'm just saying that you must have had some pretty hard times."[63]

The narrator is defensive, and likens herself to a dog that has been beaten too often. Her animal instincts are to be distrustful and cower before one who has the potential to hurt her as she has been hurt in the past. Yūichi sees the pitiful creature in her, and he knows that he must gain her trust if he is to help her overcome the pain of her past. When still with Nomura, Fumiko's response was to focus on desire to the extent that her present suffering was eclipsed. It was not until the suffering ended that she had the strength to ruminate on the pain it caused, as seen in these passages. Yūichi, and Rokubin by extension, prevents this reflection from becoming overwhelming, soothing the narrator—Fumiko by extension—and helping her reconcile her past.

Diary of a Vagabond and the works that followed it were products of a sincere yet academically unsophisticated mind, a mind driven by the energy and fervor of youth. That that mind lacked a clear focus, that it could only define its purpose in terms of what it was not, did not retard the intense desire to push forward toward unspecified goals. What did Fumiko want? Simply put, she wanted to want. Her early works are permeated by a quiet but constant drive, a voice urging the narrator to go, see, do, desire. Longing is central to *Diary of a Vagabond*'s narrator's existence; her lack of even the basics necessary for survival—clothes, food, housing—means that she need not look far to find it. Later in life, when Fumiko had gained enough wealth to support herself in a comfortable style, she found herself drawn to travel predominantly so that she could experience nostalgia and longing for home. When she had all the material goods she could want and had experienced nostalgia to the point of saturation, there was little left for her to desire, and it was at that point that her writing became dark and depressing, void of the hope and longing so prominent in her youth.

CHAPTER 3

Loneliness and Travel

Many literary critics recognize the strong theme of loneliness in Fumiko's works, but few have noted the connection between travel and loneliness. Fujikawa Tetsuji, in a short article originally published in *Bungakusha* (The Literary Scholar) in 1951, quotes an advertisement for the then newly published edition of Fumiko's complete works that mentions both loneliness and travel:

> The consistent theme in Hayashi Fumiko's works, since *Diary of a Vagabond*, has been a limitless yearning for home, which is enveloped in vagabondage and longing *similar to the melancholy one experiences on a journey.*[1]

The last portion of this quotation may have been a mere second thought—many critics discussed the forlorn images of vagrancy depicted in *Diary of a Vagabond*, and that 'vagrancy' was often associated with 'travel'—but it is an important statement. It is the first step toward understanding Fumiko's writing, even if it does not go far enough in examining the concept of 'loneliness.'

As discussed earlier, *Diary of a Vagabond* is the story of a young woman who drifts from one home and occupation to another. Fumiko's other famous novel, *Drifting Clouds*, is about a young Japanese woman who travels to French Indochina during World War II. There are also many short stories that involve travel, some but not all of which will be addressed in this chapter. Travel and the loneliness associated therein was not only a formative part of Fumiko's life, but integral to her literary art.

TRAVEL LITERATURE

In this chapter, I use the word 'travelogue' to describe what would be called *kikōbun* in Japanese. The word *kikō* (also translated as 'travelogue') has been in use for many centuries; the etymological information in the *Nihon kokugo daijiten* quotes Matsuo Bashō, and indicates that the roots of the term go as far back as the late Nara/early Heian period poetry anthology, *Man'yōshū* (Collection of Myriad Leaves). The term *kikōbun* is relatively new; the etymological information on it quotes

Mori Ōgai's (1862–1922) *Maihime* (Dancing Girl, 1890) and Natsume Sōseki's (1867–1916) *Kusa makura* (Pillow of Grass, 1906). However, the entry for *kikōbun* says that it is "the same as *kikō*," so it would seem that the only difference is that *kikōbun* is a new variation on *kikō*.[2] Fumiko wrote her travelogues in the early twentieth century so either term could apply, although it seems more appropriate to use the modern term as Fumiko was a modern writer.

The tradition of travel writing, or *kikō bungaku*, has a long history in Japanese literature. Its origins lie in some of the same works mentioned in the previous discussion on *nikki*, such as the *Manyō'shū* and Ki no Tsurayuki's (ca. 872–945) *Tosa nikki* (Tosa Diary, ca. 935), and also in some other works such as *Izayoi nikki* (A Diary of Sixteen Nights), a nun's travelogue from the Kamakura period (1185–1333), and Matsuo Bashō's *Narrow Road to the Deep North*.[3] By the time Fumiko started writing travelogues, the genre of *kikōbun* had gained considerable popularity and many writers were producing travelogues for publication.[4] Their travelogues were by no means limited to domestic journeys; although there were more written about Western Europe than any other area in the world, there were travelogues about most other regions, including China, Southeast Asia, South Asia, the Soviet Union, the United States, Australia, Polynesia, Africa, and South America.[5] The collection of travelogues in *Sekai kikōbungaku zenshū* (Collection of Travelogues from Around the World) on France alone includes works by such writers as Masamune Hakuchō, Okamoto Kanoko (1889–1939), Shimazaki Tōson, Yokomitsu Riichi, Nakamura Mitsuo (1911–1988), Ōoka Shōhei (1909–1988), Shiga Naoya (1883–1971), Uno Chiyo (b. 1897), Kawabata Yasunari, Itō Sei, Nagai Kafū, and Yosano Akiko (1878–1942).[6] With contemporaries such as these, Fumiko was certainly not a pioneer in the field of *kikōbun*.

Although travelogues were very popular in the early twentieth century, they are given little attention by both literary critics and editors. In Fumiko's case, only a small number of the travelogues she wrote were chosen by the editors who compiled her "complete" collected works. Fumiko's travelogues merit more detailed examination because travel was a governing element in much of her fiction and furthermore because travelogues show her growth as a writer and display much of her experimentation with style and structure.

THE RESULTS OF A PERIPATETIC LIFE

Despite the fact that as a child Fumiko was repeatedly forced to make new friends and adjust to new surroundings, nowhere in her writing did she ever express a distaste for her peripatetic lifestyle. She enjoyed seeing new places and meeting new people. Indeed, she knew of no other lifestyle, and continued to travel habitually even as an adult. Until 1939, she could not bring herself to spend her earnings on a permanent home, as travel took priority over settling down.[7]

Fumiko was for all intents and purposes an only child, which made for an even more isolated childhood; without siblings to play with, the young Fumiko was often left with no one but herself for company.[8] Her solitary experiences in her youth provided her with the self-sufficiency she displayed as an adult, helped her develop her imagination and provided her with the ability to entertain herself through the fictionalization of events.[9] The solitary Fumiko, left with only occasional playmates, created stories in her mind about the people she saw around her and what they were doing. This fictionalization carried over into her writing; Fumiko focused on the people around her, sometimes to the complete exclusion of the landscape.

Another, perhaps more important, result of her solitary childhood was an enhanced appreciation of loneliness. Fumiko enjoyed being alone; she savored the early morning hours, when others were all asleep, and did her best work then.[10] She also preferred to travel by herself, because traveling alone intensified the feeling of loneliness and nostalgia that she so cherished. The concepts of 'travel weariness' (*ryojō*) and 'travel loneliness' (*ryoshū*) are mentioned often in her writing (essays, travelogues, and fiction alike). A detailed discussion follows below, but for now, suffice it to say that the loneliness Fumiko experienced on her journeys was one of the most important elements of her travel experiences as a whole. Fumiko also uses the term *jōshū*, which is perhaps best translated "melancholy," as well as *kyōshū* ("nostalgia" or "homesickness") and other terms, but while she uses slightly different language in different works, the concept being expressed remains the same: loneliness on a journey.[11]

As an adult Fumiko continued to travel, and except for a few years during the height of World War II, she took a trip every year of her life. Her journeys were both domestic and international, and included such destinations as mainland China, France, England, and what was at the time French Indochina.[12] She enjoyed traveling very much, and wrote both essays about travel and travelogues of her trips.[13] In one of those essays, "Literature, Travel, Etc.," Fumiko describes in detail what it is about travel that she enjoys, and what she feels makes for the most pleasing journey.[14] In other essays, she makes note of how travel is an integral part of her life.[15]

Her travelogues range from lively accounts of encounters with foreigners to detailed records of her expenditures while abroad. The most telling and entertaining travelogues are those which she wrote either during a journey or immediately following it; these works are the least romanticized, most honest accounts of her experiences. The travelogues help illustrate how Fumiko perceived events surrounding her, and consequently shed light on travel sequences in her fiction.

TWO ESSAYS ON TRAVEL

There are two essays on travel which express the author's thoughts well: "Bungaku tabi sono ta" (Literature, Travel, Etc.) and "Tabi tsurezure" (Idle Thoughts on Travel). Both essays were originally published in 1936 in a volume entitled *Bungakuteki danshō* (Literary Fragments).[16] In the former, Fumiko discusses the acts of writing and traveling as complementary activities. In the latter, she extols the feeling of loneliness she experiences while traveling.

The important points to note in "Literature, Travel, Etc." are that loneliness is valuable to Fumiko and that she finds the loneliness experienced while traveling to be particularly pleasing. In this essay, she says that she "covets loneliness" and that "loneliness expresses the whole of me."[17] She does not say directly *why* loneliness is so important to her, but she does comment that loneliness on a journey is something that she finds extremely gratifying:

> The nostalgia and homesickness that I feel when I'm in foreign lands are so enjoyable that I could die. It's enough to make me spend days daydreaming about Japan's beauty and longing for my home.[18]

Statements such as this show that experiencing the emotion of loneliness, while disagreeable to most people, is agreeable—indeed desirable—to Fumiko.

Given that an easy way to evoke feelings of loneliness is to distance oneself from the familiar, it is not surprising that Fumiko loved to travel. Travel removed the people and landscapes that she saw everyday and replaced them with the new and unknown. Whereas many people crave companionship on a journey, to Fumiko a companion would have been an unwanted piece of the world she left behind. In "Literature, Travel, Etc.," she says that she preferred to travel alone:

> Journeys are best alone or with one companion. And when the trip is long, one should do it alone.[19]

She comments that when she does choose to travel with a companion, that companion is her mother, whose company she enjoys immensely. But the presence of another, even someone she loves, can cause difficulties. She says that when she travels with her mother, they argue quite a bit:

My mother and I fight like crazy when we travel together. She takes charge and suggests we stay at a cheap lodging house, but I'm such a pleasure-seeker that I always want to stay in a first-class inn—neither one of us yields to the other's opinion. The two of us querulously muddle along and thankfully manage to complete the journey.[20]

Disagreements about itinerary and other such travel logistics are problems she also experiences when traveling with a group:

As I don't make many plans before I set out on a journey, I enjoy carefully examining the map each new day. So, whenever I feel like traveling, I leisurely set out on my own. . . . I go where I want to go. I find group excursions immensely trying, and I rarely make plans. Whenever I do make a plan, everyone just agrees with me anyway, so what is the point?[21]

These minor distractions, such as making itineraries, are admittedly bothersome for most people, but for Fumiko they had the added drawback of requiring her to interact closely with others—specifically, people from home—to the extent that the nostalgia that she so craved would remain elusive. It would be incorrect, however, to call Fumiko a misanthrope; as will become evident upon examination of her travelogues, she enjoyed meeting new people. And in both her travelogues and her fiction, an important part of a journey is the exposure to new customs, languages, foods, and so forth; natural landscapes play a secondary role.

"Idle Thoughts on Travel" is about a domestic trip to Izu. It is a very short piece, but it reiterates some of the ideas expressed in "Literature, Travel, Etc." Most notably, Fumiko comments on the importance of traveling alone:

Journeys should only be made alone. By oneself, one can be as selfish as one pleases. For me, half-way through with my life, solitary journeys have a certain romance about them. And while I pity myself on those journeys, the travel is quite painfully enjoyable.[22]

The last sentence says that self-pity (*jibun o awaremiru*) is part of what makes a journey pleasant. This is an important point to note; in Fumiko's travelogues (particularly those written about Europe, examined below) she repeatedly writes of loneliness, of yearning to return to Japan so badly that she cannot bear the emotion. The reader's first impression is one of unhappiness and depression, but this is not entirely correct. Fumiko was experiencing unhappiness and depression, but those emotions were ones that she savored, and the process of savoring them ultimately gave her satisfaction.

The emotion of loneliness was present not only when Fumiko was traveling, but when she was writing. In another essay, not related to travel, she describes the emotion she felt while writing her novel *Lightning* in the following way:

> From the beginning of this romance, I was often struck with a kind of "thirst"—the kind one feels when reading a full-length novel—and I was swept off my feet countless times by this feeling of loneliness.[23]

In this passage, Fumiko describes her literary inspiration as "loneliness" (*sabishii kimochi*); it was the emotion that fueled her writing, and it was the emotion about which she wrote.

THE EUROPEAN TRAVELOGUES

Fumiko traveled abroad often; some trips were for pleasure and some were for the ostensible purpose of wartime reporting. These journeys informed her writing in two ways: her experiences in foreign countries were often woven into her fiction, and they were also recorded directly in the form of travelogues published in Japanese periodicals. Her most supportive publishers were the monthly magazines *Kaizō, Chūō kōron*, and *Fujin sekai* (Housewife's World).[24] It was *Kaizō* that financially supported her during her trip to Europe in 1931–32 and sent her the fare for her return to Japan.

The style of the travelogues is anything but consistent; some, such as "A London Boarding House and Other Matters," are composed of fragmented vignettes, some, such as "Pari made seiten" (Clear Skies All the Way to Paris, April, 1932) and "Pari no kozukai chō" (An Account Ledger from Paris, 1932) are detailed accounts of her travel expenses (complete with ledger entries) and others, such as "Shiberiya no santō ressha" (Third Class on the Trans-Siberian Railroad, 1932) and "Furansu no inaka" (The French Countryside, 1932) are written in an epistolary style. I feel that the travelogues of Fumiko's trip to Europe contain, as a group, good examples of each type, and so I have chosen to focus on that journey.

On November 4, 1931, at the age of twenty-eight, Fumiko set out on her journey to Paris via Korea, Manchuria, Siberia, and Eastern Europe. She arrived in Paris on December 23, 1931, where she stayed, except for a monthlong sojourn in London (January 23–February 25), until May of the following year.

Fumiko produced many essays and travelogues about her experiences on this trip both during and after the fact. The works that most express "travel loneliness" are those written during the trip. Ruminating on her travels in retrospect, Fumiko became more mechanical and journalistic about events. In the works written on location, she was more apt to be lyrical, to record every emotion, every action, and every response to events around her. This is not to say that the works written later are of no interest; rather, for the purposes of examining the effect of "travel loneliness" on Fumiko's life and works, the works written on site are more revealing.

What follows is an examination of eight travelogues about the journey to Paris.[25] In addition to Paris, they cover the Trans-Siberian railroad journey, the trip to London, and a day in Naples. The travelogues are, in chronological order of publication, "Third Class on the Trans-Siberian Railroad," "Clear Skies All the Way to Paris," "A London Boarding House and Other Matters," "Raten-ku no sampo" (A Walk in the Latin Quarter, October 1932), "Napori no nichiyōbi" (Sunday in Naples, April 1936), "Gaikoku no omoide" (Memories of Abroad, April, 1936), "Pari (no) nikki" (Paris Diary, November 1947), and "*Furansu dayori* kara" (From *News from France*, November 1948).

"Third Class on the Trans-Siberian Railroad" and "Clear Skies All the Way to Paris" are both short pieces about the train trip across the Soviet Union. The former covers the first half of the trip and the latter covers the second half. They are divided into six and five sections respectively, each section covering one or two major topics. "Third Class on the Trans-Siberian Railroad" has a more optimistic tone, in keeping with the surge of excitement Fumiko felt at the onset of this adventure. "Clear Skies All the Way to Paris" is not void of enthusiasm, but it does show the weariness that she felt after weeks on the train; she notes the squalor of the third-class compartment and its passengers, and her comments about communism and the condition of the proletariat in Soviet Russia show that whatever leftist tendencies may have remained in her mind (after disassociating herself from the anarchist poets a few years earlier) were quickly swept away by the reality before her eyes.

In the ensuing months, Fumiko wrote "A London Boarding House and Other Matters" and "A Walk in the Latin Quarter." The latter is written in diary form, much like *Diary of a Vagabond*, and covers the period January 1–24, 1932. The entries describe everyday life in Paris, and also express a growing dissatisfaction with France. The final entry is made on the day she arrives in London for a one-month stay. "A London Boarding House and Other Matters" picks up where "A Walk in the Latin Quarter" leaves off, but has a remarkably different structure. It is divided into eight sections, each unrelated to the others. The sections can best be described as vignettes, although the narrative even within each individual section is occasionally a conglomeration of disparate images. Fumiko records her thoughts in a stream-of-consciousness style, and the sequence of events may not make perfect sense to the reader. This travelogue may show some influence from the New Sensationalist School, or from the experience of seeing Cocteau, but in any case the writing style that Fumiko used here was a clear departure from anything she had written previously.

The other European travelogues, "Sunday in Naples," "Memories of Abroad," "Paris Diary," and "From *News from France*" were published after Fumiko had returned from her trip. All four share a noticeably strong element of retrospective thought. "Sunday in Naples," is more about Japan than it is about Naples. This short piece waxes nostalgic about the music that Fumiko heard during her short visit to Italy, and laments the lack of such music in Japan. "From *News from France*" discusses the writing of Shimazaki Tōson (a writer whom Fumiko admired), and reflects on Tōson's response to France in comparison to Fumiko's own impressions.[26] "From *News from France*" was written fifteen years after Fumiko's return to Japan and is a notably well organized and structured piece, which strongly distinguishes it from the travelogues written much earlier in Europe. "Memories of Abroad" was published three years after Fumiko's return and is a short piece that summarizes many of the events recorded in other travelogues. This piece is not as organized as "From *News from France*," but it does have a similar structure (i.e., it is one solid narrative, not broken into sections), and it does not express the intense emotions found in the earlier pieces. The same can be said of "Paris Diary." Given the amount of time that passed between the trip and the act of writing, it is natural that the strong sentiments and periodically random interjections of emotion typical of the earlier travelogues should be noticeably absent from "From *News from France*" and "Paris Diary." The spontaneous inspiration that is quite prominent in "A London Boarding House and Other Matters" and "A Walk in the Latin Quarter" gives way to a more somber, retrospective narrative voice. That is not to say that these two works are dry and dull reading; rather that they tend to record events in a prosaic manner, where the earlier pieces tend to be poetic.

There are a few aspects of Fumiko's travel writing that make it distinctive. The first is her description of landscapes: she rarely notes the natural landscapes that she sees on her journeys, and when she does so the description is brief. On the trip to Paris, as on other trips abroad later in her life, Fumiko saw landscapes that she had never seen before. The expanse of Siberia must have been strikingly different from anything she had ever encountered, and given that she was traveling on a relatively slow train, she must have had plenty of time to view the scenery. Likewise, the landscape of Europe was very different from Japan. Consequently, the reader might expect Fumiko to describe these sights with great interest, but in fact she does not. Fumiko's writing is almost entirely about the people that she meets, about their behavior and her interaction with them. This interaction with people who come from different cultures is very important to her, for it accentuates the distance from her home culture, and, by extension, the loneliness and nostalgia that she feels as a traveler abroad. The loneliness that Fumiko enjoyed was not one of complete isolation. She enjoyed meeting new people and purposely traveled third class in order to meet people who she felt would be more interesting than those in first or second class.[27] The natural landscape was uninteresting if uninhabited; Fumiko once said, "A landscape without people in it is boring."[28]

The people that Fumiko sees are described with crisp, short sentences. Their actions are more prominent than their physical appearances but even those actions are sparingly described. She uses few adjectives and when she uses adverbs they are more often than not onomatopoeic; such terseness emphasizes the objective observational stance of the narrator and conveys an air of reportage. This style renders the following text, even if it is the narrator's conjecture, more credible. Characteristic of most of Fumiko's travel writing are extended passages of conjecture—based only on one or two observations—about the various situations around her. For example, although Fumiko could not speak Russian, she made extensive comments on the probable thoughts of her fellow passengers on the train trip across Siberia. In the following passage, she describes a Russian woman's reaction when soldiers board the train at a stop and knock on compartment doors:

> When the soldiers knocked violently on the door, the Russian woman who was sleeping in front of me shouted something at them in a very loud voice. I suppose she was saying something like "How rude! This is a women's compartment." I tried using sign language to show her that I thought it was frightening. The Russian woman must have understood, for she said "*Da, da*" and smiled at me.[29] I ate dinner with this woman in the dining car. I really wanted to thank her somehow, but I could think of no way of doing so—on the eve of her departure, I ended up giving her a paper balloon that I had bought in Ginza. She was still playing with it the following morning, happily exclaiming "*Spasibo!*" She behaved just like a child. I had wondered if the balloon would only befit a shabby Oriental such as myself, but it was quite fitting for the Russian woman, too. She told me by sign language that she was a teacher at a girls' school—of course she was a White Russian.[30]
>
> The light green, white, and pink colored paper balloon danced about in the pure, clean landscape. The window shade was pulled down low. We arrived in Hailar at about ten o'clock, and I thought about how we would probably never meet again.[31] I wanted at least to exchange glances with this truly kind passing stranger in parting. As soon as our clasped hands parted, I peered out from the crack under the window shade and saw the retreating figure of the old woman, walking jauntily along the platform.[32]

The two women communicated by hand gestures, which could only have resulted in limited exchange at best. Nonetheless, Fumiko is sad to see her companion depart from the train. While the two became friends and were apparently quite compatible, it is safe to assume that any sort of meaningful intellectual exchange was purely supposition on Fumiko's part. She uses conjectural language when she says "apparently" and "must have been," which emphasizes the fictionalized nature of the narrative.[33]

Fumiko recognizes her own tendency to surmise about situations that she does not truly understand. Her impressions are all formed from what she perceives as an observer, not what she conceives from information that she obtains through conversations with the people upon whose lives she comments. As a result, her conclusions about the places she visits are conjecture at best. In "Clear Skies All the Way to Paris" she is disappointed by the state in which she finds the proletariat of the Soviet Union. She had expected a country in which the poor fare well, but she finds the same social injustices in Russia as in other countries. She comments thoughtfully about the state of the country, but she also notes that her deductions may not be accurate:

> I have a quite odd impression of Russia, but perhaps that is because I do not speak the language. The Russia that I knew while still in Japan is quite different from the Russia that I have come to know. Is this the same Russia that the Japanese proletariat so longs for? The Japanese peasants yearn for the places I have been to in Russia—but on Russian soil, too, the proletariat is still the proletariat. No matter what country, the privileged class is still the privileged class. There were a lot of soldiers and intelligentsia types in that three-ruble dining hall. But there were no soldiers or intelligentsia among those asleep on their feet outside in the hallway. They were almost all laborers, weren't they?[34]

Fumiko comes to conclusions about the economic and political state of the Soviet Union based on what she sees; she creates a complete scenario from one glimpse of the country. In the case of the White Russian woman, Fumiko supplies the details necessary to create a rounded friendship with someone with whom she cannot really communicate in any meaningful way. This aspect of her mental process is, I believe, greatly influenced by her childhood; a vivid imagination can be a great asset to an only child with few friends, and Fumiko's imagination likely provided her with the company that she otherwise lacked. She learned at a young age how to entertain herself, and as an adult she still enjoyed being alone, where she could interpret things to her own satisfaction. Her writing—a combination of short, precise visual observations and observer extrapolation—is the product of a mind that prefers to absorb and integrate information solitarily. She rarely writes of intellectual interaction with others; instead, she records short conversations she has with them and then proceeds to construct the meaning of the conversation within her own mind.

Fumiko's predilection for intellectual solitude is part and parcel of her penchant for loneliness. A state of loneliness was one in which she could give her own thoughts free reign, without outside interference. It was also the state in which she could be solely responsible for any conclusions or achievements. This was particularly important because Fumiko spent her life in constant doubt of her own accomplishments. She was never fully satisfied with her work, and she often expressed a desire to improve upon her writing. In her 1937 essay "My Work" she writes:

> I have written countless short pieces . . . but there are only a trifling few which I myself like. And even after reading those pieces that I like, I am not transported to a realm of bliss. . . . I sometimes feel that I have been wasting my time in fruitless endeavors for the past ten years, but if I do say so myself, I think that those ten years of preparatory work have been precisely what I needed to gain the courage and excitement that I feel within me today. . . . Somehow I feel that once I have ascertained my goals, then I can take my time and write solid works. . . . I become very angry when I receive negative criticism about any of my works. Nonetheless, I am well aware of the ugliness of my writing and thus ardently attack each new project. I may be weak-hearted, but I can also be rather determined.[35]

And later, in the same essay, she expresses dissatisfaction with her own flirtation with intellectual schools:

> [G]iven all the various [literary] schools with which I associated myself from [the beginning of my career] to the present, I am left feeling like I need an enema to cleanse myself of it all.[36]

The discontent expressed in this essay was present throughout Fumiko's life. She was never quite happy with her writing, and she purposefully dissociated herself from literary and intellectual schools of thought because, as she once said:

> I regard the ideas which I struggled to produce as my chastity, and I will not prostitute them to anybody.[37]

Fumiko was interested in reading other writers' works and learning about the various literary schools, but she would not stand for any formal connection between herself and them because she felt that such a connection would be a "prostitution" of her ideas. This intellectual isolation was also a manifestation of her desire to be alone. The same spirit that drove her to seek loneliness on a journey drove her to seclude herself from the literary intelligentsia and their trends. She enjoyed the challenge of solitary endeavors, both in travel and in writing.

Another aspect to note in Fumiko's travelogues is the juxtaposition of loneliness and happiness. Often she exclaims that she cannot stand being away from Japan, but in the sentence following that statement, she expresses a joy of life and an exuberance that starkly contrast her putative despair. In "A London Boarding House and Other Matters," she is overcome by depression and contemplates suicide, only to conclude that she is a very happy person:

> I do so want to live—things were so excruciating, I crawled into the hearth, and then closed the gas cock; when I had tried to think why I must kill myself, I could find no reason.
>
> If I ended my life here, first would come the vicious rumors of lost love. But people do not die just because of lost love.
>
> Actually, I am such a happy person. Just think about it. As a waitress in a suburban café, I've served up fried pork, and I've worked in a celluloid factory, and I've been a server in a night market butcher's stall. And I've come all the way to a foreign country on the wages from my meager scribblings.
>
> By all means, I am a happy person.[38]

The juxtaposition of happy and sad is striking; after attempting self-annihilation, Fumiko suddenly says that she is a "very happy person." There is no segue to connect the two opposing emotions, because the realization of happiness is directly related to the realization of sadness and by extension, loneliness. In other words, the suffering provides a contrast that in turns brings out into bright relief the good aspects of home and everyday life.

In "Paris Diary" Fumiko describes how thinking of the trials and tribulations of her visit to Paris gives her joy:

> [Walking alone along the Champs-Élysées] gives me a vague feeling like the tedium experienced on the open sea during a long voyage. But, for me, this voyage is an adventure. While I think about how I'd like to return to Japan and get on with my work, I take pleasure in the feeling that comes from the pain and joy that I experience by myself in this strange land.[39]

For Fumiko, the bad experiences are just as important (perhaps even more so) as the good experiences. The gratification she knows she could have if she only returned to Japan ultimately would not satisfy her; it is more important to experience the pain and nostalgia brought on by remaining in Europe. She consciously and willingly chooses to endure sadness because it is, for her, a necessary means to achieve happiness.

In the passage above where Fumiko contemplates suicide, she has a sudden change of heart because she decides that she is actually a happy person (*kōfuku mono*). In other, similar scenes, Fumiko declares that she has a strong will to live, which she uses to counter her feelings of depression and despair, as in the following entry from December 26 in "Paris Diary":

> The heights and depths of maltreatment have befallen me, but no matter what happens, I shall continue on and not give in!
> —I was crying in my sleep. It was so awful, I felt like I was tossing and turning.
> While I was moving in, I heard the sound of an accordion coming from the doorway of my room. When I got off my bed and opened the window, I saw that a young man—I think he was a street musician—was playing an accordion. There were two or three children standing by his side. I listened to the accordion with a feeling of sadness in my heart. The big building in front of my house was an elementary school, and beside the school gate was a butcher and a stonemason's shop. . . . Looking at the dull, grey sky, I suddenly wanted to return to Japan.[40]

The first sentence in the above passage (*umiyama no kashaku yo watashi ni furikakare, donna koto ga atte mo watashi wa makenai de ikiteitai*) expresses an emotion seen over and over in Fumiko's works; she uses the word *ikitai* (the volitional inflection of "to live," meaning "I want to live") here and many times throughout her essays and travelogues, and it is this word that she uses here to express a love of life. At the same time, she is overcome with melancholy at the sound of the accordion, and pauses to listen to it despite the fact that it makes her sad. Indeed, she pauses to listen precisely because it makes her sad. That sadness (*kanashii kimochi*) is desirable, for it presents a challenge and an incentive, which in turn drives her to persevere and makes her happy.

The sequence—let us call it the "loneliness, incentive, motivation" sequence—is present in both Fumiko's writing career and in her personal travels. In her writing career, she was constantly depressed about the quality of her writing and that depression inspired her to try harder. In her travels, she repeatedly chose to go on journeys by herself, which caused her to feel lonely. That loneliness enhanced the aspects of her home life that she missed most, and consequently she felt driven to write about them.

This brings us to the question of what exactly Fumiko did miss when she experienced nostalgia on a journey abroad. Besides her family (in particular her mother, with whom she had a close, loving relationship) and friends, whom almost any traveler would miss, Fumiko missed the Japanese language.[41] She was extremely fond of the Japanese language, as she expressed in "Literature, Travel, Etc.":

> The Japanese language is especially good. In French, simple words like *non* or *oui* can be used by anybody. But in Japan, even simple words like *no* and *yes* are expressed in a myriad of ways. . . . Japanese is a language inferior to none.[42]

She expressed similar sentiment in "My Horizon."[43] In her travelogues she often mentions language barriers and the disadvantages of not being able to communicate. While abroad, she finds herself reading Japanese texts that she would not otherwise have read—in "A Walk in the Latin Quarter," she records reading *Tosa Diary* at night in order to fall asleep, and she says she finds herself wanting to read in their entirety books that she did not read in Japan.[44] When a Japanese friend in Paris lends her some magazines from home, she takes special pleasure in a story by Kawabata Yasunari:

> A bundle of Japanese magazines was delivered from Mr. K. He's such a kind person. A short story by Kawabata entitled "Falling Leaves" was printed in *Kaizō*.[45] I poured over it sitting next to the stove. As I read it, I felt a nostalgia come over me, as if I could actually smell the aroma of Japan.[46] This far and away surpasses European literature, I thought.[47]

After returning home to Japan from Europe, Fumiko still vividly remembered how she was struck by the beauty of poetry written in Japanese:

> Upon my return to Japan, my thoughts centered on wanting to write some wonderful poetry. . . . While I was in Europe, I felt surprised at the beauty of the Japanese language. I felt proud of the poems written in that language, like a prospector who had struck gold.[48]

I believe that, in addition to the content, the very language of the short story caused her to become nostalgic. It must have been difficult, given her limited English and French, for Fumiko to fully appreciate particularly good writing in a foreign language. But in Japanese, it was easy to recognize good literature, and the occasional perusal of certain works struck a particularly deep chord in her soul.

Fumiko also missed the smells, sounds, and tastes of Japan. In almost every travelogue there are comparisons of Japan and the foreign country in which she is traveling in terms of the odors, the food, and the scenery. In "From *News from France*" she expresses dissatisfaction with the fact that the ditches in Paris have no smell and with the lack of exposed bare ground in the city.[49] In "Sunday in Naples" she recalls how, when she was a child, the street musicians in Japan would entertain her with sad songs.[50] In "Clear Skies All the Way to Paris" she longs to return to Japan to eat a cheap bowl of noodles.[51]

Nostalgia for Fumiko, then, was a mixture of longing for many different things, but all things associated with home. In other words, she was nostalgic for the aspects of a physical geographical location, not for a space in time. Fumiko almost never recalls the past in an idealized fashion (in comparison with the present). Her fictional characters are likewise nostalgic for places, not times, although on occasion the characters' nostalgia is expressed in such a way as to closely connect the two, as in the case of Yukiko in *Drifting Clouds* who longs for a return to past days when she lived abroad.

RYOSHŪ AND TRAVEL IN FUMIKO'S FICTION

Before examining Fumiko's use of *ryoshū* in her fiction it is important first to understand her definition and use of the term. The European travelogues illustrate well the nostalgia and loneliness directly caused by travel. When Fumiko says in those pieces that she experienced *ryoshū*, it is clear that she means "loneliness on a journey" and little else. This, however, is not the only context in which Fumiko uses the term *ryoshū*. In her fiction the word has a much broader scope of meaning, encompassing an array of sad emotions caused by a number of catalysts. Indeed, Fumiko uses *ryoshū* even in situations that have no connection to travel whatsoever. Nojima Hideyoshi notes that the word *ryoshū* appears often in *Diary of a Vagabond*, and that Fumiko uses the word in a unique way to indicate a longing but not one necessarily related to travel.[52] She uses the word to mean the general longing one feels not for any particular event or object but rather for meaningful human interaction, as in the expression "I spat out my longing (*ryoshū*) for that wretched man."[53] This *ryoshū* is a longing for a relationship that never comes to be. In another instance, Fumiko uses *ryoshū* in the expression "the longing of one's eye trained on mankind" (*ningen o miru me no ryoshū*), which, similar to the first sentence, expresses the longing for meaningful interaction with those she sees around her.[54] Nojima summarizes the use and meaning of these two expressions in the following way:

> Needless to say, "human longing" and "the longing of one's eye trained on mankind" are the expressions of a lonely person. To put it another way, *ryoshū* is none other than the lyrical expression of the loneliness of human existence.[55]

And "loneliness of human existence" is another expression for the constant longing for meaningful human interaction on the part of the individual. What is of utmost interest, however, is that Fumiko chose a word that literally means "loneliness on a journey" to mean simply "loneliness." The spatial separation of the journey is extended to all separations.

It is no coincidence that Fumiko uses words related to travel to express loneliness, nor did she do so because she lacked the vocabulary to describe loneliness in other terms. For Fumiko, travel and the nostalgia that accompanied it were unquestionably linked to human loneliness as a whole. The characters in her fiction experience loneliness in the form of nostalgia, either for places they had visited or for relationships that have been irretrievably lost. Likewise, loneliness is unquestionably linked to nostalgia. When her characters feel lonely, they feel not psychological isolation from others but rather a longing for something from which they have become physically distanced.

Two of Fumiko's short stories, "Ryojō no umi" (The Sea of Travel Weariness, 1946) and "Hatsutabi" (Maiden Voyage, 1941) exemplify the author's treatment of travel and travel loneliness. The former is not, contrary to what the title suggests, a story primarily about travel. Rather, it is about a man who, through a series of misfortunes, is driven from one way of life to another. The latter is a story about a young girl who has just graduated from school and who yearns to travel abroad instead of marrying the man chosen for her by her family.

"The Sea of Travel Weariness" is narrated by someone (identified only as "I") who knows the central character, Shida, through common acquaintances. Shida is a quiet man who is married but childless. Before the war, he was an airplane buff who owned his own airstrip. The airstrip and the airplanes are confiscated by the Japanese army during the war and so Shida moves to Hokkaidō and starts a new airstrip. This, too, is confiscated by the Japanese army and finally Shida decides to ride out the remainder of the war—although the financial means by which he does so are not clear—practicing the *shamisen* and other musical instruments. Shida is described as a "Columbus type," meaning that he perseveres even in the face of great difficulty. As a result of this perseverance, he tends to be rather solitary—this is emphasized by a narrative that tells us nothing about Shida's wife, family, or friends. One day, Shida sets out on a trip to Shizuoka, where he must tend to some business. On the journey, he meets Inoue Minoru, a nine-year-old war orphan who has been abandoned by his aunt, a single woman unable to care for him. Shida is deeply moved by the plight of the boy, who has been left alone to fend for himself. The two become friends and Shida decides that he will adopt Minoru and take him home.

The purport of this story is mainly to protest war; the sorrow and devastation in both Shida's and Minoru's lives is directly caused by the war, and Fumiko is clearly opposed to it. A secondary theme, however—as reflected in the title—is the weariness caused by both the actual journey that Shida takes to Shizuoka and the figurative journey that he and Minoru take through the hardships caused by the war. After relinquishing his airfields, Shida pushes on to find new activities to occupy himself and appears to be quite a stalwart individual, but his acquaintance with Minoru reveals a soft, nostalgic side to the tough man. This soft side is revealed in the form of sudden reflection and sensitivity until then absent in him, and it is plainly brought about by his awareness of the boy's (and his own) loneliness. Their common loneliness causes Shida to think about the meaning of war in human history, and he draws strength from his conclusions that war is wrong.

"The Sea of Travel Weariness" does not express the previously mentioned sequence of "loneliness, incentive, motivation" in the clear language that many of Fumiko's other works use, but the sequence is present nonetheless. In the closing of the story, Shida's feelings toward the war are revealed:

> People are gifted with the quality to forget that which it is convenient to forget, Shida thought, but to start such a brutal war just twenty or thirty years after the last is unbearable. He thought how wasteful it was for the young men of the air force to be dying heroes' deaths, but at the same time he felt his stomach knot up in anger at the thought that such was the nature of war. Shida fell deeper and deeper into loneliness, his burning thoughts faded away, and gradually he let himself drift into a state not far from that of an old man. But Shida's body went against the tenor of his heart, and remained young and vital. That young body would sometimes take hold of Shida's spiritually aging mind and occasionally make that mind inquire into thoughts—thoughts that were much like love. It was probably his body that made him learn to play the *shamisen*, and tinker with machines, and also made him so fascinated with the child he had taken in.[56]

In this passage, Fumiko identifies loneliness with one's spirit and optimism with one's body. This division of spirit and body is not used in any of the European travelogues, but the loneliness and happiness the two cause should be quite familiar to the reader. The "loneliness, inspiration, motivation" sequence is seen here, too: Shida's mind is overcome with loneliness; the loneliness of the mind inspires the body; and the body drives the whole person to engage in activities (playing the *shamisen*, etc.) which cause him to be happy.

Fumiko's use of the word *ryojō* (travel weariness) in the title of this piece reveals how tightly connected the idea of travel is to the emotions of loneliness and happiness. While it is true that Shida meets Minoru on a journey, the actual act of travel is not an important cause of the emotions he experiences in the story. Rather, it is the figurative journey—from the depths of loneliness in his mind to the happiness brought on by his physical body—around which the narrative revolves. For Fumiko, *ryojō* was the most appropriate term to describe Shida's feelings; they followed the same progression that her feelings often did while traveling.

Whereas "The Sea of Travel Weariness" illustrates how closely Fumiko associated travel with emotion, "Maiden Voyage" illustrates how closely she related travel to life. "Maiden Voyage" is a touching story about the coming of age of a girl, Aiko. At the opening of the narrative, Aiko has just graduated from school and is facing an arranged marriage to Sachio, a man eleven years her senior. Sachio is a former botanist who is presently studying in the law department of Waseda University. Marriage to him would mean a quiet life for Aiko, and she has reservations about the marriage because she would much rather go traveling, like her friend, Sayoko, who plans to go to Manchuria after graduation to work.

Aiko and Sayoko are best friends from school. Sayoko says that even though she is leaving for Manchuria in a few days, she wishes she could remain a schoolgirl for the rest of her life. Aiko, fated to marry soon and remain in Japan, wishes that she could travel far away.

Aiko speaks about her impending marriage (and her concerns thereof) to her stepmother, Shizuko, who tells her that she should be satisfied with the happy life she has. Aiko replies, "But this is not a happiness of my own making. I don't want to spend my life as an inn-keeper's wife."[57] Later, during a conversation with Sachio who is visiting from Tokyo, she blurts out, "To tell the truth, I'm troubled by the thought of marriage to you."[58] Sachio is startled by this statement, but he is not angry. He resigns himself to the fact that the marriage is not meant to be and shortly departs for Tokyo. He sends a telegram to Sachio's family from Okayama which reads, "Off to Tokyo. Leave alone matter with Aiko. Sachio."[59]

Three days after Sachio leaves, Aiko visits Sayoko on the eve of her departure. The attitudes of the two girls change completely; Aiko suddenly finds herself in tears at the reality that she and her friend must enter the adult world. Sayoko now finds such childishness bothersome, as she is excited about her upcoming journey.

In the final section of "Maiden Voyage," Aiko and Shizuko are riding the train to Tokyo. There is no explanation of what their business there is, but it is implied that Aiko is going to see Sachio in an attempt to convince him to marry her. Aiko finally comes to terms with herself, and realizes she is happy with her situation:

> It was a clear day, and the cherry and pear blossoms were in early bloom. As she passed along this route, Aiko wondered nostalgically if it was the same one along which Sachio's train had rumbled. She was happy that she could view her home town anew from the window of the moving train, as it provided a chance to retrospect. Aiko took *The Ten Teachings of Ekiken* from her bags and thumbed through the

book.[60] Her eyes chanced to stop on the sentence, "When the spirit is absent, one looks but does not see. One is unaware that there are things to make one brim with happiness right before one's eyes . . . " Something made her feel like smiling as she placed the book down in her lap. . . .

. . . Aiko had not a bit of sadness in her heart now. She wanted to arrive in Tokyo quickly and cry openly to Sachio. She felt now that it was somehow a shame to have cried the other day at Sayoko's house, but there was nothing she could do about it. Aiko had had no idea that she could so enjoy this thing called a train trip.[61]

Thus the train trip that she coveted so much delivers her into the life that she feared would make that trip impossible.

"Maiden Voyage" is a very short piece, but it is tightly structured to include many images of travel. There are two literal journeys (Sayoko's to Manchuria and Aiko's to Tokyo) and there are two figurative journeys (the two girls' passage from adolescence to adulthood). The literal journeys provide the stimuli that cause the girls to take the figurative journeys. The combination of literal and figurative journeys creates a text centered on movement, and throughout the piece the reader is keenly aware of the change and movement occurring in the characters' lives. It is not a static piece that describes one state; rather, it moves steadily, much in the same way as a traveler moves along a chosen route.

As in the case of "The Sea of Travel Weariness," Fumiko's choice of title for "Maiden Voyage" reflects the fact that travel imagery was an important element in her writing. Using a journey as a metaphor for one's life is not unique to her, but I feel that it is important to note how travel and travel-related emotions appear repeatedly in her writing. "The Sea of Travel Weariness" expresses the aesthetic of loneliness that Fumiko associated so closely with travel, and "Maiden Voyage" shows how similar actual travel and emotional travel can be.

Although travel had a strong influence on Fumiko's fiction writing, her treatment of travel in both of these short stories does not closely resemble that in the travelogues previously discussed. The lack of similarity, however, does not negate the idea that travel is an important factor in her work; one stimulus can certainly result in more than one type of reaction, and travel is undeniably at the heart of all the works discussed above, no matter how it is expressed. Moreover, the juxtaposition of loneliness and happiness—the two emotions brought about by travel as expressed in her travelogues but absent in "The Sea of Travel Weariness" and "Maiden Voyage"—is also present in some of her works of fiction. For the purpose of brevity, I shall limit my discussion here to *Diary of a Vagabond* and *Drifting Clouds*, but it should be noted that there are many works that express similar emotions.[62]

Diary of a Vagabond is a novel about a journey: not a conventional journey in which one leaves home, travels to a given location, and then returns home, but rather a journey in which the protagonist is constantly moving forward, with no return. The text describes her constantly wavering between the stable existence of one with a permanent home, job, and family and the life of a vagabond. She always chooses the latter over the former—she is not fired from her job, she quits; she is not evicted from her home, she chooses to move—because a stable existence would mean an end to the "loneliness, inspiration, motivation" sequence in her life. A permanent home was as foreign to Fumiko as vagabondage was to the average Japanese of the time.[63] In the opening passage of *Diary of a Vagabond*, she explains how "travel" is her "hometown":

> I learned the following song in a school in Kyūshū:
>
>> The traveler's sky
>> On a late autumn evening
>> Troubles the solitary person
>> with lonely thoughts
>> Dearest hometown
>> Beloved parents
>
> I am fated to be a vagabond. I have no hometown. My father was a dry goods traveling salesman from Iyo in Shikoku. My mother is the daughter of a hot spring innkeeper from Sakurajima in Kyūshū. My mother, having married someone from a different province, was banished from Kagoshima. The place that she and my father found in which to settle down was Shimonoseki in Yamaguchi Prefecture. I was born in the town of Shimonoseki.
>
> Born to parents who were not members of any community, I consequently had travel as my hometown.[64] Thus being a traveler by fate, I felt quite lonely as I learned this "Dearest Hometown" song.[65]

This passage may seem to imply that Fumiko longs for a hometown, but the following paragraphs tell of a happy childhood on the road. Indeed, the entirety of *Diary of a Vagabond* is flavored with a constant urge to move on. The desire for a hometown is nothing more than the same loneliness and nostalgia expressed in Fumiko's travelogues, and it is those emotions for which Fumiko yearns. She does not want those emotions (nostalgia and loneliness) to be suspended by a elimination of their cause (uprootedness); rather, she wants to perpetuate the cause (i.e., to continue to travel) in order to perpetuate the emotions. She does not feel the forlornness of contemporary Kobayashi Hideo (1902–1983), who, on the subject of hometowns, comments that "where there is no memory, there is no home. If a person does not possess powerful memories, created from an accumulation of hard and fast images that a hard and fast environment provides, he will not know that sense of well-being which brims over in the word [hometown]."[66] Like Kobayashi, Fumiko did not have a "hard and fast" environment, but did she manage to have a feeling of "well-being," one that was associated with the thrill of constant flux.

Like the European travelogues, *Diary of a Vagabond* often juxtaposes the happiness and loneliness caused by travel. In the following scene, she is riding the train home to visit her mother:

> Alone in the vestibule at dawn, my daydreams turned their back on my hometown and fled towards the city.[67] Because I have travel as my true hometown, there is no need for me to return home all decked out.[68] For some reason I was overcome with a lonesome feeling. I returned to the dark third-class car, which was like a cellar, to find some stewed seaweed and *miso* soup unceremoniously placed on a worn lacquer tray on my blanket. I felt a sort of sadness and tedium as I sat under the dim lamp among a crowd of itinerant actors, a pilgrim, and a fisherman with his children.[69] An old woman asked, "Where are you from?" when she saw that I had my hair tied up in the *ichōgaeshi* style.[70] There was also a young man who asked me, "Where're you headed?" A young mother, who was lying with her child of about two, quietly sang a lullaby that I had once heard while growing up on the road. . . .
>
> Upon this refreshing sea I was free to drink in the air, more so than I ever could fatigued and in some dirty nook in the city. It all made me think that life was a good thing after all.[71]

This passage describes the squalor of the third-class train car, then the nostalgia that Fumiko feels among the other travelers, and finally draws inspiration from both. The "loneliness, inspiration, motivation" sequence is clearly present, and the advent of travel is celebrated here and throughout the text of *Diary of a Vagabond*. It should be no surprise then that Fumiko once said, "I shall take the life depicted in *Diary of a Vagabond* and make it my cornerstone."[72]

The novel *Drifting Clouds* is the story of a young, single woman, Kōda Yukiko, who decides to join the war effort during World War II and is sent to French Indochina to work as a typist for the Japanese Ministry of Agriculture and Forestry in its field office in Dalat. While there, she falls in love with and has an affair with one of her co-workers, Tomioka Kengo. Tomioka has a wife and family back in Japan, but he tells Yukiko that he will get a divorce when he returns home and marry her. After returning to Japan, Yukiko finds that Tomioka is not interested in divorce any longer, and their relationship slowly deteriorates until it ends completely. The novel is full of nostalgic passages in which

Yukiko dreams of the days in Dalat and the happiness she found there. She longs to return to the mountains of French Indochina, where life was peaceful and quiet, and she also longs for her relationship with Tomioka as it once was, but she can have neither. Tomioka, too, thinks back fondly on his relationship not only with Yukiko but also with his Vietnamese maid, Nhu. He spends much of his time pining for these past relationships, and also dreams of past happier days with his wife. But where Yukiko remains driven by romantic memories of her past, Tomioka tries to break free by planning a double suicide with Yukiko to end their affair.

The idea to commit suicide is a spontaneous one rather than a premeditated plan. Tomioka suggests to Yukiko that the two of them go to the resort of Ikaho to spend the New Year's holidays. She has up until that point been thinking about searching out their friend Kano (toward whom she has slightly romantic inclinations) but the suggestion of travel, perhaps to experience the nostalgia of bygone days, draws her in immediately. While she thinks such thoughts, Tomioka silently thinks about her death:

> "Well, only three more days, huh?"
> "What?"
> "New Year's Day is coming."
> "Gee, New Year's Day? It had totally slipped my mind."
> "How about it? Would you like to go to Ikaho or Nikkō today?"
> "Um . . . I've never been to Ikaho, but all right. I'd like to splash around in a hot bath. Can you really go?"
> "I can if it's just for a night or two. Want to go?" Tomioka felt like a tiny little human soul floating in the sea of eternity. Wouldn't it be best, he felt at the moment, if he were to end it all with Yukiko among the dry, withered trees in the mountains. (You sit there smiling away, unaware of your imminent death at my hands . . .)[73] Tomioka watched Yukiko eat her fried noodles with a voracious appetite. Small gold plated earrings hung from her ears. Her black hair was cut short, just above the collar.
> "Won't Ikaho be cold?"
> "Yeah, but I don't care."
> "Me neither." Yukiko was cheery, just like she was a young bride discussing plans for her honeymoon. She put Kano's card away in her handbag, took out her compact, and opened up the mirror before her face.
> Tomioka contemplated the scenario of killing this woman.[74]

Although the suicide is averted, the journey is still fated from the beginning to disappoint Yukiko, who has expected the chance to reconcile her differences with Tomioka. After they have been at the inn for a few days, Yukiko realizes that it is hopeless, but instead of giving up and turning to death, she decides to return to Tokyo and continue on with her life. This passage combines Fumiko's characteristic optimism and her "loneliness, inspiration, motivation" sequence:

> Yukiko crawled along on her belly, took her watch off the bedside table and took a look at it. It was a bit past four. Last night there may have been talk of the two of them dying, but now she wasn't thinking about death at all. She thought about how senseless it would be to die in a place like this. And she thought that Tomioka was not truthfully speaking his mind. Today she would pawn this watch and go back to her home in Ikebukuro. The memories that the two of them shared from Indochina were merely fetters which called to their souls; as far as the two people sleeping here were concerned, they were dreaming in totally different directions.[75]

But Tomioka is reluctant to leave, and the two remain at the resort for a while longer. They make many attempts at a reunion, but each time one of them backs away from the other. Their emotions fluctuate incongruously, causing the relationship to be punctuated by a series of disappointed expectations. When Yukiko realizes that Tomioka is having an affair with a maid at the inn at Ikaho, she finds solace in her memories of Indochina:

> On the other side of the bed there were twenty or so volumes of forestry books piled up. On top of the books there was a pamphlet Yukiko had seen before, written in French and put out by the Lang Bian Agriculture Commission on virgin forest regions. It was unmistakably the one written by Da Biao, the Forestry Manager.[76] Yukiko was suddenly overcome by a painful nostalgia, and she took the pamphlet in her hands and gazed at the beautiful pictures of the French Indochinese forests. The tears glided naturally down her cheeks. Every picture could not but stir memories. Her eyes stopped by chance on a picture of a country house on the Lang Bian plateau, surrounded by bougainvillea and mimosa flowers. The majestic landscape of Lang Bian, encircled by mountains with a lake in the foreground, was of indescribable consolation to Yukiko now.[77]

In this passage, Yukiko is comforted by the memories of her journey to Indochina. There are many similar passages in which she fondly recalls the landscape of the area around Dalat, and all express her longing to return to French Indochina. Although she lived and worked in Dalat, the time she spent there can still be considered a "journey," in the sense that she was away from home for a period of time, after which she returned.

There is an overall sense of loss in this novel: loss of innocence, loss of love, and loss of an experience (living in Indochina) never to be had again.[78] Central to the loss is the constant memory of what was and how things have changed. The return to Japan—the end of the journey to Indochina—affects each character negatively. Yukiko and Tomioka lose the love they once shared; their co-worker Kano, who was with them in Indochina and later returned to Japan, contracts a fatal case of tuberculosis. Fumiko clearly indicates that the point of repatriation was the time when things turned sour when she says, "It was not just Tomioka who had gone thoroughly bad since he came back to Japan. Kano, too, had become a ruined man."[79]

It is important to note that Yukiko does not long for the past; before her journey to Indochina, she led an unhappy life and yielded to the sexual advances of her sister's brother-in-law, Iba Sugio, in order to avoid being thrown out of his house with no place else to live. What she longs for is the journey that took her away from that miserable existence.

The travel element in *Drifting Clouds* differs from that in Fumiko's nonfiction travelogues in that there is no indication of longing or nostalgia for Japan during the time that Yukiko is in Indochina. The longing comes, as we have seen, after the journey is over. Nonetheless, the loneliness and nostalgia that Yukiko feels are directly tied to travel; they are the result of wishing for the continuation or reestablishment of the journey. Yukiko is sure that if only she and Tomioka could return to the mountains of Indochina, their relationship would be as it was before.

In a final attempt to salvage their relationship, Yukiko decides to accompany Tomioka (who is by then a widower) to the remote island of Yaku, off the southern coast of Kyūshū. Although Yaku is not Indochina, the idea of going on a trip with Tomioka has become so important to Yukiko that she accepts the journey as an answer to their problems. It is on that journey that she falls ill with tuberculosis and dies, never to regain the happiness she once had.

ESCAPISM

Fumiko's characters often express the desire to leave their present situation and escape to a distant place, and quite often they succeed in at least a temporary flight from their problems. A journey is often the scene of dramatic plot developments and the characters hold the events of those journeys close in their hearts long after they have returned home.

The following passages demonstrate this phenomenon. Even without the context, the importance of escape is clear:

> I turned the old time table over and looked at it. I thought about how I'd like to go on a journey far away. I'd like to abandon this city of falsity and go off to breathe in the air of the mountains or the sea. (*Diary of a Vagabond*, Shinchō HFZ vol. 2, 153)

> "I've got something I'd like to talk about with you. I'd really like to go somewhere on a trip tonight." Having blurted this out, Miyamori

was surprised at his own courage. He could not stand the thought of all the mental anguish and pain that parting again would bring. (*Daini no kekkon* [Second Marriage], *HFZ* vol. 13, 353)

Tomoji wanted to rise against his father's selfishness, so he turned towards his desk, picked up a book that was sitting there, and started leafing through the pages. He wanted a taste of a life in which fresh green leaves fluttered on trees.

He wanted to set off on a boat across the wide oceans. Any country would be fine, as long as it was not this squalid place. He daydreamed about taking a little trip on a foreign ship. (*Rose of Sharon*, *HFZ* vol. 12, 185)

When I worked in a stockbroker's years ago I had seen such large bills, but this was the first time I had gazed at them in my own possession. I thought about how I'd like to take these three hundred yen and go on a long journey to a far, far away place. My father had told me to use the money for wedding preparations, but I suddenly thought of Mr. Fang, and I thought about how I'd like to see his country, China, just once. (*One Person's Life, Shinchō HFZ* vol. 8, 61)

The coldness of Kikuyo's hands was suddenly revealed for all it was. Yamamoto gently let go her hand and said, "I intend to go, with you, today, on a trip to a place where nobody knows us, and that is why I have prepared this bag. I will honorably cut off the recent arrangements for my marriage [to another woman] once we are at our destination." (*River Song, Shinchō HFZ* vol. 20, 240)

Once it had been suggested that she go to Kobe, Tomoko suddenly felt the desire to turn her back on Tokyo. She felt that there must be an interesting life, different from hers in Tokyo, in some other place. In the end of October, she shut up her second floor apartment in Tsukiji and set off with Seto on a trip to Kobe. (*Fuyu no ringo* [Winter Apples, 1950], *Shinchō HFZ* vol. 22, 25)

In each case, the character sees travel as an escape from his or her problems. In some cases, travel really does afford a solution, but in most instances it is but a temporary respite from one's troubles. The respite does, however, provide the character with the chance to distance him or herself from difficulties, and often that distance provides a helpful perspective.

The novel that is most paradigmatic in this regard is *Chairo no me* (Brown Eyes, 1949). *Brown Eyes* is about a married couple who no longer get along well together. The husband, Jūichi, wants a divorce but his wife, Mineko, refuses to grant him one. Neither spouse is happy with the marriage, but they have different opinions on what should be done. Jūichi would like to divorce and marry his mistress, Fusako. Mineko has no lover and wants to remain married as a method of exacting revenge on Jūichi. The story is told in the third person and portrays each spouse's perspective in alternate sections. The brilliance of this novel is in the portrayal of the gradual increase of tension between the two. The end of the novel sees the two still married, but despising each other more than ever.

Mounting animosity between Jūichi and Mineko cause both to leave home on trips of escape. In Jūichi's case, he travels to Ōsaka to visit Fusako, who has returned there to care for her young son. He also goes to a hot springs resort with Fusako on a whim, and it is that trip which seems to be the beginning of the end of his marriage to Mineko. Mineko disappears on her own trip to her parents' house for three days without telling Jūichi where she is going. Each time the spouses reunite after one has returned from a trip, they exchange angry words and soon after that one or the other leaves again on another journey. Distance from their home provides each with a feeling of relief, and so the desire to escape on a journey grows stronger as the bond of marriage grows weaker. One day, early in the novel, the two vie for the opportunity to leave the house:

> "I'm headed out at 8:30 today, so could you set out an undershirt and flannelette for me?" Jūichi said.
>
> Mineko patted down the floor cushion and soaked in the morning sun's rays, which were coming through the glass doors. She examined her gold-colored reading glasses. "Oh? You're going out? You didn't say anything about it last night, did you? I'm going out with Yoshimi today. Thanks to being so dependent on your meager means I've not even had enough to eat, so I thought I'd go into some sort of business with Yoshimi. Sorry, but I'll have to ask you to stay home and watch the house today."
>
> "Oh? You're going into business? That's a serious issue."
>
> "Oh really?"
>
> "Do you have to do it today?"
>
> "Today it must be."
>
> "You didn't say anything about it last night, did you?"
>
> "You are so stupid some times . . . I can't tell if you are being sarcastic or just dull-witted."
>
> "Sometimes I want to be a bit dull-witted."
>
> "You?" Mineko's brown eyes narrowed suddenly, and with the cushions under her arms, she opened the closet door with her foot. Jūichi was amazed at her dexterity, and he picked up the remaining cushions from behind her and placed them high up in the closet.
>
> "I'm really going out today. I absolutely must go," he said.
>
> "What is it you've got to do?"
>
> "I've got some important business at the boss's house."
>
> "Really?"
>
> "Really."[80]

In the end, they both leave and have the second-story boarder watch the house. The opportunity to escape is used in this passage almost like a weapon; Jūichi and Mineko know that the opportunity to leave the house is important not only to themself but to the other, too, and the chance to snatch that opportunity away is a chance to punish. Once Jūichi is out of the house, he feels an immense relief:

> He arrived at Uguisudani Station at twenty minutes to ten. It was bitter cold on the platform. Jūichi stood at the station exit in the chill, a harbinger of a long winter to come. He gazed at the dirty street as he sauntered along like a child. His happiness at the thought of being far from home and about to meet a young, beautiful woman even gave him the energy to stand in the cold for twenty minutes.[81]

Escape, and distance from home, bring Jūichi a sense of comfort and happiness. His problems are certainly not solved by running away, but the sort of temporary respite it provides is something that many of Fumiko's characters seek. And Jūichi, like those other characters, is rejuvenated by his escape. It provides him with the energy to later go home and confront the looming problem of his disintegrating marriage.

I see a connection between this sort of escapism and Fumiko's fear of ideology. When Fumiko found herself headed toward some sort of philosophical argument, she quickly steered herself clear by changing the subject or glossing over it in an indecisive manner. When life becomes difficult for Fumiko's characters, they desire an escape; when topics and concepts become difficult for Fumiko, she desires the same escape. A journey provides the escape for her characters, and a change of subject provides the escape for Fumiko. Both types of escape are distractions, and the reader may be tempted to fault Fumiko for failing to face difficulties head on, but in her fiction at least, the characters almost always return to the source of their problems after being rejuvenated by their respite.

It is clear that travel was a formative part of Fumiko's childhood, and that travel remained important to her throughout her life. Her feelings about travel are recorded in both her essays and in her travelogues, the former being slightly more analytical than the latter, but both revealing how the author felt about the subject. The emotions of *ryoshū* and *ryojō* appear often in her writing, even when actual travel is not involved. For Fumiko, travel provided an opportunity to experience these emotions, which she found pleasing and inspiring. When critics write about her work as being "sorrowful" and "nostalgic" it is the emotion of *ryoshū* of which they speak. And when they speak of her work as having "aspi-

rations" and "humor," they are describing the inspiration and consequent motivation that resulted from *ryoshū*.[82]

The importance of *ryoshū* to Fumiko was monumental; we have
seen how it affected both her travelogues and her fiction. She knew that
travel and *ryoshū* were central to her life, and she expressed this in the
prologue to a collection of travelogues published in 1939, *Watashi no
kikō* (My Travelogues):

> I have always had a feeling close to *ryoshū*, which is perhaps due
> to the fact that I have not known a permanent home since the time I
> was a little girl.
>
> I have never taken a trip that was materially luxurious, but still I
> travel quite frequently, and my memories from those journeys are the
> riches of my life. . . . I am always day dreaming about going away, if I
> had the chance, on a foreign freighter to all the little ports and towns
> in the world. When I tire of people, and am bored with worldly mat-
> ters, I think of travel. . . . Going on a trip and having the joy of grasp-
> ing the truth from the midst of the delusions that surround one in a
> strange place—for me that is a nostalgic paradise, and it makes me feel
> my familiar *ryoshū*.
>
> My spirit can only thrive in a whirlpool of *ryoshū*.[83]

CHAPTER 4

Marriage, Family, and Women's Issues

Any student of Japanese literature who has read even a little criticism on a woman writer has at some point come across the terms *joryū bungaku* ("women's literature") and *joryū sakka* ("woman writer"). What do they mean? And, more to the point, are they central to understanding Hayashi Fumiko's writing?[1] The terms unfortunately obscure more than illuminate the nature of Fumiko's and other women's work, for a number of reasons. The term "women's literature" is problematic in that it has changed referents over time. Moreover, it was imposed on literature by critics, not the writers themselves, conforming to those critics' ideals. Initially, "women's literature" referred to literature written by women. Later, in the early twentieth century, it included both literature written with a female audience in mind and literature written in something vaguely deemed to be a feminine style, although what this would be has never been definitively determined. All of these categorizations present problems, because the gender of the writer does not decide the nature of the prose, and not all female readers prefer the same sort of writing. Yet Japanese literary scholars have continued to use the terms "women's literature" and "woman writer" to refer to diverse works and authors, including Hayashi Fumiko. In many cases it may be easier for a female writer to accurately depict the life of a woman and likewise easier for a male to accurately depict the life of a man, but this does not prevent a writer from accurately and sympathetically depicting the lives of characters of the opposite sex. Certainly many writers have demonstrated such a skill, for example, Nagai Kafū (1879–1959) in his novel *Ude kurabe* (Geisha in Rivalry, 1917) and Tanizaki Jun'ichirō (1886–1965) in his novels *Tade kuu mushi* (Some Prefer Nettles, 1929) and *Sasame yuki* (The Makioka Sisters, 1944), both of whom masterfully portray their female characters. Likewise, Hayashi Fumiko portrays many of her male characters with richness and realism, as in her short story "Maihime" (Dancing Girl, 1940), which is about a man who is opposed to the marriage that his family has arranged for him, and in "Ame" (Rain, 1946), the story of a returned war veteran who has become estranged from his family and country.[2]

The gender of the author does not determine the underlying message of a novel; men can write—and have written—about issues specific to women and vice versa. Despite the distinction in Japanese between men's and women's speech, a writer is not constrained to use one or the other; a male writer is free to depict feminine speech and a female writer to depict masculine speech.[3] Nor does the author's gender determine the gender of his or her audience: plenty of women read men's novels and vice versa. Clearly the term "women's literature" is a specious one, and does not refer to an individuated concept.

The term itself aside, there is still the issue of whether Fumiko wrote feminist works. If we define 'feminist' as "of or pertaining to feminism" and 'feminism' as "advocacy of the rights of women (based on the theory of equality of the sexes)," then Fumiko was not a feminist. While Fumiko's works often focus on the political or economic injustices suffered by the protagonist, the gender of the protagonist is not usually at the heart of the matter; it would be more accurate to say that she advocates for the individual the same rights granted other individuals. But if we define feminism in broader terms, such as "of or pertaining to women and their qualities," then certainly Fumiko was a feminist. Many of Fumiko's works address problems unique to women, such as the problem of an unwanted pregnancy—the short stories "Canary" and "Ajisai" (Hydrangea, 1948) and the novel *Drifting Clouds* all have protagonists who must decide between having an abortion and giving birth to a baby they do not want (and which in some cases would be illegitimate). These are problems women face in family situations in which their desires are given second priority to men's desires. Fumiko also often depicts women on the fringes of society—women who were engaged in nontraditional employment such as factory work, and so on—and by this example indirectly promoted the idea of women branching out from household and family duties into the workplace.

Another important way in which Fumiko addressed what might be termed feminist concerns was in her reinterpretation of history. Some of her works focus on historical female figures, figures who have been given little attention but who inspired Fumiko to imagine what their lives may have been like.[4] One work that stands out is a short story entitled "Fudegaki" (Writing, 1942), about the Edo fiction writer and Neo-Confucianist Takizawa Bakin (1767–1848), most famous for his novel *Nansō Satomi hakkenden* (The Story of Eight Dogs, 1814–1832) in which he advocates strict Confucian morals.[5] Bakin had a daughter-in-law, Michi (1806–1858), wife of Bakin's only son Sōhaku (1798–1835). "Writing" is a fictional account, told from Michi's point of view, of what life was like in Bakin's household.

In order to appreciate what Fumiko does in "Writing," it is helpful first to know the historical facts as recorded by Bakin's biographers. In his biography of Bakin, based primarily on Bakin's own diaries, Leon Zolbrod describes Michi as a learned woman who became Bakin's amanuensis near the end of his life. Zolbrod also describes the relationship that the two had as initially strained but later close:

> Two letters, to Jōzai and Keisō, both dated July 4, 1840, marked O'Michi's first efforts as Bakin's amanuensis.[6] Before Sōhaku's death her life in the Takizawa household had afforded little joy. . . . O'Michi repeatedly suffered Sōhaku's abuse, and being high-strung by nature, she would sometimes withdraw to her room, refuse to eat, and finally become ill. O'Hyaku would then nurse her and Bakin offer her some medicine . . . but Sōhaku generally "refused to come near and remained as ill-tempered as ever."
>
> Bakin's poor opinion of her family must also have pained O'Michi. Initially he showed respect for her father, Genryū, and her elder brother, Gen'yū, both physicians, but Bakin later asserted that they were "quacks." He sarcastically referred to Genryū's wife as O'Michi's "mother-nun from Azabu," and he described her visits as "hateful in the extreme."
>
> [After Sōhaku's death] O'Michi and Bakin grew closer. At first, she merely prepared and marketed the medicines and kept financial records for it. Later she assumed additional responsibilities. "It would be impossible without her," he wrote on April 19, 1837. He praised her as "an unflagging worker," and she served him in many ways, large and small.[7]

As Bakin's eyesight failed him, Michi's responsibilities increased, to the point that she wrote the last chapters of *The Story of Eight Dogs* from dictation.[8] Zolbrod summarizes the relationship by saying that "in both practical and intellectual matters, they had achieved a rare partnership."[9] It is clear that without Michi's help, Bakin could not have finished *The Story of Eight Dogs*, the masterpiece of his writing career.

It is this latter point of "intellectual matters," and not the working partnership that Bakin's diaries record, which must have caught Fumiko's attention. When she sat down to tell the fictionalized story of Bakin's last years through Michi's eyes, she portrayed Michi as an oppressed woman who did not like her father-in-law, a man who felt that women and their writing were insignificant compared to men and theirs. When "Writing" opens, Bakin is already near the end of his life, suffering from bad health and nearly blind. He is obsessed with writing *The Story of Eight Dogs*, and that has taken precedence over consideration for the other members of the family. He refuses outside visitors, too, and Michi thinks to herself that he is surprisingly unhappy for somebody who is so egoistical:

Bakin sat at his desk with his glasses on. His appearance, with his left shoulder slumped down, bent towards his desk, gave the impression of a lonely person. He had repelled his family, repelled his friends, and despite the fact that he said he didn't need anybody in whom to confide, Michi could not but think that such solitude must be lonely. Even his good friend, Hanayama, had said that father was steeped in his own ego. But Michi could only think how unhappy such a man must be.[10]

Michi does not agree with Bakin on most things, especially literature. She finds his writing didactic and distasteful, and he finds the books she reads shallow and frivolous:

Bakin ridiculed Shunsui's works as trivial novels, complete garbage.[11] Bakin could not but object to the fact that such works—works which were nothing more than pictures of people's shadows—were so sought after by everyone. Kyōzan and Tanehiko were permissible, but those weak men without money or power who depicted nothing but women from the world of indolence, who persisted in writing common *genre* novels![12] Shunsui's manner of producing novels which pandered to obscene interests and then flaunting them before the public as novels written by a man was something Bakin dismissed as artisan writing.[13]

Bakin obviously feels that such vulgar writing is below the intelligence of a male writer, and he is disgusted that a man would produce such works. He tells Michi that her taste in literature leaves much to be desired, but Michi does not let her father-in-law's opinions change her choice of reading material. She tolerates his brusqueness but she is miserable living in his house and contemplates suicide at one point. Finally she finds friendship with one of Bakin's daughters, Kuwa, who is married and lives away from home, and the two of them discover that they enjoy the same books and share many of the same thoughts.[14] They are also equally poorly treated by Bakin. When he finally dies in the last scene neither Michi nor Kuwa expresses grief, although Michi is touched when Bakin bids her to sit by his side because he is lonely.

There are aspects of "Writing" that diverge from Zolbrod's biography of Bakin: Bakin's diary tells us that Sōhaku was unkind to Michi, but Fumiko depicts Sōhaku as a kind and supportive husband, one who on his deathbed tells his wife that she is "more of an artist" than her father-in-law; and nothing in Bakin's diaries indicates that Michi was unhappy enough to contemplate suicide.[15] However, many of the things Fumiko wrote of are part of established fact, such as Michi's role as Bakin's amanuensis and the way in which she ran the Takizawa household after Sōhaku's death. It is plain that Fumiko took liberties with the facts in this narrative, but what is most interesting is that in the places where she deviates from recorded history, she clearly does so in an effort to emphasize the importance of Michi in Bakin's life and the high level of literary intelligence that Michi had.[16] In this sense, Fumiko was writing a feminist short story; not only was she writing a story "of or pertaining to women and their qualities," she was writing specifically about the qualities of a woman who, Fumiko might have liked to think, was slighted by history. Her incentive in writing "Writing" was the desire to promote a positive view of a historical female figure.

MARRIAGE IN FUMIKO'S LIFE

Hayashi Fumiko wrote many works that deal with marriage; some question the validity of the institution itself, some criticize the practice of arranged marriages and some are about marriages which suffer from a loss of love. This subject matter may be one of the reasons why Fumiko's writing is so often relegated to the category of "women's literature" (marriage being a central concern to many Japanese women), but Fumiko did write some works about marriage that are told from the man's point of view and that certainly cannot be considered "women's literature," if what we mean by that is literature "of or pertaining to women and their qualities." It would be more accurate to say that, coming from a home where marriage was a rather casual relationship and having had many affairs herself before she married, Fumiko was interested in exploring what place marriage had in society and culture as a whole, not just in the female half.[17]

The marriage that she herself had with Rokubin was unconventional in that Fumiko, the wife, was the sole breadwinner in the family. Also, she tended to disappear for days at a time without informing Rokubin of her whereabouts, something that he found trying at times, although it never caused a permanent rift in their relationship.[18] Marriage for Fumiko seemed to be more of a social obligation than an act of the heart. She loved Rokubin, and she married him, but the marriage itself was more of a formal concession to societal convention than an emotional dedication of herself to her husband. She did not play the retiring role that was normally expected of a wife in those times, nor did many of the characters in her fiction.

In those works that portray characters forced into marriage by their families, or who are already married but find themselves dissatisfied with their spouses, the central issue is that of freedom of choice. These characters accept marriage as a worthwhile act, but they do not accept being deprived of their right to choose to be married. Fumiko's belief in free will made this a very important issue; precisely because people have the ability to choose, she implies in these works, they should not be

denied the use of that faculty. In *Diary of a Vagabond*, Fumiko cele-
brates the exercise of free will, but in a variety of later works she begins
to explore what happens when an individual is forced against that will.
These works also reveal a change in Fumiko's world outlook, a change
from a youthful, vigorous, *carpe diem* attitude to a more mature, sometimes pessimistic, approach to life.

QUESTIONING THE INSTITUTION OF MARRIAGE

The first group of works I would like to examine are those that question
the legitimacy of marriage itself. Most of the characters in these works
are pressured by family and friends to marry, but they can find little reason in their hearts to do so. They meditate on what marriage is for, what
society expects of each partner in matrimony, and whether such expectations and obligations have any good founding. Although their families
and friends generally see marriage as a natural act for human beings,
these characters stand back and reexamine the legitimacy of such an
assumption.

Lightning concerns a family of five: four siblings—Nuiko, Mitsuko,
Hirosuke, and Kiyoko—and their mother, Osei. Each child has a different father, but only Kiyoko is disturbed by this fact. She thinks often on
how her family's structure is psychologically harmful to its members,
how the siblings simply hate each other, and on the fact that there is little love in the family. Mitsuko becomes a widow early in the novel when
her husband, Rohei, dies of acute pneumonia. She mourns, but not
much, because he was not a faithful husband and his loss cannot be considered a great one. Nuiko is married to a man named Ryūkichi; both
characters are grating types, rarely seen in a positive light. Hirosuke
remains single and leaves his unpleasant family to become a dry-goods
seller in Manchuria.

Kiyoko is the heroine of this novel. She resists her family's proposal
that she marry a baker named Takakichi, a family friend, despite the fact
that everyone except Kiyoko assumes that the match would be most convenient. After opposing her arranged betrothal to no avail, she leaves
home and moves into her own apartment. The apartment is an oasis of
calm away from the family, and single life makes Kiyoko a happy woman.
The pressure to marry Takakichi never ceases, but neither does Kiyoko's
determination not to do so. Near the end of the novel, Mitsuko tries to
convey to Kiyoko Takakichi's sincere interest, but Kiyoko tells her sister
how she feels about marriage to Takakichi in no uncertain terms:

> "Takakichi really seems to love you, you know," said Mitsuko as
> she tossed around in bed. Kiyoko remained silent.

"He seems absolutely intent on having a relationship with you. He's got a picture of you in his wallet. He's serious about loving you, he's wholehearted about the matter . . ."

"Just thinking about it is unpleasant. Really unpleasant . . ."

"But, whatever else, he's got good work. You're so helpless, but you can always fall back on him, just like Nuiko does with her husband . . ."

"What are you saying? I'd rather spend my entire life in a convent than marry that sort of man. I wouldn't marry such a man even if I were a cripple . . . I've got a lot of things to think through about myself. I don't know yet which road I should head out on, but I do so want to live my life splendidly. I wonder if you wouldn't ask Papa in Azabu to pay for some schooling for me?"[19]

Kiyoko goes on to say that she is really not sure what she wants in life, that she is very lonely, and that not being able to have a "normal" marriage—one in which the spouses love each other—makes her wish she had never been born. She does not question the legitimacy of marriage in principle; she thinks that it would be fine if it were a match that made both partners happy. What she does question is the social pressure to marry for the sake of being married.

The protagonist in *River Song*, Kikuyo, is a young woman who has left her home in the countryside and moved to the city where she hopes to make a good life for herself. She moves in with a former teacher of hers, Hisako. Hisako, like Kikuyo, is still single and finds herself lonely without a husband, but she does not want to marry her suitor, Nozu, a man she met through her brother. One day, when Hisako is out, Kikuyo opens Hisako's diary and flips through the pages, reading some of the entries:

Sunday

I don't know what I should do, how I should live. Again yesterday I felt dizzy all day long. I keep thinking about the day I will be with Mr. Nozu. I don't know when that will be, but still I wonder what sort of aloof figure he will cut. I received a hundred yen, but I have no need for it. I'd just like to send for my mother from the countryside, and let Nobuyuki and his wife see the two of us living together.[20]

Is marriage something that people do to make their lives difficult? Is it something they do to live their lives in comfort? This is not an easy question to answer.[21]

Kikuyo reflects on how unhappy Hisako must be, but there is little she can do for her. Kikuyo does not share Hisako's strong feelings about marriage; to Kikuyo marriage is more of a curiosity, something that she will probably face later in life but not an impending necessity. Later in the novel Kikuyo has a disturbing conversation with a co-worker, Fukuoka; Fukuoka tells her that marriage is a terrible thing, and that the time one is single is the happiest time in a person's life:

> It was time for the afternoon break. Kikuyo was invited by Fukuoka to go for a walk along the canal by the Unagami Building. The two of them walked slowly along the scorching white pavement.
>
> "You're still single, so you can't sympathize with how a married woman feels," said Fukuoka rather suddenly, with no outward clue as to what she was thinking. The two of them wore the same purple striped office uniform, but Kikuyo had a younger, fresher look about her. Kikuyo walked along, gazing lazily at the white buildings in the afternoon sun.
>
> "You don't know how difficult a woman's life can be until you've gotten married . . . You must be so happy being single," Fukuoka said.
>
> "Oh, you think so? I have never once thought that I was happy. I feel lonely, like something is missing . . ."
>
> "All single women feel like there is 'something missing.' I feel sorry for young women born in this day and age. In my day, it was so pleasant being a young maid."[22]

Indeed, these words frighten Kikuyo away from hastily marrying anyone. She has a few affairs, but none of them result in marriage. By the end of the novel she is still single. There is an air of hesitation about her approach to romantic relationships; the words of Hisako and Fukuoka have made her cautious.

Hisako does eventually get married, but to a fellow teacher, Kawajiri, not to Nozu. Her life changes dramatically when she quits her teaching job to stay at home, and she finds herself quite bored when her husband is conscripted into the army, leaving her all alone. She does not regret her choice to marry, however. Near the end of the novel she reflects on how marriage has changed her life:

> Once a baby is born there will be no return to being a teacher, she thought. She had no self-confidence in her ability to raise a child well. For Hisako, there was nothing mysterious about marriage and bearing children. Thinking back on it all, she realized that the flurried feeling she had before she got married was really quite different from how she felt now, since she had settled down and developed affection for her husband.[23]

Through Hisako, Fumiko tells us that although marriage does not have to be a bad thing, it definitely does change one's life. Those changes are ominous enough to prevent Kikuyo from rushing into matrimony, although her curiosity about married life is constantly being piqued by those around her. Fumiko's message in *Lightning* and *River Song* is the same: marriage, she implies, should be for love, not social obligation. Both Kiyoko and Kikuyo remain single so the reader does not see what married life would actually bring them, but there is an underlying assertion in both works that the only morally correct marriage is one in which the individuals participate of their own free will.

In her novel *Rain*, Fumiko creates a heroine who also feels strongly about the importance of marrying by choice; she does so, but contentment is not so easily secured. In this novel, Fumiko goes beyond the issue of choice and asks whether, even if one freely chooses it, the institution of marriage provides any benefit to one's life.

Rain is the story of a young woman, Michiko, who comes from a relatively poor, rural family. After rejecting a prospective suitor chosen by her family, she marries a man from Kyōto, Ōhara, whose family is wealthy and well educated. Most of their marital strife stems from the difference in their backgrounds. The relationship grows over the years, but it is not an easy process and the two find that the simple act of marriage does not provide much of a guarantee of security: that legal bonding does not provide emotional stability.

In the opening chapters of *Rain*, Michiko's family wants her to marry a man, Shiokai, who loves her but toward whom she feels no affection. She refuses the match because of this, and the incident makes her meditate more profoundly on marriage. Her older sister (who is physically deformed due to a bad case of rickets) had a love affair years earlier, though the family forced her to break it off. Michiko knows that her sister was truly in love with her suitor, and she feels it tragic that they were compelled to separate. She wonders why society condemns love the way it does:

> As Michiko sat on the *tatami* she was struck by the sudden desire to have a boyfriend. It wasn't as if she had been told by everybody that she must not love somebody, it was just that everybody around her seemed to walk about with scary expressions on their faces, as if they certainly did not love anybody else. Michiko was totally baffled as to why love was always thought of as if it were a crime. She recalled the time when she was a schoolgirl and her crippled sister had been in love. Her sister's lover had been an elementary school teacher, but their grandfather had been so extremely angry about the affair that he hit her. Michiko had cried when she saw that. The teacher went back to his hometown in Shinshū shortly after that, and then he had been conscripted. Michiko's sister was never the same; now she would spend all day shut up in her room reading books and sewing.
>
> Why was it that people like her sister were forbidden to love? Michiko remembered what an extraordinarily good young man her sister's lover had been. And now he was off at war.
>
> Before she knew it Michiko had reached the age that her sister had been at the time, and she began to understand the bitterness that her sister had felt then. The *tatami* were warm and moist. Countless young

women had probably slept on these mats.[24] It made Michiko feel odd to think that she too would be sleeping on these mats tonight.

The love that Michiko had experienced so far was like some by-product of a moral code created by people who lived in darkness, under a horrifying law that forbade one to love another.[25]

For a while, Michiko maintains a simplistic, unsophisticated idea of marriage; she thinks that having a happy marriage is simply a matter of marrying for love, and as long as she is not enamored of another she can keep the specter of marriage at a safe distance, but when she falls in love with Ōhara, she becomes frightened by the immediacy of marriage. Suddenly she realizes that being in love has not miraculously made the concept of marriage fully comprehensible to her. Of itself, love could not handle the difficulties of dealing with her in-laws, nor could it prepare her for being uprooted and moved to a new city. Indeed, Michiko comes to the horrible realization that marriage is really more about legal, social, and economic bonds than it is about two people enjoying each others' company. On one of the first nights she spends with Ōhara, she wonders what marriage really means:

> That night, Michiko slept a deep, dreamless sleep. When she lay down on the floor she had pondered the idea of starting out on a new life together—these were novel thoughts she had never had before. Just what was this thing called "marriage"? Two young friends fall in love and have a family—this sort of marriage made Michiko a little uneasy.[26]

It makes her uneasy because it is happening so fast, and she is not sure it is what she wants. Michiko is right to be suspicious, as her marriage to Ōhara turns out to have its share of difficulties. Most of these are brought about by Ōhara's family, who eventually request that he move back home to Kyōto. The familial obligations are what Michiko finds the most trying and near the end of the novel she wishes that she could go off on her own to a place where she could work.[27] For her, marriage has very little to do with her emotional bond to her husband; that is something that would probably exist whether or not the two were officially wed. Michiko's marriage is primarily a bond to her in-laws, a bond of social obligation similar to the social obligation of an arranged marriage as depicted in *Lightning* and *River Song*.

A Family of Women is a story about a family of four women: the mother, Yukie, and her three daughters, Tokiko, Ruiko, and Hideko. Yukie would like to see her daughters married, but none of them want to be pushed in that direction. The most strong-minded of them all is Ruiko, who walks out of an arranged marriage meeting in order to be with her lover Ōtsubo, whom she later leaves because he is married with children. Hideko is the most emotionally immature of the sisters. She becomes romantically involved with a man named Seki and thinks about marrying him, but by the end of the novel still has not done so.[28] Tokiko is a war widow who would really rather free herself of all family obligations, including caring for Yukie in her old age. The feelings that Hideko and Ruiko have about marriage and family obligations are summed up in a dialogue between the two in the final scene of the novel:

> "If you get married to Seki, you should come to Atami," said Ruiko coldly.
>
> "I don't know yet if we'll be able to get married. I think that I really should be taking care of Mother. Tokiko really has no intention of living with mother . . . she's just like that."
>
> "But there's really no point in you giving up on the idea of marriage to Seki for Mother's sake. I'll look after her somehow. She's still young—the two of us can do some sort of work. Tokiko just wants her freedom. She thinks only of herself, she's the type that can't leave others alone, and I can't live with her. Mother and I can look after Reiko, and if I end up having children I'll just work my hardest.[29] I learned about relationships the hard way with Ōtsubo, and I don't intend to fall into that rut again. You should go where you belong, Hideko, to Seki's side . . ."
>
> "Yes, but, getting married? I don't know if that will make me happy or not . . . Do women ultimately find happiness when they marry? I'm not sure. Is marriage really something to which women just escape?"
>
> "Oh! If that's how you feel, then don't get married. What kind of happiness can women find, do you think?"
>
> "I think they can find plenty even if they are single."[30]

Ruiko has dismissed marriage as an option for herself, but she thinks that married life would be fine for her sister; she does not equate her failed affair with Ōtsubo with Hideko's relationship with Seki. But Hideko, despite her relative naiveté, wonders whether marriage would bring her happiness. Ruiko thinks, as she watches Hideko sleeping later, that Hideko is at the point of life when women are their happiest. She wishes that she could return to that point in her life—presumably the time before she had ever become involved with a man.

All these works, *Lightning*, *River Song*, *Rain*, and *A Family of Women* question the rationale of marriage out of obligation—marriage for marriage's sake. Fumiko stops short of a deep discussion of why such obligations exist, which is in keeping with her tendency to avoid philosophical topics, but it is clear that all the protagonists in these novels face the same basic question: Why should one marry? Is it solely a duty which one is expected to perform? Does it necessarily carry with it the burden of familial obligations?[31] Kiyoko and Kikuyo reject the institution of marriage entirely, finding no good in it. Michiko finally accepts it, only to discover that is it not what she had hoped, and Ruiko resigns herself to the conclusion that marriage is an inevitable but undesirable event in a woman's life. In these four novels we can see the development of Fumiko's philosophy of marriage, the gist of which, it would seem, is that marriage is most advantageous for the families of those getting married, and the only option—if one is to avoid such tangled familial obligations—is to remain single. It is interesting that Fumiko never wrote about a marriage such as her own, which by all accounts worked well and gave both spouses considerable freedom from traditional duties.

THE IMPORTANCE OF FREEDOM OF CHOICE

Kiyoko (*Lightning*), Michiko (*Rain*), and Ruiko (*A Family of Women*) all flee from arranged marriages. None of these novels address clearly why such a marriage is supposed to be undesirable—there is an assumption that the reader will understand implicitly—but the novel *Aware hitozuma* (Pitiful Wife, 1950) is more specific. The protagonist, Watari Keiko, is a young, single woman who at the beginning of the novel hears plenty from her married friends about how terrible married life can be. One friend is miserable with her husband, but feels she cannot leave him for the sake of her children. The other, Keiko's sister-in-law Yoriko, has no children, but still finds it impossible to abandon her marriage. Both women warn Keiko about how horrible marriage is, and Keiko feels sorry for them. Their warnings emphasize to Keiko the potential for disaster in a marriage, and while she cannot guarantee herself a future life of married bliss, she does recognize that there is at least one thing she can do to avoid unhappiness: she can choose her own spouse.

Keiko works in an office and becomes enamored of a man who works there, Tomoda. He is a rather sloppy man but Keiko finds his haphazard manners endearing and attractive because he is not like all the others in the office. Keiko and Tomoda become friends and their romance begins. Unfortunately for Keiko, her family has in the meantime been making arrangements for her to marry a man whom she has never met, Tokunori. She finds out about their plans and tries to resist, but the family is determined. They go so far as to offer Tomoda money to leave Keiko; Tomoda refuses the money and then tells Keiko what her family has done. Keiko is forced by her family to move back home, and forbidden to see Tomoda any more.

The climactic scene is one in which the family members air their opinions about the entire affair, and while it is rather lengthy it merits being quoted in full. The characters include Etsuji and Noboru (both older brothers of Keiko), Etsuji's wife Yoriko, and Taeko, Keiko's mother:

> In the sitting room were Etsuji, Yoriko, Noboru, and Mr. and Mrs. Sakai, in-laws of Taeko's from Chōfu. Mr. Sakai was the person who had brought the wedding proposal from Mr. Tokunori. By profession he was a dentist, but he was crazy about elections and when Watari Etsuji was running as a candidate, Mr. Sakai had become invaluable to the Watari family—they couldn't have gotten along without him.
>
> With the feeling that she had entered an enemy camp, Keiko went and sat down beside Noboru.
>
> At first the conversation was harmless chitchat, but it naturally turned to the matter of Keiko's marriage. Etsuji was angry with Keiko and acted as if he wanted to break off relations with her. He turned toward Taeko and purposely did not look in Keiko's direction.
>
> Yoriko was the first to speak. "We've discussed Keiko's matter among us before, but I thought it would be best to meet with her and give it further serious consideration, so I asked mother to call her here today . . ."
>
> "Mr. Sakai's father has already made all the arrangements for the meeting, and would like to know how to proceed from here. So, Keiko, we've decided that we'd like to you to save Mr. Sakai embarrassment by going to meet Mr. Tokunori . . ."
>
> Noboru was gazing out at the garden. Keiko turned to face his profile and pleaded, "But I don't think that I'll have any interest in Mr. Tokunori even if I do meet him. I understand your concern, but I don't want to meet Mr. Tokunori, and I'm going ahead with my plans with Mr. Tomoda."
>
> "Oh? With whose permission?" Etsuji asked angrily.
>
> Keiko was silent for a moment, but then she burst forth in a flood of angry words. "I am an adult. I thought I could get married without anybody's permission . . ."
>
> "Oh, I see. Did that man put this idea into your head? That may be the law, but you are a member of the Watari household. You cannot behave like a stray cat, picking and choosing what you want!"
>
> "But I thought that because I was a member of the Watari household, I would not lose my humanity and be forced to go to a place that does not please me for the sake of the family."
>
> "Hmm . . . You certainly are not speaking in a very ladylike manner. What do you think, Mr. Sakai? Like I was saying, there is no hope for this woman, so though I'm sorry to ask it of you, would you be so kind as to cut off negotiations with Mr. Tokunori? For my part, I have no intention of recognizing this autonomous marriage."
>
> Sakai smiled and said, "Well, I have a bit of a problem with that. I think things are being said rather rashly here. After we've finished eat-

ing I'd like to go to the next room and discuss this thoroughly with Keiko . . ."

"Let me repeat myself. My feelings stand on this matter, whether or not I go to the next room for a talk with Sakai . . ." Before Keiko finished speaking, Etsuji thrust his hand out in anger and struck her across the face.

"Who made you queen?! How dare you talk back like that! Give a thought to the fact that we are all opposed to your ideas. Do you have any idea how treacherous those thoughts of yours are?"

"No. Noboru said it was OK!"

"Noboru? Noboru is opposed, too!"

"Noboru is the only one who understands how I feel."

Noboru wished that the conversation would proceed as amicably as possible, but things had gotten out of hand and at this most important juncture he was the focus of everybody's attention. He turned to Etsuji.

"It's like Keiko says. Wouldn't we all be satisfied as long as Keiko is happy? Of course Mr. Tokunori has gone to a lot of trouble, and Keiko should be thankful to Mr. Sakai for his kind services, but I think it would be best if we let Keiko do as she sees fit."

"Who will take responsibility if Keiko ends up unhappy?!"

"Keiko herself, of course. That is not a responsibility for others to bear. When men and women get married, they do so on their own, don't they? They would be stupid to hold their relatives forever responsible for their own unhappiness."

Etsuji was furious and stormed off to his own room. Yoriko looked pale and said, "Noboru says that a woman should find her happiness in the way she sees fit, but I'm a woman and I don't agree. We're all angry because we care for Keiko. Shouldn't we be grateful that someone is proposing marriage?"

"That may make the family happy, but for Keiko it is a real predicament. The family just gangs up and welcomes the idea."

"Good Heavens! What a terrible thing to say! Do you think it would be good for Keiko to suffer by being married off to an obviously impoverished man?"

Noboru glared indignantly at Yoriko. "Keiko is still young. Don't you think she can stand a little hardship? The only one who's not suffering in this whole thing is you. All of us are suffering, you know. Love shouldn't be a matter of suffering or not suffering; it should be the warmth felt by two lonely people who find each other after searching the world over. The two of them love each other—who are we to gang up against them with this and that objection? I'm talking to you, too, Mother. Don't think about the indebtedness that Keiko is supposed to have toward the woman who raised her. History has repeated the parent/child cycle for thousands of years. When children are grown, they leave the nest. Just give the matter a rest."

Taeko looked like she was on the verge of tears. With a shaky, restrained voice she said, "Now, wait a minute. This isn't like you . . . Discussion of Keiko's marriage should not involve filial obligation. No matter what you say, Keiko is still a child and she knows little of the world. This fellow Tomoda wanted to meet me, but I wouldn't agree to it. I'm not saying anything in particular about this Mr. Tomoda, but I want my daughter to be placed safely in the hands of a man close to me. Keiko may be an adult, but I don't think that she is as wise a daughter as Noboru says. She is still selfish and wilful, which makes me think that she is still a child—refusing talk of marriage to Mr. Tokunori and all. It's perfectly natural that parents should be concerned about their daughter's happiness. I don't know how they do things in the West, but surely since time immemorial parents have been concerned with their children's happiness.

"In any case, I'd like Keiko to stay with me for the time being. I'd like her to quit her job. She knows nothing at all about being a housewife, so for the next year she shall learn how to sew and how to cook. If, after all that, she still has difficulty with the idea of marrying Mr. Tokunori, then I think it would be best to let her do as she pleases. Won't you agree to this, Mr. Sakai, and give us a little time? This should be just fine with Etsuji, too. I will not allow Keiko to do just exactly as she pleases. That is my parental duty. Nobody should disagree with me on this."

Keiko thought the course the conversation was taking quite an odd turn. "What? There's no way I'm quitting my job. If I spend a year learning how to sew and cook that means that Etsuji will have to support me again. I wish you all would just not consider me part of the Watari family any more. Mother and the rest of you will thank me someday for this. I will make it up to you somehow."

Yoriko had offered lunch to Noboru, but he said he had business to attend to and went on his way after stating his opinion. The *sushi* arrived and Keiko passed out plates and chopsticks to everyone, although she herself had not the slightest appetite.

As Sakai savored his beer he said, "Well, what demanding talk! It's best for Keiko to be by her mother's side for the time being. You know, Keiko, society doesn't cater to people's selfishness. You can't get along in this world by trying to prance around the demands of duty and humanity. You've got to have the spirit of cooperation. You've got to understand how your mother feels, having raised you all this time. Noboru is Noboru. First of all, that's just the sort of thing men say. When he has a daughter of his own he will remember this day and be embarrassed. 'It's nothing special that parents raise children.' Ha! What dubious notions those are! I don't agree with those words at all. This is Japan. It is not America or the Soviet Union."[32]

This family meeting makes Keiko desperate, and so she arranges with Tomoda to escape to Atami (a seaside resort) for a few days. They succeed in doing so, although they cannot truly escape the situation in which Keiko has been placed by her family. After they return home, Keiko's marriage to Tomoda is finally agreed upon, on the condition that Keiko quit her job after getting married.

The marriage is not the island of bliss that Keiko had imagined; Tomoda stays out late at night and comes home drunk. Keiko is lonely in the empty house and tries working as a typist to keep herself occupied, but the job does not interest her. Near the end of the story, she is pregnant and faces the sort of bored, trapped existence as a housewife that her friends had warned her about in the beginning of the novel.

For Keiko's family, that a young person would want to choose his or her spouse is a minor consideration; they feel an overriding responsibility for her that includes assuring a materially comfortable future. Keiko has seen and heard enough about unhappy marriages to think that taking her chances with a stranger is absurd. The right to choose (in this case, her own husband) is very important to her, something that reminds the reader of the general mood of *Diary of a Vagabond*. In both novels the importance of freedom of choice is central to the narrative. Free choice does not necessarily bring happiness, but that does not reduce its importance. When Keiko later becomes unhappy with Tomoda, she knows that she has no one but herself to blame. Although there are scenes where she breaks down in tears because of a given difficulty, there are no scenes in which she indulges in self-pity.

There are two short stories that Fumiko wrote about arranged marriage from the man's point of view, "Hana no ichi" (A Flower's Place, 1937) and "Maihime" (Dancing Girl, 1940). In both stories, the man's family decides it is time for him to marry and presents him with their decision rather abruptly. In both stories, the protagonist is mainly concerned not with the act of marriage as such, but rather with being given the chance to choose it of his own free will.

"A Flower's Place" is about a young man, Koyano Shūichi, who is the eldest son in his family. His mother died when he was young and he now lives with his father, Kōhei, stepmother, Tamiko, and youngest brother, Kōzō, who is still in his teens. The middle brother, Kuniji, dropped out of college to go to Europe and study textiles. Kuniji returns from Europe and shocks his family by taking a lover. They do not approve, but Kuniji is determined to live his life his own way and so there is nothing that the family can do. Shūichi watches his brother's actions with envy. He wishes he could be so free, but being the eldest son of the family puts an extra burden on him and he knows that his parents' expectations are high. His reaction to this family pressure is social withdrawal; we are told that when he graduated from law school he did not look for work, and at the opening of the narrative he is spending most of his time cooped up in his study at home, translating economics texts.

The family has a maid, Miyako, with whom Shūichi begins an affair. Miyako is terrified of being found out by the family, but Shūichi assures her that he intends to marry her. She knows in her heart that the family will never allow this, but she cannot bring herself to say that to Shūichi. When Shūichi's family arranges a marriage for him to a woman from Kyōto named Kawauchi Sumie, he gathers all his courage and tells his stepmother about his love for Miyako. Tamiko tells him that she will not stand for it, and that as the eldest son of the family he has responsibilities that Kuniji does not have. When Shūichi says that he wants to relinquish those responsibilities to Kōzō, Tamiko tells him that that would not be acceptable either:

> "Well, in any case, if you want to do me a favor, then leave this matter about Miyako up to me. You are too young to be talking about responsibility. Miyako could end up being a real burden on the Koyano family, and besides you are the eldest son . . ."
>
> "Well I was thinking that if this matter doesn't work itself out, Kōzō could carry on the family line and Miyako and I could start our own household."
>
> Tamiko was distraught, and tears rolled down her saggy cheeks. "No, I won't stand for it. I'm going to live a proper life. No matter what happens, Kōzō is the youngest, and on top of that he's mine.[33] I won't stand being scrutinized by all sorts of people. And the fact that it's Miyako makes it all the worse . . . Oh, if people thought that I did this on purpose to the precious eldest son, why . . ."
>
> Shūichi disdained his stepmother's concern about such shallow issues. He thought, "Just like a woman—she's got it all worked out." In his heart, he thought about taking Miyako and leaving home. If he left home, he would be living for the moment, and it wouldn't be miserable if he were with her.[34]

The family absolutely refuses to allow Shūichi to marry Miyako. They discreetly send her away, and Shūichi has no way of finding her. The family proceeds with preparations for Shūichi's marriage to Sumie. By the end of the story, Shūichi has heard from Miyako (who is staying with her family in the countryside); he suspects that she is pregnant with their child, but that she is afraid to tell him. In the final scene, he cries out in sorrow just as Sumie, to whom he is now married, comes into his study.

Shūichi is denied the right to choose his wife, and the denial makes him miserable. He yearns for his brother's freedom; not for the opportunity to go abroad (he says he has no interest in doing so), but rather the opportunity to be able to choose where to go and what to do. The thing which prevents him from doing so is social convention, which is just what pressures the women in *Lightning, River Song, Rain, A Fam-*

ily of Women, and *Pitiful Wife* to marry. Each of these characters knows that the freedom to choose is more important to them than social acceptance, and that failure would be tolerable if it were of their own making.

"Dancing Girl" has a similar theme but one main difference: in the stories discussed above, the protagonists all have some other, concrete goal toward which they strive. It might be possible to say that they reject social pressure to marry because there is another, more tempting option close at hand, and not because the right to choose is fundamentally important to them. But the protagonist in "Dancing Girl," Suekichi, does not have such a tempting second option; he does not love another, nor does he particularly want to pursue some other goal.

Suekichi is an only child and lives at home with his father and stepmother. He was working in Taiwan as an apprentice on a sugar plantation until he contracted malaria and returned to Japan to convalesce. He is of marrying age, but has not given the matter much thought, being a rather retiring sort. The story opens as he is watching the four sisters from the Nishio family (who live next door to him) practicing a dance in their garden. The vivacity of the young women strikes him, especially that of the tallest.

Suekichi's father calls him for a talk one day and shows him a photograph of a young woman named Umeko. He says that Suekichi's stepmother has suggested marriage between the two (Umeko is a relative of hers) and he asks Suekichi what he thinks of Umeko. Suekichi takes a glance at the photo, but tells his father that he does not have the mind to marry just then. His stepmother is disappointed, but does not give up hope of arranging her stepson's marriage.

One evening Suekichi goes out for a walk and when he returns to his neighborhood, he meets the tall daughter from next door. She has come home late from the movies and cannot get into the locked gate at her house. Her determined air and pragmatic demeanor—she thinks nothing of hopping over the wall—shake Suekichi from his placidity as he begins to realize that he has been too timid in life and there is much in the world for him to discover:

> When he approached the dark earthen wall of the Nishios' house, he saw the dark silhouette of somebody climbing over the wall. Sue-kichi was startled and strained his eyes in the starlight, staring through the darkness at the figure on the wall.
> "Who's there?" Suekichi said in a low, stern voice. The figure, who had both hands on the wall, was startled by Suekichi's voice and nimbly stepped down to the ground. When he drew close, Suekichi realized that it was the young daughter of the Nishio family who had greeted him so kindly earlier.

"The gate's already shut for the night," she said, shrugging her shoulders awkwardly.

"Are you by yourself?"

"Uh huh. Grandma yelled at me so I decided to get out of the house for a while. I went to the movies and now I'm home late . . ."

She was the young woman who had danced like a dying swan at the edge of the pond.

"Don't you have a doorbell at the gate?"

"Uh huh, but it has been broken for ever so long and still doesn't work." Her profile was faint, and resembled a water lily.

They had no telephone in the Nishio house, and it did not seem that one would be able to hear knocking at the gate from the distant main house.

"Aren't you Mr. Nishio's daughter?"

"Uh huh, although this is grandmother's house. It's a family of good people, except for me. I'm selfish and sometimes I can be so difficult." The young woman shrugged her shoulders, stuck her tongue out and smiled.

Suekichi bent over at the base of the wall and said, "Well, just climb on my back and get over this wall!" She took off her shoes and climbed up on Suekichi's back, up and over the wall. There was a small thumping noise as she jumped down into the garden. Suekichi paused and listened. "Thank you. Goodbye," said a small, charming voice.

That night, Suekichi just couldn't get to sleep. He could still feel the soft weight of the woman's body penetrating his bones. An owl hooted in the trees of the Suizen temple. Suekichi wondered whether she, too, was listening to that owl. The smell of dead leaves had permeated his nose when he had stooped down with both hands against the wall. His necktie had swung beneath his chin. The air had been full of late autumn, and occasionally an insect would sing out. Suekichi opened the curtain, slowly inched open the glass door and the rain shutter, and stared out at the dark garden next door.[35]

Later on, the young woman tells Suekichi that she is leaving home to go to study dance in Tokyo. Suekichi's stepmother invites Umeko to come and stay with the family, and Suekichi knows that it is only a matter of time before the two will be married despite the fact that he does not really want it. In the final scene, while Umeko is peeling a persimmon for him, he imagines how happy the young woman from next-door will be in Tokyo when her talents as a dancer are recognized. The symbolism in this scene involves goldfish in the ponds behind the house:

Suekichi went toward the windows and opened the glass door. He could see the garden next door. A puppy was lazily poking about in the sun of the expansive yard. The cockscomb and sage bloomed in all their glory, like candles put out on display.

Umeko silently started peeling the persimmons.

Suekichi gazed at the autumn landscape next door with a strange feeling of submission.

"Am I right in thinking that you are angry at me for coming here?" asked Umeko, as if she had suddenly remembered something. "Your stepmother says that the ceremony will be in early December . . ."

It was the first Suekichi had heard of the plan to have the wedding in early December. He was angry at his stepmother, for she had to know that he himself felt uneasy about this marriage. "I still have military duty I must do. We can't talk about the ceremony just yet . . ." he said brusquely, still with his face towards the garden.

"Yes, I know." Tears poured down Umeko's face as she peeled the persimmon. The tears hit her bosom and spilled onto her lap, but she made no move to wipe them away as she lined up the peeled pieces of persimmon on a plate and pierced them with a small fork.

Suekichi left Umeko there crying and went to the side of the fish ponds out back. He rolled back the reed screen which covered a pond, and there beneath it were three or four arch-shaped goldfish lazily swimming about in the water.[36]

The image of the young woman he had left in Unzen floated up before his eyes from the bottom of the pond.[37] She was headed for dance school in Tokyo, and would wait for the day when, like the goldfish, she would be chosen. How happy that young woman must be when she is dancing so skillfully . . . He walked around, looking at each pond. In every single one, there was a goldfish—some patterned, some crimson, some silver—swimming about lazily as if it were the very best fish in all of Japan.

Suddenly Suekichi remembered Umeko, crying as she peeled the persimmons, and it made him feel a distinct sadness in the bottom of his heart. How shameful it would be for him, as a man, to end up marrying her and caring for her . . . Suekichi thought he'd like to bring her along and show her the beautiful, splendid ponds and their goldfish.[38]

Suekichi feels pity for Umeko, but he has no intention of showing that pity by agreeing to marry her. To him that would be "shameful," not because he would betray some sort of masculine honor, but rather because he would be selling himself short by relinquishing his right to choose his future and, he fears, robbing Umeko of the same right. Consequently, his response to Umeko's tears is not guilt, nor is it surrender to his family's demands to marry; it is to show her the goldfish that symbolize independence and determination. He wants to share the emotion that drives him, not give it up. The last page of this story depicts the sudden transformation of Suekichi from a fatalistic man to a man who realizes he is the master of his destiny. The realization promises to take him away from his horrid existence, closed up in his house, and catapult him toward a vast realm of possibilities.

What is odd is that, despite the almost overwhelming feeling of catharsis Suekichi experiences when he decides to take charge of his life, we are never told what it is that he wants to do. Fumiko simply is not concerned with telling the reader what Suekichi's future aspirations might be. Such details are irrelevant; what is important is that the hero understands he is capable of aiming his life, of making choices. Like the narrator of *Diary of a Vagabond* and many other of Fumiko's protagonists, Suekichi experiences life in a immediate manner, rarely dealing with the past or the future but rather focusing on the present, and within the present his attention is given mostly to emotions. This centrality of immediate emotions should be familiar to the reader; we have seen it in *Diary of a Vagabond* (where it is most often expressed as a nonspecific desire to "do something") and the travelogues (where it is centered on feeling loneliness or nostalgia). It is as if Fumiko wears conceptual blinders; she does not want to see (much less explore) anything beyond her immediate surroundings. Within those surroundings what is most important is that she (or her protagonists) be enveloped in emotion—be it desire, loneliness, or whatever—so overwhelming that all else is obliterated.

Near the end of her life Fumiko suddenly changed; in the works discussed in the next section and in other works, such as *Drifting Clouds*, her characters were dramatically more mature. No longer were they headstrong, moody individuals oblivious to everything but the feeling of the moment. Now they occasionally reflected on the past, and they were able to keep their will in check long enough at least to attempt cooperation with others.

MARRIAGES GONE SOUR

Fumiko also wrote many stories about the husband-wife relationship once a marriage has soured. Given her penchant for depicting both physical and psychological violence, it is surprising that she does not include much of either in these stories. Instead, she tends to portray both partners as decent, sensitive people who would simply rather not be married any longer. Tension like that in the relationship between Jūichi and Mineko in *Brown Eyes* is present to a certain degree, but it does not escalate into ferocious confrontations. It is in these stories that Fumiko's character development is at its most subtle; the hesitation and mature concerns of each spouse reveal their personalities just as clearly as harsh speech would, but without the unpleasant, sometimes artless, violence of the earlier works.

The majority of works of this type were written near the end of

Fumiko's life. Two examples are "Kōya no niji" (Rainbows in the Wasteland, 1948) and "Ukisu" (Floating Grassplot, 1951). Both works are about marriages that have deteriorated over time; in neither story does any particular act cause discord, but rather a long chain of small events culminates in a situation that becomes unbearable for both spouses.

"Rainbows in the Wasteland" is about a couple, Tatsuo and Haruko, who were married a mere six months before Tatsuo was called away for military duty. This abrupt separation was difficult for both of them, and by the time Tatsuo returns home six years later, the two cannot simply pick up where they left off. While Tatsuo was stationed in Indonesia he had an affair with a Japanese bargirl, Hisako. He never intended to continue the affair in Japan, but once home, he cannot forget his lover, especially when a friend tells him that she, Hisako, is back in Japan, married, and with a child.

Haruko had a brief encounter with a man during her husband's absence, but she is not actively involved with him when Tatsuo returns. Still, she has been living on her own for so long that married life has no appeal to her any more and she feels that Tatsuo has become a totally different person from the man she married. One night, he overhears her talking in her sleep:

I'd like to talk to you about how I feel. I don't think either one of us is to blame, but coming through this war has made our relationship seem fragile somehow, and I can't help but feel how strange it all is. I just hung on, thinking that if only you would come back then everything would be settled, but it's been too long and that intense feeling has died. What kind of beast is war? There must be plenty of couples who are at odds with each other because of mixed thoughts like those I'm having . . . Although I haven't given my heart to some other whom I like more than you, I just don't have the wild, deep desire that I had when you were called into service. I used to dream about searching you out among all the conscripts and bringing you home . . . But six years have passed since then, haven't they? All that is gone now. My love has faded, and on the day when you first came back I had an odd feeling, like I wanted to go and hide myself somewhere. Both physically and spiritually, it's all for naught . . . Such a long time away from each other puts us in such a fix. After being separated from you at the age of twenty-four, I wasted the next six years of my life. After coming back you said that this was not the motherland you had dreamed of while you were away—is it true that the men who went to war and the women who stayed home have all changed? It may sound strange, but sleeping with you has become painful for me . . . I myself don't understand why I feel this way. When you aren't here I can vision you in my mind, but I can only see you when you were young, in the old days.

You're different now. I don't feel at all like I'm with my husband. I feel like I'm sleeping with some totally different person. What should we do? I must seem like a totally different woman to you . . . It's been three months since you came back. I've done a lot of thinking about this six-year, empty, hopeless marriage. But nothing comes of it, so I thought I'd ask you to give it some thought, too . . .[39]

This is not easy for Tatsuo to hear, but Haruko is not saying anything that he does not already know in his heart.

Neither Tatsuo nor Haruko harbor any animosity toward the other because they know that there is no one to blame for the unfortunate circumstance in which they find themselves. They also know that there is no realistic way for them to continue living together, and so their relationship comes down to figuring out the logistics of how to manage the separation. Tatsuo does not want Haruko to leave him and return to her mother's house in Nakano, and he tells Haruko as much in a feeble attempt to salvage something of his marriage:

> "How about if you try staying here, with freedom to do as you please? Don't you see that you will only be in the way in Nakano because they only have two rooms in the house? Isn't there some way for the two of us to work at this together?"
>
> Tatsuo made this suggestion, but Haruko rolled over and said that the two of them living together was just not a proper life. She went on to say that she did not hate him at all, but continuing on in this way, dragging along in this life as husband and wife, well, that was too much. She said, in a rather sullen manner, that she could not stand the thought that sometimes the image of another would be harbored in her heart, and that such unhappiness and maltreatment would be unbearable. If they had lived together for many years, there may have been occasion to comment ironically on the nature of their marriage, but given the short amount of time they had actually lived together they both knew that any irony was pointless.[40]

Dealing with the sad state of affairs is burdensome for them both, and so the process becomes an extremely slow and painful one. There is no denying that love has been lost; their interactions are gentle but businesslike, with both parties intent on being fair and just.

Haruko's brother complicates matters by telling Tatsuo that he feels his sister is being unreasonable. He encourages Tatsuo to be stricter, and he says many disparaging things about Haruko. Tatsuo cannot bring himself to follow his brother-in-law's advice, and so he must shrug off this family pressure, another instance of this theme that remained consistent throughout Fumiko's career. Tatsuo does not see any reasonable or logical reason to deny Haruko her freedom, despite what his in-laws suggest.

The fundamentally critical attitude toward the concept of marriage, as expressed in *Rain, A Family of Women, Pitiful Wife,* and *Lightning,* is absent in "Rainbows in the Wasteland." It is replaced by a somber resignation, an acceptance of unfortunate circumstances and a mature determination to overcome them. Somber resignation is also the response to marriage in "Floating Grassplot."

"Floating Grassplot" is also about a marriage that has become more of a social formality than any sort of spiritual bond. It is written in the third person, but told mainly from the husband Michitsugu's point of view. Michitsugu is depressed that his marriage has come to so little, and he contemplates suicide as a way out. He has two young children, Tokiko and Shigeichi, whom he loves dearly and who he imagines will commit suicide with him, leaving his wife, Kikuko, alone to do as she pleases. The children are unaware of their father's intentions, although they know that something is not right between their parents.

Kikuko is a very independent person and the story opens when she has been gone from the house for three days without contacting the family to tell them where she is. When she finally returns she says that she was visiting her parents, and she shows no compunction about having left abruptly without warning.

The narrative gives enough family history to explain how the family has come to be the way it is: Michitsugu had been conscripted during the war, and when he returned home he found that his place of employment had been burned to the ground. The postwar economy being slow at first, he cannot find employment and the family must depend on Kikuko, who makes money by sewing. The fact that she is the sole source of income gives her more power to do as she pleases, for Michitsugu is too concerned about the welfare of his children to alienate the one person who supports them. Being unemployed makes Michitsugu lose self-respect and self-confidence, and it is in this depressed state that we see him at the beginning of the narrative.

As in "Rainbows in the Wasteland," the spouses in "Floating Grassplot" clearly recognize that their marriage has deteriorated to the point where it has no meaning:

> Every morning, if the weather was good, Michitsugu would leave the house on the bank of the river in east Nakano and go out walking, but lately he felt that these walks were meaningless, and this he could not stand. Stuck in a whirlpool of falsehoods, an emptiness where he could not grasp even a single major reason for living, Michitsugu was nonplussed at his own fate. He felt his wife and children were to be pitied, but there seemed no way around this fated destiny. At times Michitsugu would gaze at Kikuko and wonder suspiciously if she did not wish him an early death. And her way of talking to the children

when she was tired in the evening, as if she were setting up a line of defense, made him uncomfortable.

She had passed the past few months in this dark mood, but Michitsugu could see through her act. He was sure she was up to something.

He did not know how long this empty marriage would continue on this way, but he adjusted to Kikuko's way of doing as she pleased, coolly placing himself alongside her on these train tracks of fallacy.[41] Michitsugu and Kikuko were deeply at odds, and they both probed at that discord. Kikuko seemed to be aiming at the chance to separate, and Michitsugu felt it warily in his soul.[42]

The depression Michitsugu feels is uncharacteristic of Fumiko's earlier protagonists, especially when he thinks that "there seemed no way around this fated destiny."[43] A few pages earlier, though, he expresses a more optimistic outlook on life:

Michitsugu had not, however, given up hope for himself. He had lost hope for the life he was living, but he still had a glimmer of hope, one that might be dredged out of the muddy swamp into which he had fallen. He felt a sort of easy comfort, as if the climax of desperation was just a little further beyond where he was.[44]

Still, Michitsugu is really too depressed to be saved by one small glimmer of hope. This story was written in early 1951, months before Fumiko's death, and it shows the fatalism and depression so common in the works from that time. Michitsugu has lost his faith in his ability to better his life. He believes that he has no control, that any choice he makes will have no positive bearing on his situation.

"Floating Grassplot" differs from "Rainbows in the Wasteland" in that the former does not approach marriage as a social obligation, whereas the latter does. If anything, Michitsugu sees marriage as a financial arrangement that is complicated by children. If it were not for Tokiko and Shigeichi, one can imagine Michitsugu being able to separate from Kikuko, but their presence prevents him from striking out on his own. Michitsugu does not meditate on the loss of love in his marriage, and in this sense too, he differs remarkably from Tatsuo. Both men, however, are concerned with their futures. Tatsuo wants a slow, discreet separation in order to minimize the amount of pain and embarrassment it is bound to cause. He tries to make concrete plans for the future, instead of focusing on his more immediate marital strife. Michitsugu is so concerned about the future (particularly his and his children's well-being in it) that he decides to avoid it by committing suicide.

Through Tatsuo and Michitsugu, Fumiko reveals a new phenomenon in her method of evaluating the world; a phenomenon perhaps best described as a pause, one that provides the chance to consider issues previously avoided either through escapism or selected awareness. The petulance of earlier protagonists here gives way to a more patient maturity, albeit one haunted by despair.

ILLEGITIMACY

Fumiko herself was an illegitimate child. It seems natural, therefore, that the issue appear in her fiction, but what is most notable is the fact that she does not view illegitimacy as a primary determinant of action. Although she recognizes that social pressures will influence how a bastard is treated, illegitimacy does not necessarily dictate one's future. As with most of Fumiko's characters, the illegitimate person retains his/her free will, and the individual's choices are what shape and decide his/her fate.

Fumiko usually portrays illegitimate children as misunderstood problem children who have a sort of naive wisdom about them which adults do not fully understand or appreciate. The family problems that result from the strain caused by illegitimacy are more often than not dealt with in a practical, pragmatic manner. The characters do not concern themselves with the psychological ramifications of illegitimacy (e.g., feelings of inferiority) so much as the social logistic ones (e.g., convincing others that one should be treated the same as any legitimate child).

Illegitimacy is mentioned in a good number of Fumiko's works, including *Jūnenkan* (Ten Years, 1940), *Inazuma* (Lightning, 1936), and "Hyōga" (The Glacier, 1938), but perhaps the most striking treatment of the subject is that found in *Kawa uta* (River Song, 1941). The illegitimate character in this work is Shimagi Yasuko, a young girl who is regarded as a "problem child" at school. Hisako is her teacher, and she pities Yasuko. After Yasuko loses both her parents, Hisako tries to give her extra attention only to be reprimanded by a fellow teacher at school for displaying favoritism toward one student. Still, Hisako cannot but feel for Yasuko and so she takes her under her tutelage, providing Yasuko with a place to stay and some school supplies (which Hisako pays for out of her own pocket). What Hisako does not understand is that Yasuko does not want pity, that the charity which Hisako gives her only makes her feel more lonely. Yasuko is too young to express her feelings in any but the most simplistic terms, but her values are still clear: she wants independence, she wants to be responsible for herself, and she wants to make her own decisions. She cannot bear being subjected to the control that adults want to exercise on her.

Hisako tries to explain to Yasuko that she has no choice but to conform to society's strictures, but Yasuko resists the lecture. Hisako says:

> "You must not think only of yourself. Now that you have come to stay with me there is no where else to go, so you must put all your energies into your studies. Just like I've always said, right? People are different from cats and dogs. Your mother will have no peace if you go about always putting yourself before everything else. . . . Life is difficult for everybody. Don't go thinking that you are the only one who is sad. You must not think that you alone are unhappy. You're under my care, now . . . you must gain strength from that. Mr. Kawajiri is abroad serving his country.[45] Soldiers can't just go home of their own accord when being in the military becomes unpleasant, you know. You mustn't cry over such things as this. We've all got to get along together, don't we? We've all got to take care of things at home while the others are off at war. Mr. Kawajiri would surely think poorly of you if he saw this behavior. You said you wanted to go home, but where would you go?"
>
> "I would go to Umamichi and become a maid."
>
> "My goodness, a maid? Have you thought about that? If you want to be a maid, I will send you wherever you want to go, but you couldn't do the work. But come now, if there is something you are lacking just tell me what it is. You don't understand how much I care for you, do you?"
>
> Asked if there was something lacking, Yasuko broke out into tears. She was not wanting for food or clothing, but somehow she still felt helplessly forlorn. She had made no friends at school and was left feeling that there was something missing in her life.
>
> "Come on, tell me if you lack anything. That's right, just tell it to me straight."
>
> But even though Hisako had sat her down for this direct conversation, Yasuko could not describe what it was that she found lacking. She herself found it quite odd that she was bored and lonely despite the fact that she had everything she needed. Her mind was filled with a black cloud of dissatisfaction and discontent for which she could not find words. She looked up, as if she had suddenly hit upon it, and said, "I want my own money."
>
> "Money?"
>
> "Yes, I want money to buy crayons and pencils and things."
>
> "Well, yes, but don't I buy crayons and pencils and things for you?"
>
> The crayons that her teacher had bought for her came in an ugly box and Yasuko hated them. Hisako did not understand in the least Yasuko's desire to have her own money and to buy things herself. Yasuko felt like buying things with her own money whenever she felt lonely. She wanted to buy some bread and take it to her teachers.
>
> "There is nowhere else for you to go but here. If it is money that

you want, I will give it to you. But what will become of such money
that you have for buying crayons and pencils? Things aren't easy for
me right now. It's strange that you can't understand that."

"I want to become a maid and make lots of money and give it to
everybody," Yasuko said clearly, her eyes puffy with tears. Hisako
stroked Yasuko's soft hair with her hands and felt helpless faced with
the hopelessness of Yasuko's situation. Maybe it was best to let this
child go where she wanted to go, she thought. If left on her own, perhaps she would discover the road on which she must travel.[46]

The ability to buy crayons and pencils with her own money represents
the ability to make all decisions on her own, that is, the ability to exercise free will. Hisako's pity stems from the knowledge that Yasuko lacks
a stable family, that she is poor, and that she is illegitimate. To Hisako,
these are fatal characteristics to be righted through charity. To Yasuko,
they are incidental characteristics to be righted with effort. Like so many
Fumiko characters, Yasuko does not want pity; she wants the chance to
work and support herself. Her age prevents her from being taken seriously.

One day Yasuko goes to Asakusa (the neighborhood where she used
to live) and does not come home until late at night. Hisako stays awake
and waits for her, and while she is waiting she realizes that Yasuko may
have been right all along about how to live one's life:

> Just what is making me so lonely? Everybody feels lonely at some time
> or another. But does that make it right to yield to it? One must create
> the bright spots in one's life on one's own. I've never once thought
> about children's happiness. I've always thought about children through
> the logical eyes of an adult. Yasuko said that I was a liar. I'm not sure
> exactly what she was referring to when she did, but come to think of
> it, perhaps it was because I am living inside my own world of con-
> structs. Perhaps she has seen through my facade.[47]

In this moment, Hisako realizes two things: first, that only she is responsible for seeing to it that she thrives; second, that her reasoning (up to
this point) is a false construct, that is unnecessary for, and perhaps even
harmful to, the achievement of her goals. Yasuko is not concerned with
the complications of adult society, and her abandon enables her to
thrive. Thus, Fumiko tells us, while the exercise of free will is essential
to happiness, so is the ability to forsake apparently logical constructs. It
is this kind of message that might have caused critics to describe Fumiko
as both a nihilist and an anarchist writer, although I would simply call
it Fumiko's intellectually lazy way of getting around the challenge of
defining her ethics clearly and avoiding complex constructs.

In *Ten Years*, *Lightning*, and "The Glacier" Fumiko depicts illegitimacy as destructive to family structure, but the unstable families in

these works are so more because the illegitimate characters are siblings all fathered by different men than because their parents are not married. As in *River Song*, being illegitimate is not a major concern for the characters in these works; rather, it is a hard fact—one that cannot be altered or erased—and therefore does not merit much attention or anxiety. The characters accept their births and move on with their lives, transcending the stigma of their status at least in their own minds. Compare this with the treatment of illegitimacy in Shiga Naoya's *An'ya kōro* (A Dark Night's Passing, 1937), in which the protagonist, Kensaku, agonizes for pages over the possibility that he was born out of wedlock, and one can see a remarkable difference. Where Shiga (Kensaku) cannot get past the mere thought of the possibility of being illegitimate, Fumiko's characters begin with illegitimacy acknowledged, accepted, and think it merits no further consideration.

I think that this utilitarian view of life, with its philosophically uncomplicated approach to issues that would cause much more consternation to those such as Shiga in the higher circles of society, is a large part of what made Fumiko a popular writer. The selectivity with which her characters approach problems, that is, the way they choose to focus on concrete issues not abstract ones, also conveys a sense of earnestness beyond any sort of culpability. The characters who avoid marriage for the sake of doing something else may never define that "something else," but their sincerity puts them above reproach. Likewise, the illegitimate characters who long for respect do not hold up achievements and concrete goals as proof that they deserve that respect; rather, they hold up their humanity and their abstract desires, things that, in their minds, validate their right to be freed of concrete restraints.

These characters truly reflect their creator, a woman who demanded respect solely on the basis of her earnestness. Fumiko asked that she be free to desire and free to choose, and she based her claim to these freedoms exclusively on her desire or need for them. That there were ways she could better present her case, philosophically sound arguments that, if carefully considered, could fully support her cause, was not important to her. It seemed plain to her that she was right, and that the secret to communicating this was to do so in the most simple way possible. Even in the later years of her career, despite the fact that she no longer believed much in people's ability to improve themselves, she still held that if one kept one's thoughts simple, one could not be held culpable if things went wrong.

CHAPTER 5

War and Fatalism

THE ENCROACHING DARKNESS

Some literary critics note that, after the war, Fumiko began to write "dark" works, but few of them try to define exactly what it is that makes a work "dark."[1] It cannot be the subject matter; despite the potentially depressing themes of her earlier works—poverty, unemployment, malnutrition, and so on—we have seen how a faith in will, in one's ability to chose paths for improvement and have some control over one's existence, instilled Fumiko's writing with an upbeat, optimistic air. The subject matter of the later works, many of which also are about people living in poverty, did not change significantly enough for it to be the sole "darkening" factor in Fumiko's writing. Rather, I suggest that it was a new fatalistic outlook that caused a qualitative change. Many critics quote a passage from the afterword of *Drifting Clouds* in which Fumiko says:

> I wanted to write about man's fate, a fate which could be overlooked by everyone and which flowed along in an empty void. My plan was to write . . . about a world with no plot, to write a novel peripheral to the world of novels and which could not be explained.[2]

But only one of these critics, Fujikawa Tetsuji, comes close to recognizing the important message in this statement: that Fumiko was writing about fate. Fujikawa says that all of Fumiko's novels are dedicated to the depiction of fate, but in fact this is not true of most of Fumiko's prewar works.[3] Yet Fujikawa's statement is quite true about the postwar works. Whereas the prewar Fumiko wrote about the strength of human character, the postwar Fumiko focused her attention on man's shortcomings—despondency, irresponsibility, and immorality—and underlying all these undesirable traits is a loss of faith in the efficacy of free will. Initiative, responsibility, and morality can only exist if one has free will.[4]

It is impossible to mark the time at which Fumiko's writing changed. The trend from nondeterminism to determinism is unmistakable, but there are exceptions, such as the early short story "The Oyster" in which the protagonist seems unable to help himself in any way and succumbs to environmental changes around him without so much as a struggle. And the later short story "Karasu" (Crow, 1949) is a notably nondeterministic work about a young man, Tanii Mamoru, who has lost his siblings during the war and who is not happy being a college student at Waseda University. He leaves school and home and goes on a trip to the mountains to collect his thoughts. He considers suicide, but after meeting many people whose lives are more difficult than his own he decides that suicide is not the answer, and that his life is not as bad as he thought. Tanii is quite different from the despondent protagonists in other works published around the same time, and in him Fumiko revisits the antideterministic fervor of her youth.

The loss of one's ability to choose is an intermediary step to the submission to a perceived predestined fate shown by Fumiko's later characters. Whereas the characters in *Pitiful Wife*, "A Flower's Place," and "Dancing Girl" feel depressed about having their free will curtailed when they are forced into undesirable marriages, the characters in *Drifting Clouds*, "Rain," "Fubuki" (Blowing Snow, 1946), "Nagusame" (Comfort, 1946), "The Sea of Travel Weariness," "Yoru no kōmorigasa" (Evening Umbrella, 1948), "Bones," and "Downtown" feel depressed because they believe they have no free will in the first place.

WAR WORKS

The aftermath of World War II left Fumiko greatly disillusioned, and this may have been the major reason for the qualitative change in her later works. During the war she traveled to China and Indochina as part of the Japanese war effort and saw much devastation first-hand. The two prominent works of war reportage that she produced during this time were *Battlefront* and *The North Bank Unit*. *Battlefront* is written in an epistolary format, although the letters are not addressed to anyone in particular, simply "you."[5] *The North Bank Unit* is written in a diary format, but unlike *Diary of a Vagabond*, it is purely a first person narrative as one would expect a true diary to be. Both works depict the trip that Fumiko took to China in the autumn of 1938 on which she accompanied Japanese troops for about a month. She was not spared the sight of illness and death on that journey, but it did not seem to move her unless it was suffered by Japanese troops. She visited a field hospital, and went so far as to enter the operating room before the sights overcame her and she felt faint.[6] The sad plight of some of the soldiers she met moved her to tears, and her overall experience presented such a shock to her system that she felt unable to write about it:

> How odd it is that I have no other passion in my soul save for what I feel about war. I have not given up thinking about writing further

manuscripts, but at this point I feel like those love stories will take care of themselves. I've had enough of them. All those things I wrote so fervently [in the past]—what comfort are they to me now? I don't mind if I become poor. I'll not write a thing. I received a letter [from Japan] asking me to write a poem about the nurses here, but that is something I cannot do right now. It is as much as I can do to breathe.[7]

But she did write, as the existence of the manuscripts attests. When she wrote, she often focused on individual soldiers and how the war affected them. She also wrote a considerable amount about the horses of the Japanese army (she found them admirable work animals, and felt sorry for them in the midst of the man-made war). And in a move that was quite a divergence from all her previous travel writing, she described scenery. It seems that she was eager to write about anything but the underlying mechanism that drove the war machine; at times that meant her writing showed hints of naiveté and ignorance. It is possible that government pressure prevented her from writing anything even remotely sympathetic to the Chinese, although as a civilian she would not have been under the same military orders as the writer and army corporal Hino Ashihei (1907–1960), who claimed that he had strict guidelines regarding his depiction of the Japanese Army.[8] Still, the pressure to portray the Japanese Army in a good light must have been fairly strong, and that may be the reason Fumiko did so.

Like other writers involved in reporting on the war, Fumiko wrote to put a human face on the Japanese army, to show the people back home how proud they should be of their fighting men. Despite the death and destruction that she saw in China, Fumiko incongruously comments in *The North Bank Unit* that it would be sweet to bring the children of the soldiers to the front to show them the work that their fathers were doing.[9] Emphasis on the individual, personal aspect of war would draw more sympathy from those at home than a broad, patriotic appeal for support, and it was this that the Japanese army hoped for when it engaged the services of popular writers such as Fumiko. However, Fumiko's writing, although it glorified the Japanese soldiers' spirit of camaraderie and their code of honor, also contained such gruesome passages as the following from *Battlefront*:

> War has a painful, barbaric side to it, but it also has plenty of truly splendid aspects, aspects which are excruciatingly beautiful. Once, as I was passing through a village, I heard the following conversation between two soldiers who had captured a member of the Chinese resistance:
> "I'd like to see him burn at the stake."
> "Nah, when I think about the image of [our fellow soldier] who died in Tianjia village it makes me sick to my stomach. That's really offensive . . ."

"Let's kill him like a man, with a single strike of the sword." And with that, the captured Chinese soldier died instantly, without a moment of suffering, at a single, splendid, stroke of a sword. I listened to the soldiers' conversation with a feeling of concurrence. I do not feel that this is in the least bit brutal. What are your thoughts? I'd like you to understand these soldiers' pure state of mind. The strong memory of their fallen comrade called forth their sentimentality and aroused great indignation in these soldiers' hearts.[10]

Fumiko tries to celebrate the soldiers' "pure state of mind" (*junsui na heitai no shinri*), but the image of the two men discussing the prisoner's death so dispassionately cannot help but illustrate the brutality carried out by the Japanese Army. In this sense, it is questionable whether she succeeded in her efforts to promote her country's cause. One may ask if this work might have been subversive—if she was criticizing the war with such a brutal depiction. But Fumiko never used satire in any of her works, before, during or after the war. Without a precedent or antecedent, it seems unlikely that there was a hidden antiwar message.

Fumiko did not comment publicly on her war reportage after Japan's defeat, even though her attitude toward war and its effect on the common man changed remarkably. Neither *Battlefront* nor *The North Bank Unit* were included in the 1951 collected works (*Shinchō HFZ*), and only the latter was included in the 1977 collected works (*HFZ*). The decision to omit these works was in keeping with the general trend to omit war-related writing in authors' collections, as noted by Donald Keene:

Many Japanese authors in later years felt embarrassed by the wartime enthusiasm they had voiced concerning the unique spirit of the Japanese race and similar themes, and refused to allow such writings to be included in what were supposedly their "complete works" (*zenshū*).[11]

Fumiko was no exception; her attitude towards war changed completely after the Japanese defeat. The end of the war found her stunned by the devastation war had wreaked on veterans, their families, and other civilians. And although she did not participate in the editorial decision to omit her war works from her *zenshū*, it is reasonable to expect she would have made such a choice given the chance.

The aspect of war that seems to have been the hardest for Fumiko to accept was the random distribution of suffering. One's individual merit had little bearing on whether one was killed, lost a loved one or was burned out of home or business by enemy bombing. Fumiko had spent years writing about people who worked hard and pulled themselves up by their own bootstraps; thus the idea that individual effort or involvement was meaningless naturally threw her world into turmoil. She discovered that free will seemed not to matter, as war arbitrarily distributed fortune and disaster.

In most of her postwar works, this determined fate deals misfortunes to the characters, although occasionally there are fatalistically fortunate scenes. Given this, one could argue that Fumiko did not lose her spirit of optimism, rather her depiction of it simply became more subtle in her later years. But there is a fundamental difference between the confident scenes and events of the early works and those in the later ones: in the former, when a character benefits it is usually a result of his or her own actions. In the latter, good and bad luck alike are distributed arbitrarily.

Fumiko spent August 1944 to October 1945 as an evacuee in the countryside outside of Tokyo in which the civilian population was threatened by Allied bombing. After the last years of the war prevented her and other writers from publishing due to material shortages, Fumiko one again began writing and publishing prolifically. Among those works published in 1946 were "Blowing Snow," "Comfort," "Rain," and "The Sea of Travel Weariness." In 1947, she published "Uruwashiki sekizui" (Splendid Pith) and "Kawahaze" (River Goby). In 1948 she published "Evening Umbrella," and in 1949 she published "Bones" and "Downtown."

THE PRIMACY OF SURVIVAL

All the above stories concern people who are adversely affected by the war. Most of the stories put emphasis on the random manner in which these people's lives have changed (primarily because of the war), and on the discouragement that they often feel. A comparison of these works reveals both the primacy of survival in Fumiko's worldview and also the loss of the author's faith in free will. By primacy of survival, I refer to the importance of biological existence, which is necessary before any other aspect of one's life can be an issue. Fumiko's writing reveals an underlying understanding of the importance of simply being alive in order to achieve values.

The story that perhaps best illustrates the primacy of survival is "Comfort," the story of an indigent man, Shūkichi, whose house burned down in the war and whose wife has disappeared, her whereabouts unknown to both her husband and her family. Shūkichi misses his wife, Kiyoko, and would like her to return, but he has no means of finding her. He consoles himself by enjoying the company of his friend, Fuji. The two of them go fishing, and have the following conversation:

"The world sure has changed an awful lot, hasn't it? A *kanme* of potatoes costs fifteen yen—what a world, huh?"[12]

"That's for sure. Gosh, Fuji, weren't the old days wonderful? I worked in Kinichi and on my way home I could buy a mackerel supper in the market. Bananas could be had for ten *sen*, to boot.[13] I used to eat so much I'd let out a big belch afterwards.—But now I feel just like I'm seeing a sort of monster. That monster that I was so sure would never appear has arrived, and now the world has changed completely into an extraordinary, odd, bizarre place. At least you still have your wife and kids, but with Kiyoko gone, I have nothing. All I have is the fact that I am still alive—but, you know, that's good in itself. I don't in the least feel like giving up here and dying. I never think, 'Damn it all, I'm so lonely that I'd be better off dead!' I'm mostly thankful that I haven't been thinking like that. I don't think it can be said that 'Mankind is the lord of all creation,' given that all we do is eat steamed potatoes and then throw ourselves down to sleep, do you?"

"Ah, enough of all that. Isn't it amazing that we are both still alive? . . . Let's drink to that. Let's drink and be merry."[14]

Shūkichi wanders the streets after parting with Fuji, and meets various people, one of whom is a boy of twelve or thirteen who has a brief, terse conversation with Shūkichi and then steals Shūkichi's bag and disappears into the night. Still, he reflects on how happy he is just to be alive:

As he munched on some beans, Shūkichi thought how happy he was that he himself had survived. A horrific number of people had died in Asakusa. So many people had been burned to death, and it hadn't even been due to some natural disaster. Shūkichi was almost smug with happiness at the thought of having survived it all. He was relieved that he had not fallen victim to the rain of fire that had fallen daily when the huge airplanes came. Shūkichi had not a single enemy; he had no reason to fight with those big airplanes. He knew nothing of foreign lands, and he saw no reason for so many children to join the military and go to war.[15]

He may be happy to be alive, but he is in terrible health, and he soon falls to the ground, delirious first from illness and then later the injury he sustains in his fall. There are people around him, but their voices fade into the distance, "like the cry of summer cicadas." A miserable end is at hand, but Fumiko insists on making this pitiful death an honorable one:

As the time slipped by, the night gradually grew brighter, but the city was not yet awake. As the night wore on, the light of the shiny moon moving overhead also became brighter and brighter, and the ground all around shone as if covered with snow. On the gentle slope of the embankment, Shūkichi pulled a reed mat over him. His feet stuck out, covered in tattered socks. It was a tragic way to die, but Shūkichi did it as if it were a most honorable way to die, lying face up with the mat pulled up over his head. It was not a horrible way to die, it was an entirely happy way to die. Shūkichi slept eternally like one pebble in nature's limitless realm.[16]

In sum, Shūkichi does not care about his poverty, pain, future prospects, or immediate or future gratification. Quality of life is not important; indeed, Shūkichi has convinced himself that, being a lowly creature who "eats steamed potatoes and sleeps," he deserves no more than subsistence. Fumiko wants the reader to pity Shūkichi—which one does, for he is a victim of random violence—but she also wants the reader to admire him, to believe that his death was "honorable and happy," not "horrible," which the reader cannot do. Fumiko gives us no reason to do so; instead she gives us a man who has little respect for his own humanity. He revels in his own existence, even though that existence is miserable. He aspires to nothing more than idly passing time. Still, that he does not give up all hope and commit suicide is to his credit, for it shows some recognition of the value of life.

This reverence for life was first seen in *Diary of a Vagabond*, where Fumiko made such statements as "Ah, isn't it good to be alive!"[17] It was repeated in *The North Bank Unit* with her concern over losing her own life while reporting from the battlefront.[18] Of course, the joy of living is not a unique emotion, and Fumiko's writing is not necessarily notable for her expression of it. However, the fact that life—biological existence—is essential for all other actions does have a direct connection to the importance of free will in Fumiko's works; with death comes the end of free choice; after death, the individual is incapable of making any further choices. When Shūkichi is thankful for surviving the war, he is thankful for the ability to continue to choose. The pitiful state of his existence is secondary; what is primary is that he does still exist.

The importance of life is also clearly expressed in the short story "Rain," which concerns a repatriated soldier, Kōjirō, who finds that he cannot return to his prewar life. The story opens with Kōjirō entering a bar and asking for a place to stay for the night. The proprietor tells him that all the inns in the area have closed up (due to the economic difficulties of postwar Japan), but he finally agrees to let Kōjirō stay at his place that night. The proprietor feels sorry for the veteran, for his own son has been killed in the war. Kōjirō sits and drinks, and meditates on the bitter experience he had when he returned to his home town after being discharged.

Kōjirō arrives in his hometown to find that his family had thought him killed in action, and that his girlfriend, Hatsuyo, had ended up marrying his younger brother, Sōzaburō. Kōjirō never sees these members of the family; all this information about them is passed on to him by his father, Sakutarō, who meets Kōjirō at a neighborhood inn. Sakutarō is sympathetic, but encourages Kōjirō not to return to the house, for it would cause more trouble than it would be worth.

Kōjirō then goes to Nagoya, where he tries to find work at a factory where he has been promised employment, but he finds that the factory has been burned to the ground and there is no work to be had there. He wanders about a bit, and ends up in the bar where he sits in the opening scene.

While Kōjirō tells Sakutarō about his experiences in the war, and later when he tells the barkeeper his story, the recurring theme is his determination to live. Over and over Kōjirō tells how the single goal of escaping with his life pulled him through the most difficult times of the war. When Kōjirō meets Sakutarō, they exchange the following words:

> "I'm surprised you're still alive," said Sakutarō.
> "I worked as hard as I could to make sure that I came home alive."[19]

And a few paragraphs later, Kōjirō repeats this sentiment with:

> "I was determined to live no matter what happened. I wanted to live, and to see you and Mother again."[20]

When the barkeeper asks him what being in the army was like, Kōjirō replies:

> "I guess I'm pretty happy . . . No matter what, I was determined to come back alive. I focused all my energies on that desire to live. I knew I shouldn't ever surrender to death, or think it was all over. If you're determined to live, no matter what happens, then you will do so."
> "I guess so."
> "I was called up twice, and both times I was saved by ending up in the hospital.[21] Frankly speaking, it was because I didn't want to die."
> "Ho, are such things really possible?"
> "You can't get away with any funny business in the military ranks. Both times that I was called up I thought, 'Staying alive is not going to be easy.'"[22]

The barkeeper says he is thankful that he did not suffer the same fate of death by fire that many other civilians did. He agrees with Kōjirō that death would be meaningless:

> "I sure am glad that I wasn't burned to death. It's like you say, nothing comes of death," said the barkeeper.
> "You're right there. We've got to live long lives and to assure ourselves of a world in which one can feel at home. One's life is important, after all," replied Kōjirō.[23]

Most of Kōjirō's attitudes about life are a reaction to the emphasis on death that he experienced in the army. He recalls training, in which soldiers were made to spend every day "making rafts and learning how to die."[24] The attitude of the superior officers was the opposite of the soldiers':

> Kōjirō would never forget the day that one of the superior officers yelled at a soldier who was slacking off, "If you just think you are going to die, then you are sure to be able to do this." The soldier muttered that he could do anything if he just thought that he would *live*, but if he thought that he was to *die* then it was extremely easy just to fall down and die. Kōjirō felt the same way.[25]

Throughout the story, Kōjirō reflects on the abnormality of war; it is not natural, he thinks, for people to suffer in this way, nor is it normal for death and pain to play such a prominent role in anybody's life. The fact that he survived, however, does not provide him with the unconditional happiness that Shūkichi had in "Comfort."

Kōjirō and Shūichi recognize that biological life is necessary in order for one to achieve anything else, in order to be able to make choices and affect one's future. These two protagonists do not feel their fate to have been decided; there are a number of pleasant possibilities before their eyes—for Shūkichi, the chance to spend pleasant afternoons drinking and fishing with his friend, for Kōjirō the chance to find work and build up a normal life again—as long as they are still alive. Their futures afford them hope and pleasant anticipation—the feeling they share is that life will be good for them if they can simply survive long enough to enjoy it.

As mentioned earlier, Fumiko's turn from free will to determinism did not happen at a specific point in time; it was a gradual change. During the postwar years there was a period during which both sorts of works were written, as well as works that combined the two elements. A good example of this is "Evening Umbrella," in which the protagonist, Eisuke, vacillates between feeling helpless and feeling capable. Eisuke is a war veteran, one who lost a leg in battle and now depends on his wife, Machiko, to support the two of them. The loss of mobility makes Eisuke feel useless, and he hates being unable to work. Being dependent on his wife deprives him of full control over his life; it reduces his freedom to choose. He does not have an income and this means that he is, to a certain extent, under Machiko's control. She is not a domineering or pushy woman, but that does not diminish the power she exercises over Eisuke by simple merit of the fact that she is their only source of income. She has little time to pity him, for she is busy working and visiting her lover (or so Eisuke suspects) on the side. All this leaves

Eisuke, a rational adult able to make his own decisions, deprived of the opportunity to do so. But what makes Eisuke different from Keiko in *Pitiful Wife*, Shūichi in "A Flower's Place," and Suekichi in "Dancing Girl" is that he is not fully convinced that he has the ability to control his life. He suspects it, and the suspicion grows with the progression of the narrative, but he remains menaced by the fatalistic attitude his wife exhibits.

The story opens with Machiko telling Eisuke frankly that he is not the type to commit suicide, thus emphasizing her feelings that he has so little control on his life that he is even incapable of ending it of his own accord. Eisuke is depressed by Machiko's words, and he wavers between a desire to make something of himself and the fear that such a thing is impossible.

One day Machiko leaves the house to go shopping and does not come home for hours. Eisuke becomes concerned, so he goes to the train station to wait for her. While he is there, he meets a young patrolman who is bright and cheery and who talks to Eisuke about taking initiative and improving his life. Eisuke is drawn to this young man, for he expresses a confidence in Eisuke's ability to act, something that Machiko long since ceased to do. The patrolman tells Eisuke that his injury should not stand in his way of having a livelihood:

> "Does your wound hurt?" the patrolman asked.
> "Yeah, it's bad when it gets cold like this. It's bad any time, for that matter. Stuck without a job, it's worse than being a criminal . . ."
> The patrolman replied quickly, with a smile in his eyes, "That's not true. You shouldn't think such a silly thing. You can't go thinking like that just because of one injury. You can't say that it's nothing, but if you don't find a way around it you'll always be dependent on others . . ."[26]

The patrolman is a beacon that shines light on that aspect of Eisuke's life that had been lost and forgotten: self-esteem. Eisuke clings to this ray of hope; he knows that the patrolman's daily presence would be much more beneficial to him than Machiko's, and when he finds out that the young man is looking for a room to rent, he realizes that it would make him very happy to have such a person in his house. He asks Machiko if she would be willing to take the patrolman in as a boarder, but Machiko dismisses the idea promptly; she expects her younger brother to be coming soon to attend college, and the house is not big enough to accommodate all four of them. Eisuke is gravely disappointed:

> [Eisuke knew that] there was no way Machiko's younger brother would give a cripple like himself the respect one should show an older

sister's husband. Eisuke wanted ever so much more to take in the
young patrolman than to take in his wife's brother. Eisuke's soul had
been impressed with the patrolman's kind words of faith in people.[27]

Eisuke wants to believe in his own ability, to build his self-esteem—in
essence, to believe he is capable of making choices—but Machiko does
not help him do so, nor does Eisuke expect his brother-in-law will either.
The result is that Eisuke feels smothered by the emotional attrition that
envelops his marriage and, he suspects, so many others. One day, he tells
Machiko in desperation:

> ". . . You must be bored with this sort of life. You are free to go where
> you want, you know. I won't perish. I'll be fine running a used book
> store, just like Shōkichi said.[28] I'll get by somehow. I've been depend-
> ing on you for a long time, but now I regret it. Desire and regret, I guess
> that is what you could call it . . . I can't stand going on like this."
>
> "What can't you stand?" said Machiko, licking a thread with her
> puffy, ill-colored lips, and looking up at her husband. Looking into her
> eyes, Eisuke was not sure how far he could trust his wife. He wondered
> how many couples—couples just like themselves whom fate had
> thrown together—there were out there in the night. Those fated cou-
> ples went on with their lives while suppressing even the tiniest breath.
> A formless wail sounded in the night with a terribly pitiful noise. And
> that wail, frozen just as it was, permeated the darkest reaches of mem-
> ory, a time so far past that it had become but a dream to which one
> could not return. Those fated people just silently adjusted and contin-
> ued with their lives. They had adjusted to a state of uncertainty.[29]

Silent adjustment is a form of resignation, and Eisuke feels it smothering
him. He wants to resist, but the patrolman is the only person he knows
who is willing to help him fight against it. The story ends with Eisuke
hurtling a book at the wall in an attempt to break the stagnant air
between his wife and himself. The act is desperate, and reveals to both
of them that something needs to change the frozen state in which they
have been living.

"Evening Umbrella" was one of Fumiko's last attempts at resisting
the growing fatalism of her later years. Like Eisuke, she wanted desperately to believe that there was some order and justice in the world, but
the apparently random events around her—evidence of a determined but
irrational fate manifested in the indiscriminate devastation caused by the
war—became overwhelming. Her nihilistic attitude also may be
attributable to her realization that her heart condition had become a
serious threat to her life, and that with death so close, those things which
were so important before had come to matter little now.[30] As a younger
woman, Fumiko took pride in her ability to push herself hard without
becoming ill.[31] When her body began to give way and her mortality

became a constant concern, it understandably caused her to lose much of the vigor—both physical and psychological—that had carried her through most of her life. Death was one thing over which she knew she had little control, and the realization of that lack of control contributed to her increasingly deterministic attitude.

FATALISM

The importance of life and, by extension, the importance of free will is not to be found in many other works from Fumiko's postwar period. The predominant theme in these works, as mentioned above, is a sort of fatalism. "Blowing Snow" is a typical short story of this type. It is the story of a woman, Kane, who is married and has four children. Kane's husband, Manpei, is conscripted and Kane spends a good amount of the war pining for him. One day word comes that he has been killed in action, and while Kane mourns his death she is comforted by a neighbor, Katsu. After a period of time, a romance blooms between Kane and Katsu, although Kane's love for her dead husband still lingers in her heart. Katsu and Kane live together as husband and wife (although they are not officially married) until one day Katsu comes to Kane with a look of deep concern. He tells her that he has heard that Manpei is still alive, and recuperating in a military hospital not too far away. Kane and Katsu are devastated by the news, but Katsu tells her that he will take her to see Manpei, and that he will not stand in their way. He volunteers to leave their common-law marriage, and while Kane loves him and feels for him, she cannot deny her excitement and joy at the news that Manpei is alive.

While all three characters are together at the hospital where Manpei is a patient, an air raid breaks the tense air:

> "I can't thank you enough for all you have done for my family," said Manpei to Katsu, looking over at his weeping wife.
> "No, I owe you so much. I'm just glad that you're alive. As long as you have life, there is no end to the possibilities . . . I was just thinking while I waited at the hospital gate how happy Kane and the children and the elders will all be when you get well and come back home. There is nothing for me to mind. I think I'll do as I had planned before: leave Tokyo in search of work," Katsu answered.
> Suddenly an eerie siren sounded.
> Announcements came blaring out of the radio about a coming air attack.
> Manpei instinctively squatted down. Katsu, still holding his cigarette, covered Kane and leaned up against a pillar. An air of panic enveloped the hospital. For a while, the sounds of people running about

and shouting filled the air. Manpei was frantic; the attacking planes and the near dusk on all sides clutched at his heart. He wondered how it would be for the three of them to be killed like this by a bomb.[32]

The randomness of the bombing causes panic on all sides. The air raid represents one's unknown fate, events that one cannot control, that do not reflect one's virtues or lack thereof, and that have the potential to steal one's very life away with no advance notice. Emotions had already been running high in the ward, as Manpei, Katsu, and Kane had been discussing their awkward situation as it stood—a situation that was itself created by the exogenous, fated false notice of Manpei's death. They feel helpless in the present circumstances, and the air raid brings a new wave of helplessness, one punctuated by the urgency of a life-threatening situation.

Late that night, on the way home from the hospital, Katsu tries to take his leave of Kane. The scene is desolate, and Katsu's attitude toward the entire situation is one of resignation:

> Snow whirled around them as they got off the train. It stuck to the sky and earth, bits of it blowing about wildly. Until they left the embankment the road was clear, but away from the broad embankment the world was one slate of white, and the wind blew about wildly. In the blink of an eye the snow had piled up quite high, and seemed to seize their feet as they walked along. Katsu walked in front. There was not a light to be seen, perhaps because a black-out alarm had been sounded.
>
> Suddenly Katsu stopped in his tracks and took Kane's hand. Her hand was cold.
>
> "I'll go to Tokyo, so there's no need for you to worry about me. Manpei doesn't think badly of me, and I'll find something to do, rest assured. All right?" he said.
>
> Katsu brought his mouth up close to Kane's ear, as if fighting against the wind, and spoke loudly.
>
> "Our relationship ends here."[33]

The final line in the above passage has a double meaning; the Japanese is *oretachi wa, kore made no en da sa.* The word *en* means "relation," but it also has overtones of "fate." Here it carries both meanings, as Katsu is saying that their relationship was fated to end at this point.

Katsu and Kane continue to walk in the blizzard, emotionally torn over their situation. Like the air raid, the random swirling of the snow is emphasized in this passage to add an element of randomness, representative of the unpredictable events that affect one's life. Katsu and Kane are victimized by the war (and the snow storm), and they are depicted as powerless to change their situation.

Whether it was due to the disillusionment which Fumiko experienced after Japan's defeat in the war, or to her failing health and the subsequent realization that she had not long to live, the optimism of *Diary of a Vagabond* had faded to but a glimmer of its former self by the time Fumiko wrote *Drifting Clouds*. The change of authorial attitude is first evident when one contrasts the titles of the two works; whereas the *hōrō* of *Hōrōki (Diary of a Vagabond)* can mean "doing as one pleases," "drifiting clouds"connotes no control over where one goes.

Kōda Yukiko, the protagonist of *Drifting Clouds*, has much in common with the narrator in *Diary of a Vagabond*; she is a young, single woman who needs to support herself. She has a few love affairs during the course of the novel, but none of them bring her true happiness. But while it would be incorrect to say that she shows none of the drive and determination of *Diary of a Vagabond*'s narrator, she does readily resign herself to unsatisfactory situations, and it is this point that makes her a markedly different sort of character from Fumiko's earlier creations. Yukiko's main lover, Tomioka, displays similar fatalistic tendencies. There is an increased use of the word *unmei* (fate) in *Drifting Clouds*, used to indicate something beyond the control of the characters, a concept absent from *Diary of a Vagabond*.

In the beginning of *Drifting Clouds*, Yukiko is in Tokyo, without lodging or friends. She has just returned to Japan from abroad and needs to reestablish herself in her home country. She goes to visit Iba, a brother-in-law with whom she had a love affair years ago, as she believes his house is the only place where she can stay. The thought of living with this disagreeable man and his family brings back unpleasant memories and she feels unhappy about her situation, although she thinks of it as something to which she is fated, and not something about which anything can clearly be done. One day, as Yukiko and Iba head home after an outing to Shinjuku, Yukiko wishes she could be with her lover Tomioka instead:

> Yukiko suddenly thought of the time she had spent [with Tomioka] at the Hotei Hotel in Ikebukuro, and the idea of going back to Saginomiya with Iba and sleeping next to him in that tiny room was an unpleasant one. The fact that she had gotten nothing of what she wanted, and that all she did not want seemed fatefully to surround her, left her with a dry feeling in her soul.[34]

There is an air of self-pity here, as well as a touch of anger at "fate," by which Yukiko feels victimized. Similar feelings of helplessness are expressed throughout the novel, such as in the following passage, which takes place still relatively early in the novel when she still has some hope for a resumption of her relationship with Tomioka:

> Lately Yukiko was given to weeping, and she wondered if it didn't indi-
> cate that she was starting to lose her mind. While she was crying, the
> dark shadow of uncertainty which she intuited about her immediate
> fate showed on her face.[35] That intuition told her that things were dic-
> tated to turn out a certain way. There was no deviation from that dic-
> tate. She felt that she had nothing strong on which to support herself,
> and that she had to live her life like a little stone, being kicked along
> by someone else.[36]

Clearly Yukiko does not feel in control of her life here, nor does she feel
any control is possible in the future. The yearning and nostalgia that she
feels for her former, happier days in Indochina bring comfort but also
quell any aspirations she might develop to improve her present and
future. Instead of working to better her situation, she simply indulges in
memories of more cheerful times. The reader is not meant to be critical
of this in Yukiko; rather, one is to pity and sympathize with her.

A few pages after the above passage, Yukiko meets Joe, a foreigner
with whom she has a short love affair. She meets him while she is taking a walk in Shinjuku, and interprets the serendipitous nature of their
meeting as a twist of fate:

> Yukiko went to Shinjuku with no particular motive in mind. A cold
> wind blew in the evening. With the roadside stalls and most of the
> other stores all closed up, Shinjuku was like a lonely deserted town. She
> tried her best to walk along as if she had some business there, but it left
> her feeling quite dissatisfied. She considered going back to Shizuoka,
> but seeing as she had gotten herself the little shack to live in, she also
> wondered if it wouldn't be best for her to start a new life from that
> shack. She had walked as far as the Isetan department store when she
> was called over by a tall foreigner. He asked her where she was going,
> but because she had been asked so abruptly, Yukiko merely smiled and
> stood still. The foreigner matched her stride and walked with her.
> Yukiko grew bold. The foreigner babbled along a mile a minute, but
> Yukiko remained silent and leaned up against his body as they walked
> along. She felt that her fate was slowly but surely taking a turn in a new
> direction.[37]

Joe becomes her lover and visits her often, bringing small gifts when he
does. He is kind and Yukiko enjoys his company, but the language barrier prevents her from truly falling in love with him. Still, Joe's appearance in her life is a positive sign to her; it is a gift that fate bestowed on
her when she was down and out. Her passive acceptance of his companionship, exemplified in the passage above when she silently leans
against him, is symptomatic of her passive acceptance of many events in
her life. Yukiko does show some signs of personal volition, such as in
the scene where she decides to leave Tomioka behind in the resort of

Ikaho and to continue with her own life in Tokyo. But these scenes are overshadowed by those that display a wavering of her will, an irresolution that causes her to change her mind and surrender to fate more often than not.

When Yukiko is faced with the necessity of finding some sort of employment to support herself, she cannot decide what sort of work to do, and the options all seem bleak. While she muses, she idly shakes a pair of dice that she finds sitting nearby:

> Yukiko picked up the dice which had been thrown on top of the table and shook them in her hand for a while as she sank deep into her own thoughts. She contemplated what sort of work she should do. She had lost her talent for office work. And she couldn't be a waitress. Becoming a housewife was also an unpleasant thought. She would starve if she didn't find some sort of work. Yukiko shook the dice as she wondered what sort of work to choose.[38]

The specter of chance, or fate, as manifested in the dice, haunts Yukiko's thoughts as she tries to make a decision. It is as if any choice, whether she seems to make it of her own will or not, is predestined. Again, the narrator of *Diary of a Vagabond*, in the same situation (unemployment), decides on a job rationally, not by throwing dice, the implication being that the decision is hers to make, it is not predetermined.

Despite efforts to branch off in their own directions, Yukiko and Tomioka end up together, headed for Yaku island, in the conclusion of the story. Yukiko is dying from consumption, and she is resigned to her condition. She becomes so weak that she cannot continue, and shortly after that she breathes her last. Tomioka is saddened by her death, but it seems to him to fall naturally into succession with the recent deaths of his former lover, Osei, and his wife, Kumiko. Tomioka and Yukiko display no control over the tragic events that lead to the latter's death; they know she is very ill, but they continue traveling as if something was preventing them from other courses of action.

The last paragraph sums up the fatalistic metaphysical overtones of the novel. Tomioka has just attended to Yukiko's funeral, and is faced with either returning to Yaku Island or to Tokyo. He does not have the energy to deal with the former on his own, but the latter does not offer any potential way for him to earn his livelihood:

> Tomioka thought about his own condition, which was just like that of a drifting cloud. It was a drifting cloud which could disappear at any time, in any place, without anyone knowing about it.[39]

Here Fumiko asks the reader, What does life matter? Why fret over decisions that are predestined? She tells us that we cannot know our fate, although it is set—all we can do is suffer with the knowledge that we have no control. Indeed, what disturbs both Yukiko and Tomioka most about fate is its quixotic nature. The fact that something could happen "anytime, in anyplace" is frightening, and the threat of the unknown hangs over the entire novel. That threat grows with the progression of the narrative to the point where it paralyzes the characters in a state of nonaction. Instead of seeing a world of possible opportunities, Yukiko and Tomioka see a world of possible disasters.

THE FALSE SOLACE OF RELIGION

In *Drifting Clouds*, Fumiko criticizes organized religion, which, as she depicts it, provides a false sense of control over one's fate. When the morally corrupt Iba joins a religious cult and tries to convince Yukiko that he has found salvation through his faith, Yukiko sees that the sect is a fraud, and that Iba is grasping at any chance to rehabilitate himself after a life of debauchery. Fumiko writes Iba's monologues on the subject of religion with contempt and disdain, and she makes Yukiko unable to believe what Iba says about the goodness of the sect.

Iba goes to visit Yukiko in the hospital after she has had an abortion (the child was not his—it was Tomioka's—but out of compassion for Yukiko, he pays for the procedure), and while he is there his religious rhetoric attracts some of the other women in the ward. Yukiko is appalled by his behavior:

> Iba came to visit her on the second day, but all he had to ask her was when she would be well and able to come help him [with secretarial duties]. Yukiko was extremely weak. Iba had given himself over totally to the Dainikkō sect, and he was boasting about how the money for construction costs was just pouring in from their accounting office.[40]
>
> The women whose beds were lined up along side Yukiko's in the hospital room were in no time drawn to what Iba was saying.
>
> Lying next to the wall was a woman close to forty years old named Ōtsu Shimo. She suddenly blurted out, "Would it be possible for me to join the ranks of the faithful?"
>
> Ōtsu had disposed of a child she had conceived with an older married man. She had not spoken a word about it herself, but the nurse, Miss Makita, had said that she was an elementary school teacher from somewhere near Chiba. She did not seem the type to become attached like that to some man. She had a dark complexion and was heavy set, and she was rather formal.
>
> "This Dainikkō sect—is the leader a man?"
>
> Iba grinned and said, "Of course, he is a man, and a marvelous one at that. He studied in India as a young man and has plenty of vision. He has surmounted all sorts of obstacles, and he came to Japan

to shine his light in the wilderness here. He is well known as a brave man, thanks to his long stint with the army in Malaysia and Burma. In different times, we would not be able to approach such a man. Please, come join us. All your difficulties will be erased."

"My! So the founder was originally a soldier?"

"That's right. He's a discharged soldier, which makes him all the more interesting. Fellows straight out of the military like this are naturally full of energy. He can be downright highhanded with an unruly mob . . ." Iba lowered his voice, "He's buying a car in my name. He's footing the entire bill, but I'm in charge of everything he owns . . ."

"How old is he?"

"Oh, about sixty-one or sixty-two . . . He's an amazing guy, said to have been with over a hundred women. He says that plants turn towards the sun, no matter where they grow, so he named the sect Dainikkō after that energy of life.[41] We've got over 100,000 believers now. It has the potential to grow indefinitely. His creed seems to be that by staying inconspicuous, we will be conspicuous."

Yukiko felt a little uneasy at how Iba had changed entirely from his former self into what seemed like a man gone totally mad. He seemed to have no interest whatsoever in her past relationship with Tomioka. He just wanted to take her into his confidence as his private secretary, to hire a woman with whom he had had relations in the past.[42]

Iba goes on to describe to Ōtsu Shimo how much money she needs to contribute in order to become a member of the sect, and she enthusiastically responds that she definitely wants to join. He tells her that the sect does not heal physical ailments, but rather psychological ailments; in effect, he promises happiness and an improved life. Yukiko remains unswayed, for she knows that Iba is simply running a scam. Iba never stops talking about the church and about God, but his insincerity is obvious, as in the following exchange between him and Yukiko:

> "I can't say this very loudly, but in this world the best business is religion. Religion is the way to save people. Some incredibly lost souls come to hear the teachings. All around us drugstores have sprung up, and there is a map for us at the station.[43] It's amazing. These people all happily part with their money. Religion has the power to keep people from begrudging payments. I sold that house in Saginomiya, you know. I'm buying the house of a banker in Ikegami, and we'll live together with the sect leader—how grand! The house is sort of old for 3,500,000 yen, but the building is 80 *tsubo,* the grounds are 500 *tsubo,* and there is a pond and a hill."[44]
>
> "God will make you pay for this."
>
> "God? God only looks after those with good luck. Those who are not caught in the net of luck are of no interest to God. You know, I am

quite taken with you. I'll buy you a cozy little house all your own. No matter what happens, I was your first man, and I'll never forget it . . ."
Yukiko found it all repulsive.[45]

Iba does not believe what he preaches and sells; his comment about luck indicates that he too shares Yukiko's belief that luck and fate are at the heart of one's existence. Yukiko would like to believe in the doctrines of Iba's church—because they would bring the psychological comfort that eludes her—but she cannot bring herself to do so. One day she attends one of the services:

> Yukiko sat down on a bench and listened to the parishioners singing. She tried pressing her palms together and closing her eyes, but her impatience tangled around her like a string and she could not calm down in the least. There was an admirable bundle of money before her eyes. But nowhere around her could be seen the image of God. And she could not see the ether that Iba was consuming.[46] God was nowhere.[47]

It is hopeless; Yukiko cannot believe in God. Instead she believes in "fate," which is faceless and indistinct. It is this fate—the conception of which remains conveniently indistinct in her mind—that dictates her future, not God. The vagueness of "fate" makes it intangible, and ironically that gives Yukiko more faith in it. In other words, an incomprehensible power is more acceptable than a comprehensible one. As mentioned in chapter 1, Fumiko liked the idea of faith but she did not adhere to any organized religious doctrine. Such doctrines were too complex, too logical, and too structured for her to find them appealing. Thus, both Fumiko's early vague faith in the individual's free will, and her later faith in a sort of deterministic fate were tolerable forms of religion for her.

Diary of a Vagabond and most of the earlier works espoused a sort of "live and let live" policy: it was fine for others to follow a religion or political philosophy as long as the protagonist was left alone. But a number of short stories written near the end of Fumiko's life abandon this posture; rather, they directly criticize man's attempt to comprehend and control his life and environment. For Fumiko at this time, it was no longer appropriate to blithely ignore complex philosophies; now she declared that these human constructs were not to be trusted. Most notable of these stories is a collection of children's stories published under the title *Kitsune monogatari* (The Fox's Tale, 1947), which includes "Tsuru no fue" (The Crane's Flute), "Kame-san" (Mr. Turtle), "Hirame no gakkō" (The Flounder's School), "Fukurō no dairyokō" (The Owl's Big Journey), and "Kitsune monogatari" (The Fox's Tale).[48] In the tradition of Aesop's fables, these stories use anthropomorphized animals to illustrate some vice of human nature. Although the scenarios are different, they all criticize some sort of complex human psychological construct and imply that a simplistic approach to life would be better. Yukiko's criticism of Iba's sect also falls along these lines: those involved in organized religion, she feels, are trying to build constructs to structure their lives when in reality there is no controlling one's fate. It would be best for them to acknowledge that fact and live their lives simply, without complicating them with false codes of conduct and bogus beliefs.

Ultimately, Fumiko tells her readers that the solace one may find in organized religion or philosophy is false. It is presumptuous of man to claim an understanding or comprehension of the world, for it is not his to understand, much less control. It is best, she implies (more in the children's stories than anywhere else), for man to remain meek, passive, and relatively ignorant.

FUMIKO'S THOUGHTS ON DEATH

The joy that Fumiko took in writing as a young woman all but disappeared in her middle age. Writing became a chore, something she did, it seems, more out of habit than desire. While the quality of what she produced did not noticeably suffer—if anything her ability to develop characters and structure plots became better after the war—the author herself become increasingly depressed about the ephemeral nature of a writer's popularity. She wrote about these feelings in an essay entitled "Yashi no mi" (Coconut, 1949), originally published in a collection of short stories entitled *Beef*. "Coconut" rambles a bit, but there are passages in which Fumiko talks lucidly about the futility of writing. The opening two paragraphs are one such passage:

> Writing novels has become quite tiresome of late. And it's not just because I'm getting old. I have worn down my fishing hook for ideas over the course of my twenty-year literary career. Sometimes I sit in front of the brazier, roasting dried sardines, and I think how nice it would be to just enjoy a peaceful life with a cup of *sake* in my hand. When I was young I was under the illusion that my works would live on in the world after my death, but my thoughts on that have changed entirely. It's not just limited to my works; nobody's works survive. The times now are even more rushed than today's popular novels, everything has become so fast-paced. What is written today is old news tomorrow. All one can do is spend life lying low in obscurity. A certain idea which was the hottest thing right after the war has now gradually grown old. And we, like potatoes, over the course of the years, gradually have our skin peeled away. I do not know if there is anything to this world of man; nothing but vast, vacant thoughts occupy me

each day, darkly stagnating in my heart. I realize that man's destination is none other than the crypt of anarchy.

As I sit idle at my desk my fishing hook fails to catch any fish. Everyday I greet a number of visitors, and it makes me lose my bearings. I imagine putting a sign out on the gate—what should it say? "Temporarily Closed"? "In Mourning"? The truth is that I cannot for the life of me find the urge to write. There's no point in slaving away to write something which will not survive after I'm gone. I dream about owning a small inn—to earn just enough income to put food on the table—where I could sit at the front desk with my dried sardines and drink. It wouldn't be a bad living. It wouldn't be so bad to take in some gasping author who had undertaken to write seven or eight different serialized novels, and then squeeze every last cent out of him. Such are my thoughts as I sit grinning at my desk.[49]

The cynicism and intemperance in this passage is quite uncharacteristic of anything Fumiko had written before. She ridicules herself when she imagines maltreating an author who took on too many serialization contracts (she herself was notorious for working on a number of manuscripts at once). The loss of several of her friends and contemporaries also made her reflect on death in some depth:

I have lost nine friends who were authors in the past few years: Hasegawa Shigure, Tokuda Shūsei, Yada Tsuseko, Kataoka Teppei, Takeda Rintarō, Oda Sakunosuke, Dazai Osamu, Kikuchi Kan, and Yokomitsu Riichi.[50] Everyone of these people was kind to me. My memories of them are sweet. These writers have left behind quite a few works, so the limp, helpless feeling I have that not one of their works survives is perhaps due to my own twisted frame of mind. I would like to drink a *shō* of *sake* and quietly speak the truth to myself.[51] In Masaoka Shiki's *One Drop of Ink* there is the frightening line, "As an experiment, I place a number of poisons by my bedside to see if I will drink them or not."[52] To drink them or not . . . I am a coward, and these inward thoughts of Shiki's terrify me so as I sit at my desk late at night, thinking.

Sometimes I get serious and think about my own death. When my life ends, well, that will be the end of me. I shall regret it, but that regret will only exist until the moment of death, and once I am dead I suspect it will flee at full speed to the dark underworld. And all my abhorrence of life will disappear. For a short while, I shall be fondly remembered by my friends and acquaintances. I absolutely decline to have an epitaph like Stendahl's "He lived, he wrote, he loved."[53] I think that, at the time of my death, I'd like the police or the tax office to be notified that everything I've written will cease to be printed from that day forward. I think it odd that the power of works by dead authors can exceed that of live authors. What I'm trying to say is that the works of dead authors should not continue on through the ages like ancient almanacs.

> No matter how poor the writer, reading works by a living author brings out the life in me. I get terribly depressed reading works by dead authors, and I cannot get their images out of my mind. On top of that their themes seem to fade with age. Perhaps it is due to the fact that I write novels, but in addition to the feeling that today's novels are being rapidly outpaced by the times, I feel an unbearable irritation when I read dead authors' works. Nevertheless, I know that the novels by Tokuda Shūsei and Oda Sakunosuke that I have been reading recently are not in the least bit antiquated. Among these nine recently deceased authors, there are some who have not been read at all since the end of the war. And while it is cruel, the string that connects the memory of these authors with the present day has been completely severed. There is simply nothing to be done about it.[54]

Although she contradicts herself and seems unable to make a coherent statement, Fumiko's main point here is clear; she has little faith in the ability of a literary work to stand the test of time. This feeling was apparently mostly based on her own reactions when she read novels, not an objective observation of the world of Japanese literature. (The idea that any author's works rapidly become arcane after the writer's death is absurd at best.) In any case, she knew that she had only a little longer to live, and the idea that her works would fade quickly after her death filled her with gloom. Still, there is one passage in "Coconut" that shows she had not totally lost her will to live:

> For the sake of writing novels, I want to travel everywhere and anywhere. I have a feeling that I only have a few years left to live. . . .[55] I've been thinking about going to South America lately, and I've taken to daydreaming as I look at a map of the world.[56]

The line "for the sake of novels" is a throwback to her past, when travel provided her not only with settings but also with the nostalgia which was so central to her fiction. In reality, dreaming of travel was but a pleasant distraction, for by the time Fumiko wrote "Coconut" she was too weak to make a major trip of any kind. Whether a journey would aid her in writing a novel or simply aggravate the feeling she had that her writing career was over is something that she would never find out.

By the end of her life, Fumiko was a woman stripped of everything that had made living worthwhile. She could not travel any longer, and without travel, it was more difficult to put herself in situations that brought about the nostalgia she so treasured; her emotional need to long for something could no longer be focused on a physical place ("home"). Nor could that need be focused on a utopian existence where she was left to do as she pleased (as it had been in her youth), for she had achieved that objective as much as anyone can when she became an established, independent, wealthy writer. What was there left to long for? Fumiko's answer was devastating: Nothing should be longed for, because one had no control over one's fate. Longing for something that one could not achieve brought no pleasure, only a feeling of helplessness. And with that feeling of helplessness came discouragement, despair, and resignation. It is perhaps surprising that Fumiko continued writing, instead of giving up altogether, although I think that writing had become such an integral part of her way of life that the idea of stopping would never have occurred to her. This, plus the fact that she, like most writers, needed to write in order to concretize ideas and to understand the world, kept her writing until her death in 1951 at the age of forty-eight.

CONCLUSION

Hayashi Fumiko's provenance helped launch her to fame, but even without the serendipitous reception of *Diary of a Vagabond*, she would have eventually made her mark. By providing her audience with breezy interpretations of even the most squalid situations, she was filling the gap left by her contemporaries, who were busy focusing either on the nature of their own individuality or the plight of the working class in a newly industrialized Japan. Fumiko showed that Western influence in the modern age did not need to bring angst to the Japanese, for she produced *Diary of a Vagabond* based on a Western model, with a protagonist who lived in a Westernized Tokyo but who was not daunted by existential epistemological or social concerns. Although she did ask herself what the nature of literature should be, she did not dwell upon this question within her works themselves.

Although immediately following the publication of *Diary of a Vagabond* Fumiko's novels suffered from problems of structure and characterization, her short stories intimated an ability to produce outstanding work. The characters in these stories were three-dimensional, and lived a world familiar to much of her audience. She portrayed them speaking and acting, not contemplative and immobile, and although she never mentioned it in her essays on writing, it is clear she subscribed to the "show" (and not the "tell") school of expression. She created role models for other youths born in poverty, and showed that one's origins need not dictate one's success or failure in life. Throughout her entire career, she remained a nonconfrontational author, avoiding the academic controversies that divided many of her colleagues; in the few cases in which she was criticized for not following some dictate, as in the criticism that *Diary of a Vagabond* was not proper *lumpen* literature, she simply denied any didactic or homiletical intent.

Moreover, Fumiko did not depict abject poverty for its shock value. She reveled in the idea of creating "the literature of poverty," but not because she saw it as expressive of an inequality or injustice. Quite to the contrary, the "literature of poverty" was a beautiful thing that addressed her childhood and concretized the abstract images in her mind from that time, helping her comprehend and appreciate them further. She resented those critics who insisted on categorizing her as a leftist writer, for she felt politicization detracted from literature's purer essence and prevented one from arriving at man's true nature. Her choice of rough vocabulary, extensive use of dialect, and relentless honesty in showing life with all its scars was simply second nature to her. It was the world she knew, and the only one that she was capable of depicting.

Although Fumiko is certainly one of the most prominent "women writers" of the early and mid-twentieth century, there is no direct evidence that she intended herself to be a major actor in the feminist movement of the time. She published in some of the periodicals considered "women's magazines," such as *Women and the Arts* and *Housewife's Friend*, but this in itself does not place her in the feminist camp. True to her tendency to avoid political discussions, nowhere in her essays does she mention feminism as a political action. However, the example she set in her own life could not but be an inspiration to other women of the time; she had a flourishing career, fame, fortune, and a happy marriage. And her literary characters, although often not as successful as their creator, tend to disregard the social and cultural restraints preventing them from pursuing their dreams. Tradition means little if anything to them, and they question social obligations as apparently arbitrary and nonsensical. Both Fumiko and her characters were fundamentally pragmatic, and often chose the most commonsensical path to their goals.

The desire one feels in the process of achieving one's goals was a central theme in Fumiko's life and her works, a theme that reflects the traditional aesthetic of longing. Fumiko sought to enhance her own sense of desire by separating herself from the familiar in order to accentuate the longing. Desire inspired her to act, not to ruminate. Likewise, her characters have concrete goals in their lives; they do not mentally wander around the narrative, contemplating their existence. Fumiko associated her longing with travel, which was an integral part of her life, so much so that her expression of longing and loneliness is usually couched in terms of the emotions related to traveling. If she had been confined to one region of the world, or of Japan, during her life, the nature of her literature would have been dramatically changed. As it is, her characters are constantly moving both mentally and physically, reflecting the author's search for happiness, contentment, and nostalgia.

The turn at the end of her life from optimistic to pessimistic themes still maintained much of her earlier style. Her characters, such as Yukiko in *Drifting Clouds*, still strive for goals, still travel in search of those goals, and still come from the lower classes. The main difference is in their attitudes toward the efficacy of their own actions. This change may have been a natural reaction on Fumiko's part to advancing age and deteriorating health; gone were the inspirations of youth, the deprivations that spurred her initial works, and the challenge of overcoming

her social and economic background. She had a fine home, a loving husband and son, financial security, and acceptance in the *bundan*. There
was little left for which to yearn, yet she had so accustomed herself to
working at an almost inhuman pace that slowing or quitting altogether
was impossible. Even though her last works are often considered her
best, her essays show us that at the end of her life she felt derisive toward
her work, and mused about leaving it behind.

The public memory of Hayashi Fumiko will probably rest on the
reputation she established with *Diary of a Vagabond*: the poor young
woman living in straitened circumstances. Initially, this seemed a shame
to me, for there was so much more to the writer and her works. In retrospect, however, it would seem that she would have wanted it that way,
for it was the values she established in her early life with which she most
strongly associated.

APPENDIX

The following are translations of three essays by Hayashi Fumiko, "Watashi no Chiheisen" (My Horizon, 1931), "Bungaku, Tabi, Sono Ta" (Literature, Travel, Etc., 1936), and "Watashi no Shigoto" (My Work, 1937).

MY HORIZON[1]

A long time ago, a certain woman critic commented on my work in the following way:

> Because I have criticized Hayashi Fumiko's works (most notably *Diary of a Vagabond*) as *lumpen* pieces, there are many people who think that I speak slightingly of her artistry. Certainly, Fumiko's works lack volition. Despite the fact that her works are studded throughout with poems that shine like gems amidst the prose, they lack the power of real-life situations. For this reason her works are, as far as proletarian literature is concerned, second-rate.

I read her criticism with deep shame. She says that my work lacks volition, but that is probably due to the fact that in this particular case [*Diary of a Vagabond*] I was writing a piece that does not follow in the path of proletarian literature. I never put up a sign advertising *Diary of a Vagabond* as any particular type of literature, or belonging to any certain artistic school. Indeed, this must be why she said that it lacks volition. But then, just what *is* volition?

She may consider my work to be "second-rate proletarian literature," but I have never carried the proletarian banner; it is precisely proletarian literature that I oppose. Furthermore, as to her saying that my works lack the power of real-life situations, I would like to throw these words right back at her. The landscape within one person's field of vision is not representative of that in everyone's field of vision. I write with the intention of coming to grips with real life as it appears to me personally. I often discover strange words in my sentences. I compose extremely raw nihilism between the lines. Perhaps as a result, my work is sometimes seen as *lumpen* literature, or literature that lacks volition, or literature that runs away from reality.

I must confess that I am a proponent of nihilism. Thus I do not follow the latest trend like everybody else, nor do I suddenly change my mind about things. To this day, I have never stolen someone else's style. To give away one's carefully tempered thoughts is simply to throw pearls to swine. I regard the ideas which I struggled to produce as my chastity, and I will not prostitute that to anybody. Thus, I shall never call my own works proletarian literature. Neither, of course, will I label them as part of any given literary school. Men of letters, as spokesmen of society, are able to create works from every point of view for every cause, but I fear that the word "spokesman" will never apply to someone uneducated like myself.

In the early 1920s, during the time that I often visited Ōsugi Sakae at his home, I was constantly thinking about political movements and art; sleeping or waking, my mind was bursting with ideas.[2] If I had not the slightest talent as a writer or any love of the arts, perhaps I would have joined the ranks of the proletarian movement long ago. When I was a young woman—perhaps even now—there was an extremely savage progressive quality to my emotions. I had a naive obstinacy and paid no attention to anything besides what I wanted to do myself. To this day, I maintain the same lifestyle and my work is thus forced to bear the name of *lumpen* literature. I will live the rest of my life by the ideas that are born by my actions. In the future, my work will doubtless receive many different kinds of shocks, but at those times, I will rest easy not imitating others. Rather, my work will flourish by virtue of the things that I choose to do myself.

The term "proletarian literature" in Japanese really means "the literature of poverty." If one talks about the literature of poverty, then my works certainly fit into that category. The foreign word "proletarian" reeks of the intelligentsia and ideology. But the literature of poverty! In all its meanings, my work is the literature of poverty. Thank goodness for the Japanese language! But the term "literature of poverty" also has a *lumpen*-esqe quality. The magical spell of language causes a strange chasm in meaning in cases such as these.

Up until now I have written my work in the form of prose. I make much use of *katakana* in my sentences; I convey my volition with these phonetic markings, using them to strengthen the reader's eye. *Katakana* is usually used solely as a gloss to indicate the reading of a foreign word, but in my case, the more difficult words there are in a sentence, the more I have tried to write them just using *katakana*. Perhaps it is because I began by writing poems, or perhaps it is because my eyes become so tired when the characters are packed closely on the page, but in any case those diacritical marks that normally appear between the lines in other texts end up in the main body of my works.[3]

Why did my writing become this way? Once, when I held many different jobs, I wanted to write down many different thoughts. But when one has a job, reading and writing can become difficult. During such difficult times, even if I was exhausted, I still wanted to write something— I couldn't stand it if I didn't write. I then expressed this pent-up emotion in the form of poems and prose.

Recently I have been reading Yokomitsu Riichi's work. There is no space between his words, nor wasted breath between his sentences. I was tired upon the first reading. Upon the second reading I felt a sort of attraction toward his work, and by the third reading I had great respect for his style. Yokomitsu's style is something that I could not achieve even if I tried over the course of decades. I wonder if there is anybody in the world of proletarian literature who has such a firmly rooted style? I have thought of trying to write my "literature of poverty" in this sort of dense style, using much *hiragana*, but for me it is still quite a difficult task.

Once I fall under the spell of language, I cease to be able to write— pushed by a progressive urge—like I did before. Ozaki Akira called my work "literature of the soul," a term that I gratefully accept.

I want to use my own style to describe my own perception of reality. My goal is to reach many readers. There are probably many writers who would feel satisfied if just one or two readers understood what they wrote, but I am not one of them. I must target a large audience. Even proletarian writers write dry, highbrow novels that are difficult for even a college graduate to understand. Their message probably goes right over their reader's head. The great number of those who produce works that are exactly like advertisements, works that one would not want to read more than once, are proletarian writers who want solely to convey their ideas to their few colleagues, and one has the feeling that there is not one heart-felt emotion in their work. The media loves the proletarian writers, but from those writers' drive to write comes a commercialism and corruption that results in work that fails to draw readers.

It is because I believe this that I read Kobayashi Takiji's work with reverence.[4] The author is not heroic in his work nor is he pompous. Kobayashi's works are pieces of literature that anybody can understand and they have a certain freshness no matter which one one reads. Recently I have also been reading Balzac and rereading Chekhov. I may not understand their difficult ideas, but I enjoy their works. I think this is because in both Balzac's and Chekhov's works there is an element of reality that does not make fun of the reader. When I read a novel that has this sort of quality, I feel like I've struck water in the desert. Such an experience leads me to think that proletarian *romanticist* literature might be all right.[5] On the other hand, I couldn't write proletarian *political* literature even if I turned somersaults.[6]

I want to write seriously about the world I come from—the world of poverty—in a very nostalgic style. If I can do this well, I will have fulfilled my role in life. The world of literary robots pains me. Robotic works do not suit me.[7] Born a human being, I am happy if I can write about the pain of humans and the nostalgia of the times. I distance myself from lofty schools of thought, and I try to ride through life on the strength of my convictions and enthusiasm.

As I am exposed to various ideologies, in my ignorance I often paralyze myself by being too demanding of them. If I don't understand an idea after hearing the discourse a hundred times, it drives me to produce something from within my heart which grasps reality in a way that the discourse does not. Although the result may be absurd, I endeavor to do so.

I am truly in a confused state.

May 1931

LITERATURE, TRAVEL, ETC.[8]

It may sound strange to say that at the tender age of thirty I want to pursue the simpler things in life, but I hold the mystery of mother nature dear and gradually have come to find worldly things distasteful. Lately I have been enjoying reading the poems of Han Shan.[9] Perhaps I am infatuated with escapist literature. I like the following poem:

> In this world there are people of many affairs,
> Widely learned in all sorts of knowledge and views
>
> But they don't know their original true natures;
> Thus they are turned from and far from the Way.
>
> If they could understand the true work,
> For what use this display of false hopes?
>
> With one thought understand your own mind,
> And you open the Buddha's knowledge and views.[10]

Whenever I see all the multitalented, busy people around me, I spitefully recall this poem. Lately I have taken to traveling alone whenever I have the time. Since I profess that everyday family life needs but a bit of *komemiso*, I have no desire to build an expensive house. It is enough for me if I can live my life by working a bit here and playing a bit there.[11] There are people who tell me that I should think about building my own house and settling down, but I hate the idea of building a house or amassing wealth. The feeling one experiences while building a house and the feeling one experiences once the house is completed are both troublesome. I think it would be odd for someone like me, who is always running about and who can barely afford to buy one or two pillarbeams, to build a little modern house. People who can relax after they build their own house are quite rare. I think that after one or two years have passed, they probably get fed up with it all and can't stand to bear the burden anymore. Whenever I start planning to build a house, I end up spending all the money on travel.

Up until this point in time I have had no problems living my life the way I want to—it is perhaps because of this that I can say this—and I enjoy being semiliterate; this enjoyment has made me what I am. Right now I support myself by writing novels. Although I still cannot believe that someone like me, with mediocre talents and poor education, can support herself writing novels, I find that uncertainty indescribably enjoyable. My health and my good nature are second to none. A long time ago, I was known to sleep in abandoned houses, and slept well even when I slept on dirt floors. Even now I rarely catch cold even when I'm wearing thin clothing, and I think nothing of staying up all night for two or three days at a time. Once I set in on my work, I can't eat a thing; all I can do is diligently face the paper before me. But perhaps this state of being is one that only other writers can understand. How pleasing it is! Writing a novel is as pleasing as having one's lover waiting for one. I've enjoyed reading since I was a child, and it is because of this pleasure that I have endured this far, not doing myself in. I am a true optimist and I hate gloomy things; despite that, I dedicate myself to loneliness. I feel I have come this far through the hunger and longing I have for literature. Even now, my goals are constant hunger and constant longing. I'm not very fond of trying out new things with other people. I think that, once I'm thirty-five years old, it would be nice to retreat to the mountains and stare vacantly at the sky. Then, I think that I would surely summon great strength to work. I am so full of ambition that my selfishness borders on being disgusting. My work, which has no definite object, takes two forms: newspaper novels and diaries.[12] I've been keeping a diary for about five years now. I keep to writing one page every day for my newspaper novel, although there are days when I manage to write three or four pages. I cannot simply lounge about until the mood to write strikes me, like the writers of old would do. Lounging about would make me stupid. There is no point in imposing stupidity upon stupidity.

No matter how difficult it may be, I make it a point to sit myself down at my desk at least once a day in an effort to grow accustomed to such a routine. For someone of mediocre ability, there is no recourse but hard work. I've heard that the tennis star Moody once took two years off in order to recuperate, and then once having done so she was once again very competitive, but I think that such a long hiatus would not be appropriate for a novelist.[13] If a writer works briefly and then takes a long break—perhaps a two- or three-day trip—without constantly observing the world and constantly thinking about it, then when it comes time to "compete," she will end up staring vacantly into space. Genius was spoken of in the times before cultural development, but now resolute common sense is what it takes. This is true for any road one chooses to follow. It is not genius that I covet now; rather, I long for correct recognition on a road of plentiful common sense.

I respect people like Bashō, who was full of common sense. He was indifferent to worldly gain, and had a character that was pure and penetrated by a splendid emptiness. His taste for the simple and quiet things in life reveals his inner spirit and is representative of the same taste for such things that all Japanese have within ourselves.[14] When he set off on his trip to the north, he was appreciative of but embarrassed by all the farewell gifts that his neighbors gave him. For him, it was quite awkward that things had come to that.

Although I said that I covet loneliness, I cannot remain indifferent to worldly gain. I don't want to build a home or amass wealth, but I do want to travel to my heart's content and I don't want to worry about being able to supply my family with *komemiso*.[15] I have finally paid off my financial debts. Good work and good travel are what I long for. I want to go to India. I want to go to China. And of course there is France, too. The nostalgia that I feel when I'm in foreign lands is so enjoyable that I could die. It's enough to make me spend days daydreaming about Japan's beauty and longing for my home. The Japanese language is especially very good. In French, simple words like *non* or *oui* are used by everybody. But in Japan, even simple words like *yes* and *no* are expressed in myriad ways. The phrase *"horeta yowami ja yurushanse, nushi to ukina mo miyō ga ja to"* is full of vibrant and beautiful words; Japanese is a language inferior to none.[16]

I have come to enjoy composing poems and songs upon my return home from far away. A while back, when I was off hiking by myself near the great waterfall in the mountain pass between the regions of Musashi and Sagami, I had the uncontrollable urge to sing.[17] The new Kōshū road to Yose winds along the valleys, and I could hear the babbling of the nearby river. Looking down, I saw the luxuriant and bushy tops of the cedar trees all in a row, and I could see the Todani and Ashigara mountain ranges.

> The waterfall
> Clouds in the shade of trees in a mountain pass
> Crawl along the base of the pine-covered cliff

I think this is an odd poem, but it is the genuine article that sprung forth from my soul while I was up in the mountains, so even though it is rather warped it is still adorable. Reciting this poem about a waterfall reminds me of a poem by Yosano Akiko:

> A waterfall scatters into mist in the mountains of Kaigane
> The crimson leaves of the cherry trees at Obana no tai

What a splendid verse, endowed with such character! It is clearly Akiko's work, and I have committed it to memory, along with the following poem:

> The *tatami* of a mountain villa and the
>   mountains in Kai province all in a row,
> Create the autumn peaks of Ashigara

This poem is the one I enjoy the most of all. I think the expression, "The *tatami* of a mountain villa and the mountains in Kai province all in a row" is splendid indeed. Modern writers are accustomed to using such dry expressions, but I think they should consider turning to the expressions used in poems and songs. I may be opinionated in saying so, but I would like to speak my mind. When I gazed down the Kōshū road from behind Shinjuku station—I was really thinking about a rough trip through a cloud of dust—I found it fascinating that the flow of the road is much like the flow of a river. When I walked past the front of the imperial tomb in Tama and entered the town of Fuchū, I saw scarlet myrtle blossoms under the eaves of every house. Proceeding beyond the race track and over the bridge, I entered the city of Hachiōji. This place feels more like a single avenue than it does a town; it seemed to be just right for a single streetcar line. Then I climbed along the foot of Mt. Takao and to the great waterfall. There sits the Kōshū border marker, and the bleached white road peacefully trails off down to the town of Yose.

At a teashop, I ate the lunch I had brought along and then eventually made my way back from Yose to the Kobotoke pass. Gazing at the clear mountain stream touched me deep in my heart as the image flooded my eyes. Someday when I have the time, I think I would like to go to the ruins of Sennin Taitei in Hachiōji or the Shinkaku Temple in Yokoyama Sanda where Bashō's "Frog Mound" is located.

I also like Todori, which is part of the Imperial Household Forestry Bureau reserve. At the waterfall there, I drank the mountain stream water to my heart's content, and then I cooled my face with a damp handtowel. I felt profoundly happy to be alive and healthy. Water, the earth, the sky . . . they always make me feel good. As I don't make many plans before I set out on a journey, I enjoy carefully examining the map each new day. This prepares me to set out on my own at my own pace whenever I feel the need to leave town. I think it a great stroke of luck that I am not some gloomy housewife whose life revolves around her husband's wallet. When I come home from a day trip, I find it hard not to go off to the kitchen and keep working away. My family laughs at me when I say that I must have been a puppy in a former life. I go where I want to go. I find group excursions immensely trying, and I rarely make plans. Whenever I do make a plan, everyone just agrees with me anyway, so there's really no point in making a plan in the first place.

This summer, I have only made a day trip to the great waterfall, but once autumn arrives, I would like to take a three-week holiday with my mother with the following itinerary: we would leave for Kōshū from Shinjuku, go from Shiojiri in Shinshū to Tajimi, Nagoya, through Yokkaichi to Tsuge, Kizu, Kyōto, Ayabe, around Fukuchiyama to Tottori, Matsue, Izumo Imamachi, Iwami Masuda, Yamaguchi, Kogunasa, and Shimonoseki. Such a spree would be delightful. My mother and I fight like crazy when we travel together. She takes charge and suggests we stay at a cheap lodging house, but I'm such a pleasure-seeker that I always want to stay in a first-class inn—neither one of us yields to the other's opinion. The two of us querulously muddle along and thankfully manage to complete the journey, but there's no need for me to be haughty and have reservations about traveling with my mother. The kind of trip that I really hate is the lecture tour. I'm rarely asked to do one, but there is nothing as embarrassing, hateful, and ludicrous as a lecture tour. Journeys are best made alone or with one companion. And when the trip is long, one should do it alone. Last year I went to Hokkaidō and Karafuto by myself on a one-month journey and I stayed at merchant inns—it was very interesting. Writing this may make it seem to the reader as if I work and travel with ease, but actually it is very difficult for me to write novels. It is pleasurable and painful. There are even days when I think I would be better off dead. I travel because writing becomes intolerable. Because I would be greatly troubled if my mother died in my absence, I make it a point to take her along with me on short trips. I have been with my husband for seven or eight years now, and when he returned from military duty in the reserves, I went to meet him and we traveled together. We probably seemed like an odd couple to others, but we intend to travel into our old age, complete with walking canes. I travel with a feeling of self-indulgence; I revel secretly in the joy of youth and of being a writer. When I face difficulties that seem insurmountable, I escape it all by spending every cent I've got on travel. When I have trouble writing, it makes me feel all the more like taking a trip. I think that a two- or three-day trip for relaxation is good for one's physical health. The good and bad memories of a journey, like a jar of rice wine, are the kinds of things that one buries in the ground, to unearth and enjoy at a later date.

Lately I have been gazing at the passing autumn clouds, and the desire to travel among the shadows of the mountains wells up uncontrollably inside me. Although the weather may be sizzling hot when I travel, the journey helps me make progress in my work. I don't like the practice of going to a resort to escape the summer heat of the city. I passed this summer in the heat of Tokyo, working intermittently in the cool morning hours. This, too, is a part of the simple and quiet life that I seek.

MY WORK[18]

I am a kind of itinerant writer, one who does not belong to any one literary group. Over the past ten years, I have produced a varied lot of works, but the odd thing is that none of them have ever drawn much of a readership. I was recently reading Kawabata Yasunari's *My Specimen Room*, which he wrote some time ago, and I found myself envious of his ability to create such a superior piece of writing.[19] Although I try to live my life to the fullest, none of my works have such a fastidious tenacity as Kawabata's works. Looking back, I think that I have made the life I depicted in *Diary of a Vagabond* the foundation stone of my life. Although I have somehow managed to get this far with nothing but this rather rough literary spirit of mine, any relief I feel is tainted by a bit of anxiety. I feel that if I relax my grip a bit, I will soon end up drowning. It is not that I feel writing an explanatory essay on past works to be unpleasant. It is simply that I do not know what words to use now in order to describe the dreamy and foolish works which I wrote in the past. What marks my writing is that I write with all my soul and that I entrust my readers with the final judgment of the piece.

I respond to others through my work. I speak my true feelings. I run up against many different obstacles in my work—last year was no exception. My writing can generally be divided into three periods: the *Diary of a Vagabond* period, the "A Record of Honorable Poverty" period, and the "The Oyster" period.[20] Although I suffered many hardships while writing these and other works, such hardships become the flesh and blood of my writing and provide me with a feeling of placidity. I am left with no desire to buckle down and write something of grand proportions.

The piece with which I have struggled the most as a writer is the novel *Lightning*, which was published serially in this magazine.[21] I did not have the energy to complete this novel properly, and to this day it is not one of my favorite pieces. From the beginning of that romance, I was often struck with a kind of "thirst"—the kind that I feel when writing a full-length novel—and I was swept off my feet countless times by a feeling of loneliness. *Lightning* was a fresh breeze for me, but as that breeze was born from the foul winds that produced "The Oyster," it made me feel as if I had died in a battle between myself and my works.

I have written countless short pieces from the early "The Accordion and the Fish Town" to "The Snapping Turtle," which I wrote this year, but there are only a trifling few that I myself like.[22] And even after reading those pieces that I like, I am not transported to any realm of happiness. This leads me to think on occasion that I am a strange writer.

It's not as if I don't occasionally feel that I have been wasting my time in fruitless endeavors for the past ten years, but if I do say so myself I think that those ten years of preparatory work have been precisely what I needed to gain the courage and excitement that I feel within me today. I want to work with abandon. When I recently had my fortune read, I was told that if I hurried my work I would die an early death, but that did not make me want to slow down. I felt so busy that I would simply burn up if I tried to stand still. Somehow I feel that once I have ascertained my goal I can take my time and write solid works.

I become very angry when I receive negative criticism about any of my works. Nonetheless, I am well aware of the ugliness of my writing and thus ardently attack each new project. I may seem weakhearted, but I can be rather determined.

I am not much of a stickler when it comes to holding fast to the plot of a story. Rather, I am a bit cowardly about plot construction. When a coherent, trunklike idea comes to mind, I enjoy making branches and leaves to adorn it. And I feel successful if major allusions spread out from the text.

I have recently been indulging in some works by Mori Ōgai. His writing is perfectly structured, with no unseemly protrusions. When I write a novel, I set up an Ōgai novel like a music stand in front of me and when I'm parched, I read it. When I am tired, I reread it. But I am an unskillful writer, and even with such a splendid music stand I cannot drink in even a little bit of the expression and basic movement of thought that it provides. It's just that I want to write something that could be considered my life's work, and now I feel that I am ready to do that. It may sound strange for me to say so, but I feel that the joy and pain of my work are beginning now.

Ultimately I would like to be a sideline writer; I do not like the idea of making my works into time-honored classics. I have been thinking about publishing a collection of selected works, but I think that it would be read and quickly discarded, both the reader and the author relieved to have it over with. I don't want to stay in this kind of world; I would like to go on a new, refreshing pilgrimage. I think that in a selected collection of my works, I would put *Diary of a Vagabond* at the beginning, but given all the various schools with which I associated myself from that time to the present, I am left feeling like I need an enema to cleanse myself of it all.

> My happy youth will begin today.
> The color of the distant sea, the color of the distant sky.
> They are freshly painted in my eyes today.
> It's good to be alive!
> Alive I take deep breaths of happiness
> I'm so glad to be alive.

Now I'm at the point of breaking down and crying. I've worked too hard up until this point . . .

After coming this far, there is no pulling back. I must advance steadily. I want to live. I want to live and write good works.

I cannot write an explanatory essay on my early works. Those are written and done with. What commentary could I possibly add to them? I, the author, do not know, so the pieces must speak for themselves. Isn't that for the best?

The other day I was listening to Dvořak's "Slavonic Dances." They are pieces which fill my heart with intense resounding vibrations. They make me feel totally content. They make me aspire to write my next piece with sincerity. I cannot seem to rest.

NOTES

INTRODUCTION

1. Dates given after titles indicate date of publication and in the case of a work that was serialized, date of publication of the complete piece, unless otherwise noted. English translations of all titles and publication dates are given at the first mention of the work and omitted thereafter. *Food* was published posthumously.

The title of the volume is *Hayashi Fumiko*, the series name is *Chikuma Nihon bungaku zenshū* (Tokyo: Chikuma shobō, 1992). There are a total of fifty authors represented in this collection. The stories included in the *Hayashi Fumiko* volume, in the order presented, are *Ao uma o mitari* (I Saw a Pale Horse, 1929 [abridged]), "Fūkin to uo no machi" (The Town of Accordions and Fish, 1931), "Sakana no jobun," (Preface to Fish, 1933), "Seihin no sho" (A Record of Honorable Poverty, 1931) *Nakimushi kozō* (Crybaby, 1935), "Dauntaun" (Downtown, 1949), "Gyokai" (Seafood, 1940), "Kaki" (Oyster, 1935), "Kawahaze" (The River Goby, 1947) and "Yaen" (Wild Monkey, 1950).

2. Of note, Janice Brown recently published *I Saw a Pale Horse*, a translation of both Fumiko's early poetry in the eponymous collection and poetry selections from *Diary of a Vagabond* (Ithaca, N.Y.: Cornell University Press, 1997). Joan Ericson also recently published commentary on Hayashi Fumiko in the context of being a *joryū sakka*, along with a partial translation of *Diary of a Vagabond* (*Be a Woman: Hayashi Fumiko and Modern Japanese Literature* [Honolulu: University of Hawaii Press, 1997]).

3. *Diary of a Vagabond* and *Food*, respectively.

CHAPTER 1. LIFE OF AND INFLUENCES ON THE AUTHOR

1. There is a large collection of writing on the subject of Fumiko's life, larger than what has been written about her literature. The fascination with Fumiko's life is understandable, given the fact that her first and possibly most successful work was the autobiographical novel *Diary of a Vagabond*. Since its publication, readers have been eager to know more about the life portrayed on its pages. And despite the fact that soon after the success of *Diary of a Vagabond* Fumiko earned enough from royalties to permanently remove herself from the life of poverty for which she had become famous, she is to this day most often remembered as someone who lived a hard life. One of the problems with this is that the information provided in *Diary of a Vagabond* and other autobiograph-

ical works is not always a faithful record of real events as recorded both by the author herself in essays and other miscellany and by those who knew her during her lifetime. The result is a large collection of conflicting information that itself has become the subject of various studies. While I feel it is important to know about the life influences of any writer, I want to avoid the mire of conflicting facts that surround Fumiko as much as possible, and so here I acknowledge that the body of my biography is based on one main source: the annotated chronological table compiled by Imagawa Eiko, which is published in volume 16 of the Bunsendō *Hayashi Fumiko zenshū*. Other sources, when used, are appropriately cited. I chose Imagawa's table for two reasons: first, it is much more detailed than other tables of its kind, which leads me to believe that it was more carefully compiled; second, while none of the chronological tables contain bibliographic notes, making it difficult to check their accuracy, Imagawa's has proved consistent with what crosschecks I have run on dates and other facts. On the other hand, I do not claim that Imagawa's table is the authoritative source above all other sources; it simply is one of the best choices for a brief overview of the author's life.

2. Moji was incorporated into Kita Kyūshū in 1963. Her family registry says that she was born on December 31 in Moji, Fukuoka Prefecture. However, there is conflicting information about her birth: her mother says that she was born in June. In *Diary of a Vagabond* and in *Hitori no shōgai* (One Person's Life, 1939), she says that she was born in May. In *Pari (no) nikki* (Paris Diary, 1947) she says that she was born on May 5th. For details on her birth date and related family events, see Wada Yoshie's "Hayashi Fumiko: Shusshō no nazo" (Hayashi Fumiko: The Riddle Surrounding Her Birth) in *Kindai joryū bungaku: Nihon bungaku kenkyū shiryō* (Tokyo: Yūseidō, 1983), 131–36; "Pari (no) nikki," (Paris Diary) in *Shinchō HFZ* vol. 8, 152. The title of "Pari (no) nikki" is alternately cited with and without the particle *no* so I have chosen to place it in parentheses. The version used for this book is the one found in *Hayashi Fumiko zenshū*, and does not have the particle.

3. They sold Chinese-style herbal medicine (*kampōyaku*).

4. Fukuda Kiyoto, *Hayashi Fumiko: Hito to sakuhin* (Tokyo: Shimizu shoin, 1966), 14.

5. *Shinchō HFZ* vol. 2, 178–79.

6. Inoue Takaharu, *Hayashi Fumiko to sono shūhen* (Kokubunji: Musashino shoin, 1990), 13.

7. Fukuda Kiyoto, *Hayashi Fumiko: Hito to sakuhin*, 12–13.

8. *Shinchō HFZ* vol. 2, 5.

9. Inoue Takaharu, *Hayashi Fumiko to sono shūhen*, 16.

10. Ibid., 23–24.

11. Ibid., 24. Inoue says that Fumiko herself told this story to his mother, Inoue Yoshiko, who in turn related it to him.

12. Ibid., 26.

13. For an example, see Itagaki Naoko's biography, *Hayashi Fumiko* (Tokyo: Tōkyō raifusha, 1956), 24–25.

14. *HFZ* vol. 4, 288.

15. *HFZ* vol. 4, 288.

16. The scene in *One Person's Life* that describes her first assignation with Koizumi is found in *Shinchō HFZ* vol. 8, 80.

17. Takemoto Chimakichi, *Ningen Hayashi Fumiko* (Tokyo: Chikuma shobō, 1985), 25–29. Takemoto quotes other established biographers of Fumiko, and then provides his own evidence. Chapter 6 in Takemoto's book also discusses the father-daughter relationship and includes correspondence between the two.

18. Imagawa Eiko (*HFZ* vol. 16, 288) quotes Nakahara Masao from *Hayashi Fumiko to Shimonoseki*.

19. The Imagawa chronology says that she read Goethe's, Mérimée's, and Prévost's works in the *Eruteru sōsho* (Werther Library), a collection of foreign works in translation published by Shinchōsha from 1917 to 1927. The translations of these works were by the following: *L'Histoire du Chevalier des Grieux et de Manon Lescaut* by Hirotsu Kazuo (1891–1968), *Carmen* by Fuse Nobuo (1892–?), and *Die Leiden des jungen Werthers* by Hata Toyokichi (1892–1956). (*Nihon kindai bungaku daijiten*, vol. 6, entry for *Eruteru sōsho*.)

20. See Itagaki Naoko, *Hayashi Fumiko no shōgai: Uzushio no jinsei*, 63–67, for more information on Fumiko's school days.

21. Itagaki Naoko describes her as a near-sighted girl who sat in the front row in order to see the board better (Itagaki Naoko, *Hayashi Fumiko no shōgai: Uzushio no jinsei* [Tokyo, Daiwa shobō, 1965], 64–65).

22. Here the word "scent" is *nioi*, the same word that is translated as "smell" in previous passages. In all of these passages the Japanese word is the same: *nioi*.

23. Passage (e) falls into both the first and the third categories, as it recalls a character and causes the personal recollecting to feel nostalgia.

24. A "shoe attendant" was a job in which she was responsible for arranging and caring for the shoes that customers at some establishment would leave at the door upon entering the building.

25. Up until this point, Fumiko had written her name in *katakana*. The name that Kobayashi suggested was pronounced the same but written differently, in *kanji*. Fumiko adopted the new characters and used this pen name the rest of her life.

26. Fukuda Kiyoto, *Hayashi Fumiko: Hito to sakuhin*, 52.

27. Ibid., 47–48.

28. Itagaki Naoko, *Hayashi Fumiko no shōgai* (Tokyo: Daiwa shobō, 1965), 86–91.

29. The *Nihon kindai bungaku daijiten* describes *The Two of Us* as a "poetry magazine" (*shi zasshi*) that was an "eight-page pamphlet" (*hachi peeji no panfuretto*). See entry for "Futari" in volume 4.

30. There are two particularly violent scenes: one on page 229 and the other on page 247 in *Shinchō HFZ* vol. 1.

31. Fumiko's relationship with Nomura, as well as her other lovers, is discussed in detail in Muramatsu Sadataka's "Hayashi Fumiko no dansei henreki" in *Sakka no kakei to kankyō* (Tokyo: Shibundō, 1964), 202–17.

32. *Shinchō HFZ* vol. 5, 88–89.

33. *Shinchō HFZ* vol. 5, 101.

34. *Shinchō HFZ* vol. 13, 180–81.

35. *Shinchō HFZ* vol. 13, 204–5.

36. *Shinchō HFZ* vol. 2, 247.

37. This name, "Rokubin," is not really his given name. When asked by Inoue about how he happened to have such an odd name, he replied that his real name is "Masaharu," but that the characters used to write "Masaharu" are easily mistaken for those used to write "Rokubin." Over the course of time, Rokubin accepted the fact that people read his name incorrectly. Rokubin told Inoue, "Everybody calls me 'Rokubin,' so that will do fine" (Inoue, *Hayashi Fumiko to sono shūhen*, 276).

38. For more background on the establishment of *Women and the Arts* and other works published in it, along with commentary on *Diary of a Vagabond*, see Takami Jun's "Zen josei shinshutsu kōshinkyoku" in *Shōwa bungaku seisuishi 1* (Tokyo: Bungei shunjūsha, 1958), 179–202.

39. Mori Eiichi, *Hayashi Fumiko no keisei: Sono sei to hyōgen* (Tokyo: Yūseidō, 1992), 55–56.

40. Of the fifty-six published works cited in the Imagawa chronology between 1928 and 1930, only four were selected to be included in the *Hayashi Fumiko zenshū* (HFZ). Between 1931 and 1932, only 9 out of 59 works were included in the *zenshū*. The percentage of included works increase gradually over the following years, but one can see by these numbers that many of Fumiko's early works have been ignored by editors, presumably because the quality of writing is substandard.

41. In the *zenshū* only 7 of the 34 poems were reprinted. See *Shinchō HFZ* vol. 1, 7–25.

42. Mori Eiichi, *Hayashi Fumiko no keisei: Sono sei to hyōgen*, 18.

43. In the prologue, Fumiko wrote, "Here I have collected all the poems from the past ten years of which I am fond." (Mori Eiichi, *Hayashi Fumiko no keisei: Sono sei to hyōgen*, 18).

44. One could consider this the Japanese government, as Taiwan was a colony of Japan at the time. Likewise, given Taiwan's colonial status, this trip was not technically a trip to a foreign country, but given that Taiwan was culturally and historically not part of Japan, and that it ceased to be a colony after a fifty-year period, I shall here consider it a foreign country for all intents and purposes.

45. Mukden is present-day Shenyang.

46. For examples of sources, see Donald Keene's *Dawn to the West: Japanese Literature in the Modern Era*, 1141 and Fukuda Kiyoto's *Hayashi Fumiko: Hito to sakuhin*, 62.

47. Inoue Takaharu, in his biography of Fumiko, describes Fumiko showing up at his family's house on the morning of November 8 and announcing that she was leaving for Europe. Inoue writes, "My mother ran out to greet her and Fumiko said, 'Yoshiko, I'm going to Paris, France! . . . What a surprise, eh?' It was entirely unexpected and all Yoshiko could say was, 'Really?'" (Inoue Takaharu, *Hayashi Fumiko to sono shūhen*, 33).

48. Fukuda Kiyoto, *Hayashi Fumiko: Hito to sakuhin*, 65.

49. The essay is entitled "Ro Jin tsuioku" (A Reminiscence of Lu Xun), in *Kaizō*, Tokyo: Kaizō sha, April 1937.

50. This journey is recorded in many sources on Fumiko. The dates given here are from the Imagawa chronology in *HFZ* vol. 16, 294.

51. See translation of "Bungaku, tabi, sono ta" (Literature, Travel, Etc., 1936) in the appendix.

52. Donald Keene, *Dawn to the West: Japanese Literature in the Modern Era* (New York: Henry Holt, 1984), 1142.

53. Imagawa records Fumiko's destinations and travel dates in detail in her chronology, *HFZ* vol. 16, 295.

54. Fukuda Kiyoto, *Hayashi Fumiko: Hito to sakuhin*, 66–67.

55. *HFZ* vol. 16, 107.

56. Fumiko wrote a short essay entitled "Kane" (Money, 1939) in which she describes a debt collector coming to her house to collect on a debt that her late father had incurred twenty years earlier. She was quite upset when she found that Kisaburō designated her, at the time eleven years old, as the guarantor on the debt. The fact that her parents' debts could come back to haunt her after so much time was very disturbing to her, and she writes that she reproached her mother for being involved in such an act. (See "Kane" in *Shinkyō to fūkaku* [Tokyo: Sōgen sha, 1939], 109–11.)

57. This is recorded in two places: the final section of part 2 of *Diary of a Vagabond* (*Shinchō HFZ*, vol 2, 181–86) and "Little Viewpoint" (*HFZ* vol. 16, 105–11). The latter is almost identical to the former except for a few editorial changes.

58. Richard H. Mitchell, in his study of censorship in Japan, notes that "Writers did not need to publish to come within reach of police power; a favorite police charge against authors was to accuse them of contributing funds to the Japanese communists (a violation of the Peace Preservation Law). Kobayashi Takiji was arrested on this charge in January 1931, as was Hayashi Fumiko in 1933." The Peace Preservation Law (Chian iji hō) was a 1925 law that called for imprisonment of "anyone who has organized an association with the objective of altering the *kokutai* [national polity] or the form of government" (Richard H. Mitchell, *Censorship in Imperial Japan* [Princeton, N.J.: Princeton University Press, 1983], 271–72, 196–97).

59. "A Night of Dreams" in *Shinchō HFZ* vol. 11, 69.

60. See the translation of her essay, "Watashi no chiheisen" (My Horizon, 1931) in appendix for more detail.

61. *HFZ* vol. 12, 189.

62. *HFZ* vol. 12, 191.

63. *HFZ* vol. 13, 215–16.

64. I have found no evidence that Fumiko did so, although that does not eliminate the possibility that she might indeed have done so without ever writing about it. Given Fumiko's penchant for writing about herself, her life, and her work, however, this seems a remote possibility at best.

65. *Shinchō HFZ* vol. 1, 62.

66. *Shinchō HFZ* vol. 1, 63.

67. *Shinchō HFZ* vol. 8, 38–39.

68. This journal, published posthumously, was kept from 1943 through 1947. It is apparently factual and true to the author's life.

69. *Shinchō HFZ* vol. 11, 56. The last sentence of this passage is *Nihon no bukkyō wa, mō ichido, kangaenaosarenakereba naranai to omoimasu.* Fumiko means that the attitudes that Japanese have come to have toward Buddhism should be reexamined and changed.

70. *Shinchō HFZ* vol. 2, 23.

71. *Shinchō HFZ* vol. 20, 39.

72. *Azuma* refers to cheap cloth satchels in which women carried cigarettes. *Shinchō HFZ* vol. 3, 199.

73. "Watashi no shigoto" (My Work, 1937), *Shinchō HFZ* vol. 19, 246.

74. Isogai Hideo, *Hayashi Fumiko* (Shinchō nihon bungaku arubamu, vol. 34 [Tokyo: Shinchōsha, 1986]), 69.

75. *Bundan* means "literary world" or "literary establishment." This was not a formal group, but rather a generally recognized group of writers who were considered accomplished in their art.

76. As quoted by Mori Eiichi, *Hayashi Fumiko no keisei: sono sei to hyōgen,* 131.

77. *HFZ* vol. 10, 22.

78. *HFZ* vol. 10, 26.

79. *HFZ* vol. 10, 33–34.

80. *HFZ* vol. 16, 131–32.

81. Dennis Keene identifies these two writers' works as main influences on Yokomitsu's "The Machine" (Dennis Keene, *Yokomitsu Riichi: Modernist* [New York: Columbia University Press, 1980], 167–71).

82. See Dennis Keene, *Yokomitsu Riichi: Modernist,* 79–80, for a partial translation of the essay that Yokomitsu published in the first issue of *Bungei jidai* (Literary Age), the organ of the New Sensationalist School. Keene says of this essay: "the article is remarkable for its incompetent usage of the vocabulary of aesthetic theory."

83. Donald Keene, *Dawn to the West: Japanese Literature in the Modern Era,* 650–51.

84. Translation by Dennis Keene, *"'Love'" and Other Stories of Yokomitsu Riichi* (Tokyo: University of Tokyo Press and Japan Foundation, 1974), 51.

85. *Shinchō HFZ* vol. 2, 68.

86. Dennis Keene argues that it is impossible to "transfer the reality of objects without the secondary existence of the writer's mind or feelings interposing between the objects and the reader" (*Yokomitsu Riichi: Modernist,* 81), although this is what Yokomitsu claimed he was trying to do. Keene says, "What instead mediates is a sensibility that attempts to be as empty as possible, a mind which refuses as far as possible to give meanings to objects in the world, or to work out the connections between them; a stunned and exhausted consciousness which has decided to give up, but still a consciousness totally imposed upon all it apprehends. Language mediates between men and the objects of their world, and there is no possible way to prevent this from happening."

87. "A London Boarding House and Other Matters" in *Chūō kōron* (April 1932), 260.

88. In this short section alone there are the following terms: *tōkii* (talkie), *furan (franc), chibusu* (typhoid), *toramachikku hoteru* (traumatic hotel), *ran-*

debū (rendezvous), mekishiko (Mexico), *sairento* (silent), *nesupa (n'est-ce pas),
toranku* (trunk), *adeyū (adieu), subuniiru* (souvenir), and *konpuranpa (comprends pas).*

89. Because this is written phonetically in *hiragana,* it is impossible to tell
if Fumiko meant this to be *comprend pas* or *comprends pas,* a difference in con-
jugation that would indicate the subject of the action ("he/she" or "I").

90. Here the *kanji* for *hayashi* ("forest") is glossed *baa,* for the French
bois. "A London Boarding House and Other Matters," 260–61.

91. Translated by Dennis Keene in *Yokomitsu Riichi: Modernist,* 167.
Keene's footnote says that this was "a widely-quoted recollection made after the
Pacific War." See Hirano, *Shōwa bungakushi* (Tokyo: Chikuma shobō, 1963),
87; Odagiri Susumu, *Shōwa bungaku no seiritsu* (Tokyo: Keisō shobō, 1965),
249ff.

92. *HFZ,* vol. 16, 113. This is the only specific reference to Yokomitsu
Riichi's writing that Fumiko made, but there are photographs that show the two
of them meeting on two separate occasions in 1935 (See Isogai Hideo, *Hayashi
Fumiko: Shinchō nihon bungaku arubamu,* vol. 34 [Tokyo: Shinchōsha, 1986],
68, 70) and also a letter that Fumiko sent to Yokomitsu in 1936 recommending
a hotel in London (Isogai Hideo, *Hayashi Fumiko,* 70), which show that she had
a given amount of interaction with him.

93. "The Spring" is the story of a young married woman, Kuniko, who
has an extramarital affair with a man named Jinzai. The story suffers from trying to contain too many secondary plots, but the lack of cohesion is compen-
sated for by the large amount of intrigue: Kuniko's husband never knows about
her affair, nor does he know that he is not his child's real father. Kuniko meets
Jinzai in Paris, where her husband is stationed, and the foreign setting gives the
affair an exotic air. Kuniko is taken into police custody in connection with her
lover, who, it turns out, is a criminal wanted by the authorities.

"Lightness and Darkness" is about a young woman who is forced into an
arranged marriage by her family. She does not like her relatives very much, but
she learns during the course of the story to cope with her circumstances and to
take a firm stand for things that are important to her. It is a more mature story
than "The Spring" and does not depend on sensationalism to maintain the
reader's attention.

94. Dennis Keene, *Yokomitsu Riichi: Modernist,* 167.

95. In "Shūsei sensei" (Master Shūsei, 1947), *HFZ* vol. 16, 53.

96. In "Itarutokoro aoyama ari" (Green Mountains All Around, 1947) in
HFZ vol. 16, 133.

97. Mori Eiichi has written at length about the influence that Shūsei had
on Fumiko in his book *Shūsei kara Fumiko e* (Kanazawa: Nōtō Insatsu, 1990),
156–88. See this for comparative excerpts from both author's writing, as well as
important quotations from Fumiko's essays that mention Shūsei.

98. Sōseki as quoted by Hirano Ken in "Kaisetsu" in *Tokuda Shūsei shū,*
vol. 4 of *Shinchō Nihon bungaku* (Tokyo: Shinchōsha, 1973), 294.

99. As summarized from part II of Mori Eiichi's *Shūsei kara Fumiko e.*

100. Uno Kōji used temporal layering extensively in his novels *Kura no
naka* (In the Storehouse, 1919) and *Yume miru heya* (A Room for Dreaming,

1922). The narratives in both move from present to past and back to present again.

101. "Footprints" is "Ashiato" (1910); "The Story of a Prostitute" is "Aru baishōfu no hanashi" (1920).

102. "The Folding Satchel" is "Ori kaban" (1926).

103. The Japanese here for "argumentation" is *rikutsu*, which could also be translated as "theory," "logic," or "reason." Fumiko is alluding to what Sōseki said about Shūsei's writing having no philosophy, but what was a negative comment on Sōseki's part is repeated here as a positive one.

"The Stubby Spirit" is "Chibi no tamashii" (1935). The entire quote is found in *HFZ* vol. 16, 56.

104. Mori Eiichi's arguments are well structured with copious quotations, all fully annotated with bibliographic information. He presents much more material than would be appropriate to address in this section, but the work is admirable and deserves the interested reader's attention. (See *Shūsei kara Fumiko e*, 155–88.)

105. *HFZ* vol. 16, 141–44.

106. *Hokugan butai* (The North Bank Unit, 1939) in *HFZ* vol. 12, 262. A soldier asks Fumiko how Rokubin is, and, touched by the soldier's thoughtfulness, she replies that he is still stationed in a hospital in Utsunomiya.

107. Donald Keene, "The Barren Years: Japanese War Literature" in *Monumenta Nipponica*, XXXIII. (Tokyo: Sophia University Press, 1978), 70.

108. Keene uses the Wade-Giles romanization system for Chinese names, where I use the Pinyin romanization system. Thus, Peking is Beijing, Hankow is Hankou, and Nanking is Nanjing.

109. Donald Keene, "The Barren Years: Japanese War Literature," 84. For more information on the Information Section of the Cabinet and the Pen Unit, see Richard H. Mitchell's study of censorship in Japan, *Censorship in Imperial Japan*, 286–87, 294–95.

110. She reports in *The North Bank Unit* that malaria was commonplace and that the soldiers she met considered it a routine sort of disease to contract (*HFZ* vol. 12, 278). Inoue Takaharu also mentions that Fumiko herself contracted malaria (*Hayashi Fumiko to sono shūhen*, 74).

111. This passage, written by Fumiko, is translated and printed in a pamphlet published by the Hayashi Fumiko Memorial Hall, but bibliographic information has been omitted. (Hayashi Fumiko, Hayashi Fumiko Memorial Hall Pamphlet, 1992, Shinjuku, Tokyo.)

112. Hayashi Fumiko Memorial Hall pamphlet.

113. Rokubin continued to live in the house after Fumiko's death until his own death in 1989. In accordance with his will, it has since been converted into the Hayashi Fumiko Memorial Hall, a private museum.

114. Donald Keene, "The Barren Years: Japanese War Literature," 68.

115. "Below the Equator" was the only work Fumiko published from Southeast Asia that was included in *HFZ*. The Imagawa chronological table in *HFZ* vol. 16, 303, incorrectly lists "Sumatra—Island of the Western Wind" as "Sumatora—Seinan no shima." The original text, published in *Kaizō* in June and July 1943, is entitled "Sumatora—Seifū no shima."

116. For statistics on the number of publishers permitted to continue publishing and other details on government controls of the publishing industry beginning in 1943, see Richard H. Mitchell's *Censorship in Imperial Japan*, 332–35.

117. The letter is reprinted in *Hayashi Fumiko to sono shūhen*, 273–75.

118. Rokubin does not provide Hanzawa's given name in his letter to Inoue Takaharu. He merely describes Hanzawa as "a friend of [Fumiko's]." (Inoue, *Hayashi Fumiko to sono shūhen*, 274.)

119. Inoue Takaharu, *Hayashi Fumiko to sono shūhen*, 272–76. In his letter to Inoue, Rokubin expresses puzzlement at why Fumiko constructed such fictions about her son. He also notes that Tai's biological mother was a student at a girls' finishing school and his biological father a journalist.

120. I have made efforts to avoid using Fumiko's fiction as source material for this biographical chapter, but the lack of bibliographical information in most Hayashi Fumiko biographies leaves me in doubt as to their original sources. In some cases it is clear that the biographer has used *Diary of a Vagabond* as a source, and those have been noted with a footnote in this text. I have tried to use only those "facts" that have outside proof to substantiate them, such as Fumiko's efforts to make Kisaburō retire, and his refusal to do so.

121. Inoue Takaharu, *Hayashi Fumiko to sono shūhen*, 85, 273.

122. Of note, "Kaeru" (The Frog, August, 1936, in *Akai tori*), "Ehon" (Picture Book, June 1936, in *Bungei tsūshin*), and "Kurara" (Clara, June 1935 in *Bungei*).

123. *Anderusen dōwa* (Andersen's Fairy Tales), in *Sekai dōwa shū* (Fairy Tales of the World), (Tokyo: Akane shobō, 1950). This is a collection of eight of Andersen's children's stories, including "The Little Mermaid" and "The Ugly Duckling."

124. *A Family of Women* was published serially in *Fujin kōron* (Women's Review) from January to August 1951. Waves was published serially in *Chūō kōron* from January to July 1951. Both works were published in a separate volume with the sole title *Waves* by Chūō kōron sha in July 1951. *Food* was published serially in *Asahi Shinbun* from April to July 1951 and published as a separate volume by Asahi shinbun sha in October 1951.

125. The Japanese for "solid works" is *shikkari shita mono* ("My Work," *Shinchō HFZ* vol. 19, 246).

126. "My Work," *Shinchō HFZ* vol. 19, 247.

CHAPTER 2. THE OPTIMISM OF THE EARLIER WORKS

1. Theater and film productions include: March–May 1971, March–April 1974, August–October 1981, September–December 1983 (all at the Geijutsu-za Theater). Film versions include: June 1935 (PCL Studios), April 1954 (Tōei Studios), September 1961 (Tōhō Studios), September 1962 (Tōhō Studios). (Kumazaka Atsuko, "Hayashi Fumiko," in *Gendai bungaku kenkyū: Jōhō to shiryō*, Hasegawa Izumi, ed. [Tokyo: Shibundō, 1987], 453.)

2. In most publications of *Diary of a Vagabond*, there are three main parts. The first two parts make up the novel *Diary of a Vagabond*, and the third

part is the novel *Diary of a Vagabond, Continued*. Many *taikei* and *zenshū* collections omit part three altogether. In the present study, section numbers are not mentioned in references, and quotations from *Diary of a Vagabond, Continued* are simply identified as being from *Diary of a Vagabond*.

3. *Shinchō HFZ* vol. 2, 5.

4. Donald Keene, *Dawn to the West: Japanese Literature in the Modern Era*, 1141.

5. *Oxford English Dictionary*. The definition of the Japanese word *nikki* (diary) is similar: "To collect together the events and thoughts of one day, affix a date, and on that day or shortly thereafter make a record; said record" (*Nihon kokugo daijiten*, Nihon daijiten kankōkai, ed. Tokyo: Shōgakukan, 1975).

6. *Shinchō HFZ* vol. 2, 94–95.

7. Presumably, Fumiko is referring here to why a man would choose Ohisa over Okimi, one of the other working girls.

8. *Shinchō HFZ* vol. 2, 145–46.

9. "*Matsubabotan: Hayashi Fumiko bunko* atogaki" (Postscript to *Rose moss: Hayashi Fumiko library*, 1949) in *HFZ* vol. 16, 272.

10. Mori Eiichi, *Hayashi Fumiko no keisei: sono sei to hyōgen*, 71–72.

11. In ibid., 72. Original source: "*Seishun no denki*" *Hayashi Fumiko* (Tokyo: Tsuru shobō, 1967).

12. As quoted by Mori Eiichi, *Hayashi Fumiko no keisei: sono sei to hyōgen*, 94. Original source: "Hayashi Fumiko to sono sekai," in *Fujin kōron*, June 1953.

13. I do not mean to indicate that Bashō was writing necessarily truthful accounts of his actions. Both he and Hayashi fictionalized much of the action in their "diaries." This does not mean that the format of the work ceases to be that of a diary, however.

14. *Shinchō HFZ* vol. 19, 38–39.

15. "Itaru tokoro aoyama ari" in *HFZ* vol. 16, 130.

16. *HFZ* vol. 16, 114.

17. *HFZ* vol. 16, 111.

18. *HFZ* vol. 16, 113.

19. Donald Keene, *Dawn to the West*, 1139.

20. *Shinchō HFZ* vol. 2, 216.

21. *Shinchō HFZ* vol. 2, 220.

22. *HFZ* vol. 16, 130.

23. For a summary of the *junbungaku* vs. *taishūbungaku* debates, see Matthew C. Strecher, "Purely Mass or Massively Pure? The Division between 'Pure' and 'Mass' Literature" in *Monumenta Nipponica* 51.3: 357–74.

24. "*Hōrōki II Hayashi Fumiko bunko* atogaki," in *HFZ* vol. 16, 269.

25. Hayashi quotes a critic who calls her work "second rate" in her essay "My Horizon," *HFZ* vol. 16, 111, but she does not identify the critic by name.

26. This politicization is one in which the author not only is aware of class structure (as defined by Marx), he also specifically focuses on the "proletariat" in an effort to expose injustices inflicted upon the poor working class. For a more detailed discussion of proletarian literature in Japan, see Donald Keene's *Dawn to the West: Japanese Literature in the Modern Era*, 594–628.

27. The Webster's Third New International Dictionary defines *nihilism* as "a doctrine or belief that conditions in the social organization are so bad as to make destruction desirable for its own sake independent of any constructive program or possibility."

28. Itagaki Naoko, *Hayashi Fumiko*, 159.

29. Ibid.

30. "My Horizon," in *HFZ* vol. 16, 112.

31. Nietzsche as quoted in Johan Goudsblom's *Nihilism and Culture* (Oxford: Basil Blackwell, 1980), 11 (translation quoted from *The Will to Power*, Walter Kaufmann, trans. [New York, 1967], 318).

32. Takeuchi Seiichi points to Masamune Hakuchō's (1881–1958) works as being the most nihilistic pieces of the times. He also discusses Iwano Hōmei (1873–1920), Kunikida Doppo (1871–1908), and Tayama Katai (1872–1930) as nihilists, but more in the sense of individualism than of writing "in vain." Takeuchi Seiichi, *Jiko chōetsu no shisō: Kindai nihon no nihirizumu* (Tokyo: Perikan sha, 1988), 184–282.

33. Takeuchi Seiichi, *Jiko chōetsu no shisō: Kindai nihon no nihirizumu*, 204.

34. *HFZ* vol. 16, 112.

35. The Japanese is *taihen na nihirisuto da naa*.

36. "Tsurukusa no hana" (Flowers on a Vine, 1935), *Shinchō HFZ* vol. 4, 69.

37. The Japanese for the last line is *sō nanimo nihirisuchikku ni kangaenakute mo ii deshō?* "Meian" (Lightness and Darkness, 1936), in *Shinchō HFZ* vol. 5, 262.

38. *Penetrating the Book of Changes*. A Song dynasty text. The author, Zhou Mao-shu (1017–73), is alternately known as Zhou Dun-yi and Zhou Lian-xi. A pioneer in Neo-Confucianism, Zhou was heavily influenced by Daoist texts. Fumiko here actually quotes Zhou's other famous text, *Tai-ji-tu shuo* (An Explanation of the Diagram of the Great Ultimate). She does not include quotation marks, although I have, and I have used Wing-tsit Chan's translation of the text. For more information on Zhou and a complete translation of both his *Tong-shu* and *Tai-ji-tu shuo* see *A Source Book in Chinese Philosophy* by Wing-tsit Chan (Princeton, N.Y.: Princeton University Press, 1963), 460–80.

39. *One Person's Life*, in *Shinchō HFZ* vol. 8, 116. My translation of philosophical terminology is based on that of Wing-tsit Chan in *A Source Book on Chinese Philosophy*.

40. The Japanese is *ne kara no nihirisuto*.

41. The Japanese is *watashi wa nihirisuto tte kirai yo*.

42. *Jūnenkan* (Ten Years, 1940), in *Shinchō HFZ* vol. 21, 76.

43. Quote from Wing-tsit Chan, *A Source Book in Chinese Philosophy*, 460.

44. *Shinchō HFZ* vol. 19, 280.

45. *HFZ* vol. 1, 434.

46. *HFZ* vol. 1, 320.

47. For more detail on anarchist theory, see *The Essential Works of Anarchism*, Marshall S. Shatz, ed. (New York: Quadrangle Books, 1972).

48. Hirabayashi Taiko, "Sehyō to kanojo: Hayashi Fumiko no tame ni," in *Kindai joryū bungaku*, Nihon bungaku kenkyū shiryō sōsho series (Tokyo: Yūseidō, 1983), 75.

49. David Kelley, *Nature of Free Will* audiotaped lecture series (San Francisco: Laissez Faire Books, 1990). Kelley identifies three kinds of determinism: (1) environmental determinism, which holds that the primary determinants of action are causes in the external environment; (2) psychological determinism, which holds that the primary determinants of action are psychological factors, such as thoughts, feelings, and desires; and (3) physiological determinism, which holds that the primary determinants of action are neural events in the brain. For my purposes in this study, when I refer to "determinism," I refer exclusively to environmental determinism.

50. In *Shinchō*, March 1933, 70–71.

51. *HFZ* vol. 16, 243.

52. *Shinchō HFZ* vol. 2, 55.

53. *Shinchō HFZ* vol. 2, 55.

54. *Shinchō HFZ* vol. 2, 217.

55. *Shinchō HFZ* vol. 2, 239.

56. *Shinchō HFZ* vol. 2, 7.

57. This phrase means "As for me . . ." The "beauty" of the language is in the first-person pronoun, *uchi*. The example Hayashi gives of her own speech has the same meaning but uses the personal pronoun *washi*. I have left these phrases in the original, as English has but one first-person pronoun and cannot convey the difference.

58. Hayashi says that the children would not stop calling her the daughter of the "new stupid general" (*shin baka taishō*), a character she previously mentions as a creation of Charlie Chaplin. The reference is obscure, as none of Chaplin's films had such a character. (*Shinchō HFZ* vol. 3, 18–19.)

59. *Shinchō HFZ* vol. 3, 26.

60. *Shinchō HFZ* vol. 3, 122.

61. *Shinchō HFZ* vol. 3, 123–24.

62. *Shinchō HFZ* vol. 3, 106.

63. *Shinchō HFZ* vol. 3, 115–16.

CHAPTER 3. LONELINESS AND TRAVEL

1. Fujikawa Tetsuji, "Hayashi Fumiko ron," in *Kindai joryū bungaku*, Nihon bungaku kenkyū shiryō series (Tokyo: Yūseidō, 1983), 91 (emphasis added).

2. The Japanese for "same as *kikō*" is *kikō ni onaji*.

3. These are all mentioned in the entry for *kikō bungaku* in *Nihon kindai bungaku daijiten*, Odagiri Susumu, ed. (Tokyo: Kōdansha, 1977).

4. See *Sekai kikōbungaku zenshū*, Shiga Naoya, Satō Haruo, Kawabata Yasunari, Kobayashi Hideo, and Inoue Yasushi, eds. (Tokyo: Horupu shuppan, 1979). This is a wide-ranging anthology of travelogues from around the world.

5. According to the *Nihon kindai bungaku daijiten*, improved mass trans-

portation after World War II (and the consequent increase in leisure travel by the common man) caused travelogues to lose their literary nature and become more pragmatic, travel-guide type of works (see entry for *kikō bungaku*).

6. As collected in *Sekai kikōbungaku zenshū*, vols. 1 and 2 (France), Shiga Naoya, Satō Haruo, Kawabata Yasunari, Kobayashi Hideo, and Inoue Yasushi, eds.

7. "Literature, Travel, Etc.," in *HFZ* vol. 10, 33. In her essay "My Memoranda" she also says that although some people suggested that she publish her own magazine, she would much rather spend her money on travel to China (*HFZ* vol. 10, 276). This attitude seems to have lasted until she and Rokubin built the house in Ochiai in 1941.

8. Kataoka Yoshikazu also notes that "Having . . . moved seven times in the course of four years from one lodging house to another, and having also been compelled each time to change schools, the girl acquired not even a single friend." (*Introduction to Contemporary Japanese Literature*, 193.) This information was apparently taken directly from the opening chapter of *Diary of a Vagabond* in which Fumiko describes her childhood.

9. See discussion below about Fumiko's depiction of events aboard the Trans-Siberian Railroad.

10. See Fumiko's essay "Everyday Life" (in *HFZ* vol. 10, 21–29) for a description of her everyday life and work habits. [Note: this essay is dated February 5, 1935, but was not published until April 10, 1936, in the collection *Bungakuteki danshō* (Literary Fragments).]

11. *Jōshū* is a neologism of Fumiko's making.

12. A summary of her international travel is as follows: Taiwan (1930), China (Shanghai, Manchuria, etc., 1931), China, Soviet Union, France, and England (1931–1932), Manchuria (1936), Shanghai and Nanjing (as a reporter for *Asahi Shinbun*, 1937), Shanghai (1938), Manchuria (1940), Korea (1940), Manchuria (1941), and French Indochina and Singapore (1942). For a complete listing of specific dates of these and Fumiko's domestic travels, see the Imagawa *nenpu* in *HFZ* vol. 16, 287–310.

13. For clarity, I would like to define 'essay' and 'travelogue': an essay is "a composition of moderate length on any particular subject, or branch of a subject" and a travelogue is "a lecture about places and experiences encountered in the course of travel; hence a film, broadcast, book, etc., about travel" (definitions from the *Oxford English Dictionary*, 2nd ed., prepared by J. A. Simpson and E. S. C. Weiner [New York: Oxford University Press, 1989]). I would define these terms further by saying that an *essay* contains one major point of focus that is discussed in a relatively clear, organized manner, and also contains a conclusion at the end. A *travelogue* is a collection of vignettes unified solely by the fact that they are from the same journey.

14. See appendix for a translation of this essay.

15. See "Tabi tsurezure" (Idle Thoughts on Travel), in *HFZ* vol 10, 91–92, and "Tabi dayori" (News from a Journey), vol. 16, 34–39.

16. Tokyo: Kawade shobō, 1936.

17. "Covets loneliness" is *wabimi o motomeru*, *HFZ* vol. 10, 35. "Loneliness expresses the whole of me" is *kodoku o zenga to shite iru*, *HFZ* vol. 10, 34.

The reader may note that neither the word *ryojō* nor *ryoshū* are used in these phrases, but I feel that my translation is true to the original meaning. The word *zenga* is a neologism created by Fumiko; I have rendered *zenga to shite iru* here as "loneliness expresses the whole of me."

18. *HFZ* vol. 10, 35. The word for 'loneliness' here is *kyōshū*.

19. *HFZ* vol. 10, 36.

20. "Literature, Travel, Etc.," *Shinchō HFZ* vol. 19, 40.

21. *HFZ* vol. 10, 36.

22. *HFZ* vol. 10, 92.

23. *HFZ* vol. 10, 242.

24. Here "most supportive" means the magazines that published the largest quantity of Fumiko's work, not necessarily those that paid her the most. Publisher information from the Imagawa Chronology in *HFZ* vol. 16.

25. These are by no means all of the travelogues that Fumiko wrote. For reference, it is worth noting that many of Fumiko's works on Europe were published in one volume, entitled *Santō ryokō ki* (A Record of a Journey in Third Class [Tokyo: Kaizōsha, 1933]). The volume *Literary Fragments* also contains some of these travelogues. Still others were published in various periodicals, but never republished in book form. For a detailed list of publications, see both Imagawa's chronology and catalog of works in *HFZ* vol. 16, 283–360.

26. Tōson spent the years 1913–1916 abroad.

27. In both "Third Class on the Trans-Siberian Railroad" and "Clear Skies All the Way to Paris," Fumiko ruminates on the differences between first and second class and third class. While she admits that third class is dirtier and perhaps less comfortable than first and second class, she enjoys the camaraderie of third class very much. In "News from a Journey" she says, "Traveling [by third class]—and this is no exaggeration—is so enjoyable. It just wouldn't be the same if I rode in a second class compartment" (*HFZ* vol. 16, 35).

28. "Tabibito" (The Traveler, 1941), in *HFZ* vol. 5, 305.

29. In the original text, the words "*Da, da*" are written phonetically in *katakana*. I have left this quotation, and all others, in Russian to retain the flavor of the passage.

30. By "White Russian," Fumiko means Caucasian, not anti-Communist.

31. Hailar is a city in modern-day Inner Mongolia (an autonomous region of the People's Republic of China), close to the Mongolian border.

32. *HFZ* vol. 10, 248.

33. The verb used is *deshō*, indicating supposition on the author's part. While this inflection is often used to soften sentence endings, it is clearly used to indicate conjecture in this and other similar passages.

34. "Clear Skies All the Way to Paris," in *Kaizō*, April 1932, 26.

35. "My Work," in *HFZ* vol. 10, 242–43.

36. "My Work," in *HFZ* vol. 10, 243.

37. "My Horizon," in *HFZ* vol. 16, 112.

38. "A London Boarding House and Other Matters," *Chūō kōron*, April 1932, 264–65.

39. *HFZ* vol. 4, 416.

40. *HFZ* vol. 4, 361.

41. Two places where she expresses this love are in "Paris Diary" (*HFZ* vol. 4, 415) and "A Walk in the Latin Quarter" (*Kaizō*, October 1932, 226). In the former, Fumiko says that her mother is the only person in the world who really understands her. In the latter, Fumiko apologizes to her kind parents for being such an unfilial child.

42. *HFZ* vol. 10, 35. The words "*non*" and "*oui*" in this passage are written with the characters for *ina* and *daku* and glossed *non* and *ui* respectively.

43. *HFZ* vol. 16, 113. Fumiko says "Thank goodness for the Japanese language!" (*nihon no kotoba no, nan to arigatai koto de arō ka*) in her discussion of the term '*lumpen* literature.'

44. "A Walk in the Latin Quarter," 223.

45. The Japanese title is *Ochiba* (1931).

46. The word here for "nostalgia" is *ryoshū*.

47. *HFZ* vol. 4, 380.

48. As quoted by Nakamura Mitsuo, "Hayashi Fumiko ron," in *Kindai joryū bungaku*, Nihon bungaku kenkyū shiryō sōshō series (Tokyo: Yūseidō, 1983), 100.

49. *HFZ* vol. 16, 43.

50. *HFZ* vol. 10, 119.

51. "Clear Skies All the Way to Paris," 23.

52. Nojima Hideyoshi, "Hayashi Fumiko: hito to sakuhin," in *Shōwa bungaku zenshū: Hayashi Fumiko*, vol. 8, 1050.

53. The original Japanese is *Watashi wa ajikinai otoko no ryoshū o hakisuteta*, as quoted from *Diary of a Vagabond* by Nojima Hideyoshi, "Hayashi Fumiko: hito to sakuhin," 1050.

54. From Fumiko's *Creative Notebook*, as quoted by Nojima Hideyoshi, "Hayashi Fumiko: hito to sakuhin," 1050–51.

55. Nojima Hideyoshi, "Hayashi Fumiko: hito to sakuhin," 1051.

56. *HFZ* vol. 5, 468.

57. *HFZ* vol. 5, 252.

58. *HFZ* vol. 5, 255.

59. *HFZ* vol. 5, 256.

60. *Ekiken jikkun* (The Ten Teachings of Ekiken) is a work by Kaibara Ekiken (1630–1714), who was an early Edo Neo-Confucianist. He is best known for his early-eighteenth-century work *Onna daigaku* (Greater Learning for Women), a didactic work that prescribes proper behavior for women. *The Ten Teachings of Ekiken* is a collection of his "teachings" (*kyōkun*) compiled posthumously in 1893 by Nishida Keishi. (*Nihon koten bungaku jiten* [Tokyo: Iwanami shoten, 1983]. See entries for "Kaibara Ekiken" and "Ekiken jikkun.")

61. *HFZ* vol. 5, 258.

62. Of note, "The Accordion and the Fish Town," *Rain*, and *Uruwashiki sekizui* (Splendid Pith, 1947). "The Accordion and the Fish Town," is an upbeat, optimistic story about Fumiko's peripatetic childhood. *Rain* and *Splendid Pith* are both about men who return from military duty and who, leaving behind unbearable home lives, find solace in travel.

63. Then and even now, association with one's hometown (*furusato*) is very strong in Japan. Unlike Americans, who do not put much importance on one's

birthplace, Japanese tend to feel a strong connection to their birthplace even if they only lived there for a brief period of their life.

64. When Fumiko says that her parents were "not members of any community," she implies that they could neither consider their birthplaces as their "hometown" (because they had been disowned by their families), nor could they consider Shimonoseki as their "hometown" because they were not born there. When she says that her "hometown was travel," she means that although Shimonoseki was her birthplace, it could not officially be considered her "hometown" because her parents did not belong to that community. The original Japanese sentence is *kokyō ni irerarenakatta ryōshin o motsu watashi wa, shitagatte tabi ga furusato de atta.*

65. *HFZ* vol. 1, 255.

66. Kobayashi Hideo, "Literature of the Lost Home," translated by Paul Anderer in *Literature of the Lost Home: Kobayashi Hideo—Literary Criticism, 1924–1939* (Stanford: Stanford University Press, 1995), 48.

67. The vestibule (*dekki*) is the section between cars where passengers board.

68. The implication here is that, because the town where her mother lives is not her real hometown, she does not need to impress the townspeople by giving off the air of affluence. There is an allusion here to remark attributed to the Chinese general Xiang Yu, "Not to return to one's old home after having become rich and famous is like going out at night dressed in brocade. Who will know you are wearing it?" (translation by Helen Craig McCullough in *Genji and Heike: Selections from* The Tale of Genji *and* The Tale of the Heike (Stanford: Stanford University Press, 1994), 355ff. n17).

69. The word here for "tedium" is *tabigokoro*, which means "the tedium of a journey."

70. A "butterfly" coiffure.

71. *HFZ* vol. 1, 329.

72. As quoted by Fujikawa Tetsuji, "Hayashi Fumiko ron," 92.

73. The use of parentheses to set off the narrator's thoughts from the main text here may be an influence from Kawabata Yasunari, with whom Fumiko was good friends. The works in which Kawabata used this method include "Hari to garasu to kiri" (Needles, Glass, and Fog, 1930) and "Suishō gensō" (Crystal Fantasies, 1931). The works in which Fumiko used this method include "Hana no ichi" (A Flower's Place, 1939), "Dancing Girl," and *Drifting Clouds.* Kawabata did not use this method for long, but Fumiko continued to use it throughout her writing career. Kawabata was not the first to use this method in Japanese literature; Donald Keene points to Itō Sei's 1930 translation of James Joyce's (1882–1941) *Ulysses* (1922) as the original place such a method was used in Japanese literature (Donald Keene, *Dawn to the West: Japanese Literature in the Modern Era*, 798).

74. *Shinchō HFZ* vol. 16, 91–92.

75. *Shinchō HFZ* vol. 16, 104–5.

76. This romanized spelling is an approximation of an unidentified Vietnamese place name that Fumiko recorded in *katakana.*

77. Hayashi Fumiko, *Drifting Clouds* (Tokyo: Yūseidō, 1953), 221. The

tense of the final sentence is purposely ambiguous, giving the impression that Yukiko is simultaneously in the past and the present.

78. The text tells us that, due to world events (i.e., Japan's declining strength in the Pacific basin), it will never again be that Japanese government employees will be stationed in Indochina.

79. *Drifting Clouds* (Tokyo: Shinchōsha, 1953), 235.

80. *Shinchō HFZ* vol. 15, 35.

81. *Shinchō HFZ* vol. 15, 38.

82. "Sorrowful" is *aishū*, in Kamei Katsuichirō as quoted by Kawamori Yoshizō, "Hayashi-san no shōsetsu," in *Kindai joryū bungaku*, Nihon bungaku kenkyū shiryō sōsho series (Tokyo: Yūseidō, 1983), 82. "Nostalgic" is *kyōshū*, as found in Kawafuku Tokinori, "Hayashi Fumiko *Bangiku* ni tsuite," in *Kindai joryū bungaku*, 88. "Aspirations" is *kōjōshin*, as found in Itagaki Naoko, *Hayashi Fumiko*, 159. "Humor" is *yūmoa*, as found in Yamamoto Kenkichi, "Hayashi Fumiko" in *Chikuma gendai bungaku taikei: Sata Ineko, Hayashi Fumiko shū*, vol. 39 (Tokyo: Chikuma shobō, 1978), 537.

83. *HFZ* vol. 16, 216.

CHAPTER 4. MARRIAGE, FAMILY, AND WOMEN'S ISSUES

1. Joan Ericson has traced the history and development of "Women's Literature" in great detail in her study of Hayashi Fumiko, thus I will make only brief mention of it here. Ericson chronicles the history of the terms *joryū sakka* and *joryū bungaku* (women's literature) in her Ph.D. dissertation (Columbia University, 1993) and in "The Origins of the Concept of 'Women's Literature'" in *The Woman's Hand: Gender and Theory in Japanese Women's Writing*, Paul Schalow and Janet Walker, eds. (Stanford: Stanford University Press, 1996), 74–115.

2. "Rain" should not be confused with Fumiko's novel by the same title published in 1942.

3. The distinction between male and female speech is not, therefore, akin to the theory that women have been forced to use language as men have created it, whereas if women were left to their own devices they would have created a different language.

4. In addition to "Writing" discussed below, see the novel *Shin'yodogimi* (The New Yodogimi, 1950), about the life of Toyotomi Hideyoshi's (1536–1598) concubine, Yodogimi (1567–1615). She was Oda Nobunaga's (1534–1582) niece and the mother of Hideyoshi's only two children, Tsurumatsu (1589–1591) and Hideyori (1593–1615).

5. The emphasis in *The Story of Eight Dogs* is not exclusively on Confucian morality, but it should be noted that one of the five basic social relationships designated by Confucianism is that of "husband to wife," that is, the wife as subordinate to the husband. As in most traditional religions and philosophies, women were considered inferior to men in Confucianism.

6. Tonomura Jōzai (1779–1847) and Ozu Keisō (dates unknown), were friends of Bakin's. Here Zolbrod writes Michi's and other women's names with the honorific prefix O-.

7. Leon M. Zolbrod, *Takizawa Bakin* (New York: Twayne Publishers, 1967), 130–31.

8. Ibid., 131.

9. Ibid.

10. *Shinchō HFZ* vol. 10, 143.

11. Tamenaga Shunsui (1790–1843) was a late Edo author of prose narratives on love (*ninjōbon*).

12. Santō Kyōzan (1769–1858) was a late Edo writer of drama. He was the younger brother of Santō Kyōden (1761–1816), whose work he continued after Kyōden's death. Ryūtei Tanehiko (1783–1842), late Edo writer of prose fiction and drama. Thought to have read Bakin, he himself also wrote and practiced the martial arts.

13. The Japanese for "flaunting them before the public as novels written by a man" is *otoko no kaku shōsetsu toshite seken e furimawashiteiru*. The implication here is that Shunsui was writing for the sole purpose of making money and continuing his profession, and not for artistic ends. (*Shinchō HFZ*, vol. 10, 144.)

14. Kuwa (1800–?) was the youngest of Bakin's three daughters. Zolbrod gives little information on her, but does say that she was married to an artist and physician, Atsumi Sadashige (Zolbrod, *Takizawa Bakin*, 98).

15. Information from Bakin's diary in Zolbrod, *Takizawa Bakin*, 100, 130. Quote of Sōhaku in *Shinchō HFZ* vol. 10, 149. Sōhaku compliments Michi on her ability to get along with Bakin, and on her ability to be persistent with him. He concludes with *chichiue yori mo, o-mae no hō ga yoppodo geijutsuka da*.

16. Zolbrod does note that Michi was literate: "Besides being a hard worker, O'Michi was cooperative, and above all, literate. . . . Her ability to read with understanding [*Nansō Satomi hakkenden*] is all the more unusual because nothing indicates that [Bakin's wife] or Bakin's daughters could read more complicated literature than chapbooks, the usual reading fare for women." (Zolbrod, *Takizawa Bakin*, 99.) However, Zolbrod does not describe her as the literary genius that Fumiko portrays.

17. Fumiko's biographers sometimes use the word 'marriage' (*kekkon*) when they record her liasons with Okano Gun'ichi, Tanabe Wakao, and Nomura Yoshiya. This is apparently a euphemism for 'affair,' as there is no evidence that she ever made any formal wedding vows with these men.

18. Itagaki Naoko, *Hayashi Fumiko*, 81.

19. *Shinchō HFZ* vol. 5, 105.

20. Nobuyuki is Hisako's brother.

21. *Shinchō HFZ* vol. 20, 27.

22. *Shinchō HFZ* vol. 20, 181.

23. *Shinchō HFZ* vol. 20, 281.

24. Michiko has just recently moved into her own room, an attic room rented out to her by an old woman. It is the type of room that probably has been rented out to many single, young women before.

25. *Shinchō HFZ* vol. 21, 151–52.

26. *Shinchō HFZ* vol. 21, 171–72.

27. *Shinchō HFZ* vol. 21, 201.

28. Fumiko died while writing this novel, and so it is impossible to tell if Hideko was meant to be married.

29. Reiko is Tokiko's daughter.

30. *Shinchō HFZ* vol. 18, 269.

31. In the author's case, she apparently did not face these problems herself because Rokubin changed his name to hers and was registered in her family registry. His family lived in Shinshū, and although Fumiko and Rokubin visited them on occasion, there is no record to indicate an intense family tie. Her marriage was not "typical," and perhaps for that reason she was fascinated by those that were.

32. *Shinchō HFZ* vol. 14, 105–9.

33. Kōzō is the only one of the three children that is Tamiko's biological son.

34. *Shinchō HFZ* vol. 7, 19.

35. *Shinchō HFZ* vol. 9, 172–73.

36. The Japanese for "goldfish" is *ranchū*, a variety of fish that have rounded backs and that Fumiko raised in the pond at her house in Ochiai.

37. The "young woman" is the girl from the Nishio family.

38. *Shinchō HFZ* vol. 9, 177–78.

39. *Shinchō HFZ* vol. 13, 107–8.

40. *Shinchō HFZ* vol. 13, 115–16.

41. This is an allusion to the opening scene of the story in which the son, Shigeichi, poses a riddle to his father to which the answer is "railroad tracks."

42. *Shinchō HFZ* vol. 17, 199.

43. The Japanese here is *dō ni mo, kono shukumeiteki unmei wa kaiketsu no shiyō ga nai no da.*

44. *Shinchō HFZ* vol. 17, 197.

45. Mr. Kawajiri is Hisako's husband, who taught at the same school until he was conscripted.

46. *Shinchō HFZ* vol. 20, 273–75.

47. *Shinchō HFZ* vol. 20, 281.

CHAPTER 5. WAR AND FATALISM

1. Fukuda Kiyoto dedicates a chapter entitled "Kurai jidai no moto de" (The Origin of the Dark Years) to this topic, in which he discusses changes in Fumiko's life that may have affected her literature (Fukuda Kiyoto, *Hayashi Fumiko: hito to sakuhin*, 69–85), and also a critical section entitled "Kurai sakuhin" (Dark Works) in which he notes specific works (*Hayashi Fumiko: hito to sakuhin*, 161–64).

Itagaki Hiroko also notes that the number of Fumiko's "dark" works with a "nihilistic outlook" grew steadily after the war (Itagaki Hiroko, "Hayashi Fumiko," in *Kindai nihon joseishi 3* [Tokyo: Kagoshima kenkyūjo shuppan, 1972], 174).

2. *HFZ* vol. 16, 281. Critics who quote this passage include Fujikawa Tetsuji, "Hayashi Fumiko ron," 93; Nakamura Mitsuo, "Hayashi Fumiko ron," 102; Yamamoto Kenkichi, "Hayashi Fumiko," 539.

3. Fujikawa Tetsuji, "Hayashi Fumiko ron," 93.

4. "*Rinraku* atogaki," *HFZ* vol. 16, 245–46.

5. Hayashi occasionally uses the pronoun *anata* in the text.

6. *HFZ* vol. 12, 237.

7. *HFZ* vol. 12, 252.

8. Donald Keene quotes from Tanaka Sōtarō, *Hino Ashihei ron* (Gogatsu shobō, 1971), 34: "[Hino] insisted that he had been obliged to write under these specified conditions: 1. The Japanese Army must never be described as losing a battle. 2. The kinds of criminal acts which inevitably accompany warfare must not be alluded to. 3. The enemy must always be portrayed as loathsome and contemptible. 4. The full circumstances of a [military] operation must not be disclosed. 5. The composition of military units and their designations must not be disclosed. 6. No expression of individual sentiments as human beings is permitted to soldiers." (Donald Keene, "The Barren Years: Japanese War Literature," 76.)

9. *HFZ* vol. 12, 295.

10. *Battlefront* (Tokyo: Asahi shinbun sha, 1938), 91–92.

11. Donald Keene, "The Barren Years: Japanese War Literature," 67.

12. A *kanme* is a unit of measure equal to approximately 8.72 pounds.

13. A *sen* is a currency unit equal to 0.1 yen.

14. *Shinchō HFZ* vol. 10, 229.

15. *Shinchō HFZ* vol. 10, 233.

16. *Shinchō HFZ* vol. 10, 234.

17. *Shinchō HFZ* vol. 2, 69. The Japanese is *Aa, yappari ikiteiru koto mo ii mono da to omou.*

18. *HFZ* vol. 12, 214.

19. *Shinchō HFZ* vol. 10, 14.

20. *Shinchō HFZ* vol. 10, 14.

21. Kōjirō means that he ended up in the hospital after being conscripted, not before.

22. *Shinchō HFZ* vol. 10, 9.

23. *Shinchō HFZ* vol. 10, 22.

24. The Japanese is *mainichi ikada o kunde shinu kunren o saserarete ita.*

25. *Shinchō HFZ* vol. 10, 13.

26. *Shinchō HFZ* vol. 13, 13. In translating from this work, I have taken the liberty of indenting for quotations and new paragraphs. The original has few indentations and is written in the same style as Yokomitsu Riichi's *The Machine.*

27. *Shinchō HFZ* vol. 13, 16.

28. Shōkichi is a peripheral character who is a common friend of both Eisuke and Machiko.

29. *Shinchō HFZ* vol. 13, 16.

30. I use 'nihilistic' here to mean a rejection of logic and a spurning of rational constructs.

31. For an example, see her essay "Nichijō no seikatsu" (Everyday Life, 1939), in *Shinkyō to fūkaku*, 148–51.

32. *Shinchō HFZ* vol. 10, 188.

33. *Shinchō HFZ* vol. 10, 188.

34. *Shinchō HFZ* vol. 16, 66.

35. The word for fate here is *yukusue.*

36. *Shinchō HFZ* vol. 16, 71.

37. *Shinchō HFZ* vol. 16, 73.
38. *Shinchō HFZ* vol. 16, 130.
39. *Shinchō HFZ* vol. 16, 254.
40. It is not clear what sort of building the sect is erecting, although a new church seems likely.
41. The characters in the name "Dainikkō" mean "turn toward the great sun."
42. *Shinchō HFZ* vol. 16, 155–56.
43. The implication here is that the new drugstores have been opened in response to the cult members' demand for healing medicines prescribed by the church.
44. A *tsubo* is a measurement of area, equal to 3.954 sq. yds.
45. *Shinchō HFZ* vol. 16, 159.
46. Earlier in the story there is a scene in which the sect leader says, "Please drink a mouthful of the ether in the air. There is quite a lot of 'toward the sun' ether pouring into my hand" (chapter 46, *Shinchō HFZ* vol. 16, 175).
47. *Shinchō HFZ* vol. 16, 196.
48. Translations of these stories are in "Five Fables by Hayashi Fumiko" by Susanna Fessler in *Studies in Modern Japanese Literature: Essays and Translations in Honor of Edwin McClellan* (Ann Arbor, Michigan: Center for Japanese Studies, 1997), 369–85.
49. *Shinchō HFZ* vol. 17, 57.
50. Dates for these writers are as follows: Hasegawa Shigure (1879–1941), Tokuda Shūsei (1871–1943), Yada Tsuseko (1907–1944), Kataoka Teppei (1894–1944), Takeda Rintarō (1904–1946), Oda Sakunosuke (1913–1947), Dazai Osamu (1909–1948), Kikuchi Kan (1888–1948), and Yokomitsu Riichi (1898–1947).
51. A *shō* is a liquid measurement equal to 1.8 liters.
52. *One Drop of Ink* (*Bokujū itteki*) was a collection of Masaoka Shiki's (1867–1902) miscellany published in 1901 (*Nihon kindai bungaku daijiten: kijō han* [Tokyo: Kōdansha, 1992]).
53. The epitaph is one that Stendahl (Born Henri Beyle, 1783–1842) imagined for himself and is from his novel *Souvenirs d'egotisme* (Memoirs of an Egotist, 1832). The original is "visse, scrisse, amo." (*European Writers: The Romantic Century*, vol. 5, Jacques Barzun, ed. [New York: Charles Scribner's sons, 1985], 343–45.)
54. *Shinchō HFZ* vol. 17, 59–60.
55. In the section omitted here, she talks about her heart condition, and how she had given up drinking but could not kick her two-pack-a-day cigarette habit, despite the fact that she had been told by her doctor to do so.
56. *Shinchō HFZ* vol. 17, 63.

APPENDIX

1. The original text is in *HFZ* vol. 16, 111–15.
2. Ōsugi Sakae (1885–1923) was an anarchist radical who was killed by police after the Kantō earthquake in 1923.

3. Fumiko uses *katakana* here when she writes the word "difficult."

4. Kobayashi Takiji (1903–1933) was a prominent novelist in the proletarian literature movement. Apparently Fumiko felt his work was notably better than other contemporary proletarian writers.

5. Fumiko uses the term *puroretariya romanchishijimu* for "proletarian romanticist literature."

6. Fumiko uses the term *puroretariya seiji bungaku* for "proletarian political literature."

7. Fumiko uses the word *robotto fū na sakuhin* for "robotic works."

8. This was published by Chūō kōron in the collection of essays entitled *Bungakuteki danshō* (Literary Fragments) in April 1936. The original text is in *HFZ* vol. 10, 33–37. In order to convey the rather haphazard style that Fumiko uses in this essay, I have preserved paragraph divisions where they were in the original text, with the exception of Han Shan's poem, which I set apart from the main text even though Fumiko does not. The reader may notice that Fumiko's "paragraphs" are actually many paragraphs in one.

9. Han Shan was a Tang dynasty (618–907 A.D.) monk who was also known for his poetry.

10. Translation by Robert G. Henricks in *The Poetry of Han-Shan: A Complete Annotated Translation of* Cold Mountain (Albany: State University of New York Press, 1990), 238.

11. *Komemiso* is a kind of fermented soybean paste, considered simple food.

12. Fumiko is referring to novels that are published in serialized form in newspapers, a common way for fiction to be published in Japan.

13. Here Fumiko refers to Helen Newington Wills Moody Roark, an outstanding U.S. tennis player who was the top female competitor in the world for eight years (1927–33 and 1935).

14. The word Fumiko uses here for "quiet things in life" is *wabimi*.

15. Fumiko means here that she does not want to worry about providing daily necessities for her family.

16. The beauty of this phrase is in the colloquial and dialectic language it uses, not in the actual meaning (which is about being infatuated), so I have left it in the original Japanese. It is not apparent if Fumiko quotes the passage from some other work, or if she creates it here to serve as an example. The dialect is from the Onomichi area in Hiroshima Prefecture.

17. The trip that Fumiko proceeds to describe here is through the outlying western reaches of the Tokyo district. Although she fails to mention it, it seems likely that she took a train or car from Shinjuku to somewhere near Hachiōji and then continued her journey on foot.

18. This essay was first published in the August 1937 volume of *Bungei*. The text is in *HFZ* vol. 10, 241–44. This essay has the subtitle *jisaku annai sho* (A Guide to My Works).

19. *My Specimen Room (Boku no hyōhonshitsu)* was published in 1930.

20. These three periods are named after major works by Fumiko by the same name. Roughly, the periods are 1928–1931, 1931–1935, and 1935–1937 respectively.

21. *Lightning* was published serially in *Bungei* January to September (omitting August), 1936.

22. "The Snapping Turtle" (Suppon) was published in 1937. In this essay, Fumiko uses *hiragana* to write the title, but the story was originally published with the title written in *kanji*.

BIBLIOGRAPHY

PRIMARY SOURCES

Books

Hayashi Fumiko. *Hayashi Fumiko, Uno Chiyo, Kōda Aya shū*. In *Gendai nihon bungaku taikei*, vol. 69. Tokyo: Chikuma shobō, 1969.

———. *Hayashi Fumiko zenshū*, vols. 1–23. Tokyo: Shinchō sha, 1951.

———. *Hayashi Fumiko zenshū*, vols. 1–16. Tokyo: Bunsendō, 1977.

———. *Santō ryokō ki*. Tokyo: Kaizō sha, 1933.

———. *Sensen*. Tokyo: Asahi shinbun sha, 1938.

———. *Shinkyō to fūkaku*. Tokyo: Sōgen sha, 1939.

———. *Sōsaku nōto*. Tokyo: Kantō sha, 1947.

———. *Tai-Ō ki*. In *Hayashi Fumiko senshū*, vol. 6. Tokyo: Kaizō sha, 1937.

———. *Ukigumo*. Tokyo: Shinchō sha, 1953.

Short Stories, Travelogues, Commentary

Hayashi Fumiko. "Fukurō to shinju to kichin-yado," in *Kaizō*, August 1930, pp. 17–24.

———. "Furansu no inaka," in *Shinchō*, August 1932, pp. 28–33.

———. "Gaikoku kara nihon o miru," in *Shinchō*, December 1932, pp. 142–71.

———. "Gaitō no hiru—Shinjuku tenbō," in *Chūō kōron*, February 1931, pp. 215–17.

———. "Hinkei," in *Kaizō*, May 1935, pp. 46–66.

———. "Kafe hyaku-banashi," in *Kaizō*, August 1931, pp. 19–26.

———. "Komado," in *Kaizo*, September 1934, pp. 150–53.

———. "Kōrogi no nikki," in *Chūō kōron*, June 1937, pp. 282–90.

———. "Mashūko kikō," in *Kaizō*, August 1934, pp. 280–89.

———. "Ochiai machi yamagawa ki," in *Kaizō*, September 1933, pp. 110–19.

———. "Onna no shōgai," in *Chūō kōron*, February 1937, pp. 334–36.

———. "Ōshima yuki—Izu no tabi kara," in *Kaizō*, May 1933, pp. 162–74.

———. "Pari made seiten," in *Kaizō*, April 1932, pp. 21–33.

———. "Pekin kikō," in *Kaizō*, January 1937, pp. 11–21.

———. "Raten-ku no sanpo," in *Kaizō*, October 1932, pp. 218–27.

———. "Rondon no geshuku—sono ta," in *Chūō kōron*, April 1932, pp. 258–65.

———. "Sensō yomimono," in *Chūō kōron*, October 1937, pp. 354–56.

———. "Shi no senshi," in *Bungei*, October 1938, pp. 290–91.

———. "Sumatora—seifu no shima," in *Kaizō*, June/July 1943, pp. 87–95 (June) and pp. 107–11 (July).

——. "Taiwan no subuniiru," in *Kaigai*, June 1930, pp. 76–79.

——. "Taiwan o tabi shite," in *Nyonin geijutsu*, March 1930, pp. 88–93.

——. "Washi," in *Kaizō*, June 1933, pp. 69–89.

——. "Watashi ga moshi Kachiusha de atta naraba," in *Shinchō*, March 1933. pp. 70–71.

——. "Yukai naru chizu: Tairiku e no hitori tabi," in *Nyonin geijutsu*, November 1930, pp. 52–57.

——. "Yukigari," in *Chūō kōron*, February 1937, pp. 50–71.

Works in English Translation

Hayashi Fumiko. "Bones." Tr. by Ted Takaya in *The Catch and Other War Stories*. Tokyo: Kōdansha International, 1981.

——. "Borneo Diamond." Tr. by Lane Dunlop in *Autumn Wind and Other Stories*. Rutland, Vt.: Charles E. Tuttle, 1994.

——. "Downtown." Tr. by Ivan Morris in *Modern Japanese Literature*. New York: Grove Press, 1956.

——. *Drifting Clouds*. Tr. by Yoshiyuki Koitabashi and Martin C. Collcott. Tokyo: Hara shobō, 1965.

——. *Diary of a Vagabond*. Tr. by Joan Ericson in *Be a Woman: Hayashi Fumiko and Modern Japanese Literature*. Honolulu: University of Hawaii Press, 1997.

——. *I Saw a Pale Horse & Selections from Diary of a Vagabond*. Tr. by Janice Brown. Ithaca, N.Y.: Cornell University East Asia Program, 1997.

——. "A Late Chrysanthemum." Tr. by Lane Dunlop in *A Late Chrysanthemum: Twenty-one Stories from the Japanese*. San Francisco: North Point, 1986.

——. "Lord Buddha." Tr. by Kenneth Rexroth and Ikuko Atsumi in *Burning Heart*. New York: Seabury Press, 1977.

——. "Song in Despair." Tr. by Ichiro Kono and Rikutaro Fukuda in *An Anthology of Modern Japanese Poetry*. Tokyo: Kenkyūsha, 1957.

——. "Splendid Pith." Tr. by Sakae Shioya in *Western Humanities Review* 99.9 (Summer 1952) and 99.12 (1953).

OTHER SOURCES CONSULTED

Sources in Japanese

Fujikawa Tetsuji. "Hayashi Fumiko ron." In *Kindai joryū bungaku* (Nihon bungaku kenkyū shiryō sōsho series). Tokyo: Yūseidō, 1983, pp. 90–95.

Fukuda Kiyoto and Endō Mitsuhiko, ed. *Hayashi Fumiko: Hito to sakuhin*. Tokyo: Shimizu shoin, 1966.

Hara Shigerō. "Hayashi Fumiko." *Kokubungaku,* January 1969, pp. 160–61.

Hirabayashi Taiko. *Hayashi Fumiko*. Tokyo: Shinchō sha, 1969.

——. "Sehyō to kanojo: Hayashi Fumiko no tame ni." In *Kindai joryū bungaku (Nihon bungaku kenkyū shiryō sōsho* series). Tokyo: Yūseidō, 1983, pp. 75–76.

Hirano Ken. "Kaisetsu." In *Tokuda Shūsei shū*, vol. 4 of *Shinchō Nihon bungaku*. Tokyo: Shinchō sha, 1973.

———. *Shōwa bungakushi*. Tokyo: Chikuma shobō, 1963.

Imagawa Eiko. "Nenpu" and "Chosho mokuroku." in *Hayashi Fumiko zenshū*, vol. 16. Tokyo: Bunsendō, 1977, 283–360.

Inoue Takaharu. *Hayashi Fumiko to sono shūhen*. Kokubunji (Kyūshū): Musashino shobō, 1990.

Isogai Hideo. *Hayashi Fumiko: Shinchō nihon bungaku arubamu*, vol. 34. Tokyo: Shinchō sha, 1986.

Itagaki Hiroko. "Hayashi Fumiko." In *Kindai nihon joseishi 3*. Tokyo: Kagoshima kenkyūjo shuppan, 1972, pp. 144–77.

Itagaki Naoko. *Fujin sakka hyōden*. Tokyo: Mejikaru furendo sha, 1954.

———. *Hayashi Fumiko*. Tokyo: Tōkyō raifu sha, 1956.

———, ed. *Gendai no esupuri: Hayashi Fumiko*. Tokyo: Shibundō, 1965.

———. "Hayashi Fumiko." In *Meiji, Taishō, Shōwa no joryū bungaku*. Tokyo: Ōfusha, 1967, pp. 214–33.

———. *Hayashi Fumiko no shōgai*. Tokyo: Daiwa shobō, 1965.

———. "Hayashi Fumiko: Sakufū no kōjō to hatten." In *Kokubungaku kaishaku to kanshō*. Tokyo: Shibundō, 1972, pp. 101–4.

Kamiya Tadataka. "Hayashi Fumiko." In *Nihon no dada*. Sapporo: Kyōbun sha, 1987, pp. 172–79.

Kasai Zenzō. *Ko o tsurete* in *Gendai nihon bungaku taikei*, vol. 49. Tokyo: Chikuma shobō, 1943, pp. 12–23.

Kawabata Yasunari. *Kawabata Yasunari zenshū*. Tokyo: Shinchō sha, 1982.

Kawafuku Tokinori. "Hayashi Fumiko *Bangiku* ni tsuite." In *Kindai joryū bungaku* (Nihon bungaku kenkyū shiryō sōsho series). Tokyo: Yūseidō, 1983, pp. 86–89.

Kawamori Yoshizō. "Hayashi-san no shōsetsu." In *Kindai joryū bungaku* (Nihon bungaku kenkyū shiryō sōsho series). Tokyo: Yūseidō, 1983, pp. 81–83.

Kindai joryū bungaku (Nihon bungaku kenkyū shiryō sōsho series). Tokyo: Yūseidō, 1983.

Kumasaka Atsuko. "Onnen toshite no joryū bungaku: Hayashi Fumiko to Okamoto Kanoko." In *Kokubungaku*. Tokyo: Gakutō sha, October, 1974, pp. 79–83.

———. "Hayashi Fumiko." In *Gendai bungaku kenkyū: Jōhō to shiryō*, Hasegawa Izumi, ed. Tokyo: Shibundō, 1987, 452–54.

Kusabe Kazuko. "Miyamoto Yuriko, Hayashi Fumiko no buntai: Sono sanbunsei to jojōsei." In *Kindai joryū bungaku* (*Nihon bungaku kenkyū shiryō sōsho* series). Tokyo: Yūseidō, 1983, pp. 108–13.

Miki Kiyoshi. "Tabi ni tsuite." In *Jinseiron nōto*. Tokyo: Shinchō sha, 1954, pp. 132–38.

Mori Eiichi. *Hayashi Fumiko no keisei: Sono sei to hyōgen*. Tokyo: Yūseidō, 1992.

———. *Shūsei kara Fumiko e*. Kanazawa: Nōtō insatsu, 1990.

Muramatsu Sadataka. "Hayashi Fumiko no dansei henreki." In *Sakka no kakei to kankyō*. Tokyo: Shibundō, 1964, pp. 202–17.

Nagai Kafū. *Towazugatari.* In *Gendai nihon bungaku taikei,* vol. 24. Tokyo: Chikuma shobō, 1943, pp. 143–79.

Nakamura Mitsuo. "Hayashi Fumiko ron." In *Kindai joryū bungaku* (Nihon bungaku kenkyū shiryō sōsho series). Tokyo: Yūseidō, 1983, pp. 96–103.

Nojima Hideyoshi. "Hayashi Fumiko: hito to sakuhin." In *Shōwa bungaku zenshū: Hayashi Fumiko,* vol. 8. Tokyo: Shōgakukan, 1988, pp. 1049–52.

Odagiri Susumu. *Shōwa bungaku no seiritsu.* Tokyo: Keisō shobō, 1965.

Sekai kikōbungaku zenshū. Shiga Naoya, Satō Haruo, Kawabata Yasunari, Kobayashi Hideo, and Inoue Yasushi, eds. Tokyo: Horupu shuppan, 1979.

Shibaki Yoshiko. "*Chairo no me* kaisetsu." In *Kindai joryū bungaku* (Nihon bungaku kenkyū shiryō sōsho series). Tokyo: Yūseidō, 1983, pp. 104–7.

Shiga Naoya. *Anya kōro.* In *Shiga Naoya zenshū* vol. 5. Tokyo: Iwanami shoten, 1973.

Shiina Rinzō. "Hayashi Fumiko no hito to sakuhin." In *Kindai joryū bungaku* (Nihon bungaku kenkyū shiryō sōsho series). Tokyo: Yūseidō, 1983, pp. 84–85.

Takami Jun. "Zen josei shinshutsu kōshinkyoku." In *Shōwa bungaku seisuishi 1.* Tokyo: Bunger, 179–202.

Takemoto Chimakichi. *Ningen: Hayashi Fumiko.* Tokyo: Chikuma shobō, 1985.

Takenishi Hiroko. "*Hayashi Fumiko shū* kaisetsu." In *Kindai joryū bungaku* (Nihon bungaku kenkyū shiryō sōsho series). Tokyo: Yūseidō, 1983, pp. 114–22.

Takeuchi Seiichi. *Jiko chōetsu no shisō: Kindai nihon no nihirizumu.* Tokyo: Perikan sha, 1988.

Tamiya Torahiko. "Hayashi-san no sakuhin." In *Kindai joryū bungaku* (Nihon bungaku kenkyū shiryō sōsho series). Tokyo: Yūseidō, 1983, pp. 79–80.

Tanabe Seiko. "Isha no bungaku." In *Chikuma Nihon bungaku zenshū: Hayashi Fumiko.* Tokyo: Chikuma shobō, 1992, pp. 458–65.

Tsuchiya Kazuo, ed. *Onomichi to Hayashi Fumiko: Aru joryū sakka no kokyō no kiroku.* Onomichi: Onomichi shiritsu toshokan-nai Onomichi dokusho kai, 1974.

Ueda Fumiko, Ozaki Akira, and Yagi Akiko. "*Ao uma o mitari* hyō." In *Kindai joryū bungaku* (Nihon bungaku kenkyū shiryō sōsho series). Tokyo: Yūseidō, 1983, pp. 73–74.

Wada Yoshie. "Hayashi Fumiko: Shussei no nazo." In *Kindai joryū bungaku* (Nihon bungaku kenkyū shiryō sōsho series). Tokyo: Yūseidō, 1983, pp. 131–36.

Washio Yōzō. "Hayashi Fumiko to iu 'onna.'" In *Kaisō no sakkatachi.* Tokyo: Aogaerubō, 1970.

Yamada Yūsaku, ed. *Joryū bungaku no genzai.* Tokyo: Gakujutsu tosho shuppansha, 1985, pp. 90–93.

Yamamoto Kenkichi. "Hayashi Fumiko." In *Chikuma gendai bungaku taikei: Sata Ineko, Hayashi Fumiko shū,* vol. 39. Tokyo: Chikuma shobō, 1978, pp. 533–40.

Yokomitsu Riichi. *Kikai, Haru wa basha ni notte.* Tokyo: Shinchō sha, 1969.

———. *Yokomitsu Riichi zenshū.* Tokyo: Kawade shobō shinsha, 1981.

Sources in English

ALA-LC Romanization Tables: Transliteration Schemes for Non-Roman Scripts. Randall K. Barry, ed. Washington, D.C.: Library of Congress, 1991.

Apter, David E. and Sawa Nagayo. *Against the State: Politics and Social Protest in Japan.* Cambridge, Mass.: Harvard University Press, 1984.

Brown, Janice. "The Celebration of Struggle: A Study of the Major Works of Hayashi Fumiko." Ph.D. diss., University of British Columbia, 1985.

Chan, Wing-tsit. *A Source Book in Chinese Philosophy.* Princeton, N.J.: Princeton University Press, 1963.

Ericson, Joan E. "Hayashi Fumiko and Japanese Women's Literature." Ph.D. diss., Columbia University, 1993.

————. "The Origins of the Concept of 'Women's Literature.'" In *The Woman's Hand: Gender and Theory in Japanese Women's Writing.* Paul Gordon Schalow and Janet A. Walker, eds. Stanford: Stanford University Press, 1996, pp. 74–115.

European Writers: The Romantic Century, vol. 5. Jacques Barzun, ed. New York: Charles Scribner's Sons, 1985.

Fessler, Susanna. "Fumiko's Fables." In *Studies in Modern Japanese Literature: Essays and Translations in Honor of Edwin McClellan.* Ann Arbor, Michigan: Center for Japanese Studies: 1997.

Forsythe, Ruth Hyland. "Songs of Longing: The Art of Hayashi Fumiko." Ph.D. diss., University of Minnesota, 1988.

Gorky, Maxim. *The Lower Depths,* Laurence Irving, trans. London: The Gresham Press, n.d.

Goudsblom, Johan. *Nihilism and Culture.* Oxford: Basil Blackwell, 1980.

Hamsun, Knut. *Hunger.* Robert Bly, trans. New York: Farrar, Straus & Giroux, 1967.

"Hayashi Fumiko Memorial Hall." A pamphlet published by the Hayashi Fumiko Memorial Hall, Shinjuku, Tokyo, 1992.

Henricks, Robert G. *The Poetry of Han-Shan: A Complete Annotated Translation of* Cold Mountain. Albany: State University of New York Press, 1990.

Japanese Literature in Foreign Languages 1945–1990. Compiled by the Japan P.E.N. Club. Tokyo: Japan P.E.N. Club, 1990.

Kataoka Yoshikazu, ed. *Introduction to Contemporary Japanese Literature.* Tokyo: Kokusai bunka shinkōkai, 1939.

Keene, Dennis. *Yokomitsu Riichi: Modernist.* New York: Columbia University Press, 1980.

Keene, Donald. *Dawn to the West: Japanese Literature in the Modern Era.* New York: Henry Holt, 1984.

————. "The Barren Years: Japanese War Literature." In *Monumenta Nipponica,* 33. Tokyo: Sophia University Press, 1978, pp. 67–112.

Kelley, David. *Nature of Free Will.* Audiotaped lecture series. San Francisco: Laissez Faire Books, 1990.

Kobayashi Hideo. *Literature of the Lost Home: Kobayashi Hideo—Literary Criticsm, 1924–1939.* Paul Anderer, trans. Stanford: Stanford University Press, 1995.

Kōdansha Encyclopedia of Japan. Tokyo: Kōdansha, 1983.

Maupassant, Guy de. *A Woman's Life.* H. N. P. Sloman, trans. London: Penguin Books, 1965.

Miner, Earl, Hiroko Odagiri, and Robert E. Morrell. *The Princeton Companion to Classical Japanese Literature.* Princeton, N.J.: Princeton University Press, 1985.

Mitchell, Richard H. *Censorship in Imperial Japan.* Princeton, N.J.: Princeton University Press, 1983.

Modern Japanese Literature in Translation: A Bibliography, compiled by the International House of Japan Library. Tokyo: Kōdansha International, 1979.

Schnitzler, Arthur. *Theresa: The Chronicle of A Woman's Life.* William A. Drake, trans. New York: Simon & Schuster, 1928.

Shatz, Marshall S., ed. *The Essential Works of Anarchism.* New York: Quadrangle Books, 1972.

Strecher, Matthew C. "Purely Mass or Massively Pure? The Division between 'Pure' and 'Mass' Literature." In *Monumenta Nipponica,* 51.3. Tokyo: Sophia University Press, 1996, pp. 357–74.

Tanaka Yukiko, ed. *To Live and To Write: Selections by Japanese Women Writers 1913–1938.* Seattle, Wash.: The Seal Press, 1987.

Tolstoy, Leo. *Anna Karenina.* David Magarshack, trans. New York: New American Library, 1961.

———. *Resurrection.* Louise Maude, trans. Oxford: Oxford University Press, 1928.

Yokomitsu Riichi. *"'Love'" and Other Stories.* Dennis Keene, trans. Tokyo: University of Tokyo Press and Japan Foundation, 1974.

Zolbrod, Leon M. *Takizawa Bakin.* New York: Twayne Publishers, 1967.

INDEX